W9-CBX-445

APPLIED ECONOMICS

APPLIED ECONOMICS

Thinking Beyond Stage One

THOMAS SOWELL

Revised and Enlarged Edition

A Member of the Perseus Books Group
New York

Published in 2009 by Basic Books,
A Member of the Perseus Books Group
First edition published in 2004 by Basic Books

Books published by Basic Books are available at special discounts for bulk purchases in the United States by corporations, institutions, and other organizations. For more information, please contact the Special Markets Department at the Perseus Books Group, 2300 Chestnut Street, Suite 200, Philadelphia, PA 19103, or call (800) 810-4145, ext. 5000, or e-mail special.markets@perseusbooks.com.

A CIP catalog record for this book is available from the Library of Congress.

ISBN-13: 978-0-465-00345-7
LCCN: 2008932670

Printing 10, 2021

To Professor Arthur Smithies, who taught me to think beyond stage one

CONTENTS

PREFACE

This is the revised and expanded edition of ***Applied Economics***. There is a new chapter on the economics of immigration, and existing chapters have much new material, such as an analysis of the economics of organ transplants in the chapter on the economics of medical care and an explanation of some of the "creative financing" behind the subprime mortgage crisis in the chapter on the economics of housing.

Despite its title, this is ***not*** a book designed for economists to use in applying their expertise. It is a book to enable anyone, with no prior knowledge of economics, to understand some of the key economic issues of our time— medical care, housing, discrimination, and immigration, for example. Because these are political, as well as economic issues, we will need to consider what incentives and constraints apply to political decision-making, as well as those which apply to economic decision-making.

Economics requires thinking beyond the immediate consequences of decisions to their long-term effects. Because politicians seldom look beyond the next election, it is all the more important that voters look ahead— beyond stage one— rather than voting for a candidate or a policy that they will end up regretting later. This book stresses long-run repercussions to decisions and policies.

It is helpful to have something of a sense of humor when considering economic policies. Otherwise, the study of these policies and their often painful, and sometimes disastrous, unintended consequences can get to be too depressing or you can get too angry. Save your anger until you are inside the voting booth on election day. In the meantime, enjoy the process of getting more understanding of issues and institutions that affect your life and the future of the country.

Because this is a book for the general public, the usual footnotes or endnotes are omitted. However, for those readers who want to verify what is said here, or to read further on some of the subjects covered, the sources of the many facts discussed here are listed in the back of the book. Many, if not most, of those facts were gathered for me by my extraordinary research assistants, Na Liu and Elizabeth Costa. The former also created the computer files from which this book was directly printed and the latter did the copy-editing.

THOMAS SOWELL
The Hoover Institution
Stanford University

APPLIED ECONOMICS

Chapter 1

Politics versus Economics

> *I don't give a good goddamn* what *Milton Friedman says. He's not running for re-election.*
>
> *President Richard Nixon to a White House aide*

While economic principles are important, economic actions take place within a framework of laws and government policies that are shaped by political principles, which may or may not be consistent with economic principles. The interaction of political and economic incentives makes the study of economic policy issues more challenging— and more revealing— than a study of either economic or political principles in isolation.

POLITICAL VERSUS ECONOMIC DECISIONS

People tend to respond to the incentives and constraints confronting them, whether they are in the marketplace or in politics. However, those incentives and constraints are very different in these different situations, so it can hardly be surprising that voters tend to behave differently than consumers, and politicians tend to behave differently than sellers of goods and services.

Voters

Economic decisions and political decisions are made in different ways, even when the same person makes both kinds of decisions, for example as a consumer and as a voter. Virtually no one puts as much time and close attention into deciding whether to vote for one candidate rather than another as is usually put into deciding whether to buy one house rather than another— or perhaps even one car rather than another. The voter's political decisions involve having a minute influence on policies which affect many other people, while economic decision-making is about having a major effect on one's own personal well-being. It should not be surprising that the quantity and quality of thinking going into these very different kinds of decisions vary correspondingly. It has been said of many laws and policies that "the devil is in the details." But, if most voters are not likely to look into those details, many devilish results can be expected from legislation and policies that look good at first glance, when packaged with inspiring rhetoric.

Politics and the market are both ways of getting some people to respond to other people's desires. But people whose professional careers are in politics operate under different incentives and constraints from those whose careers are in the economy. Consumers choosing which goods to spend their money on have often been analogized to voters deciding which candidates to elect to public office. However, the two processes are profoundly different. Not only do individuals invest very different amounts of time and thought in making economic decisions versus political decisions, those decisions are inherently different in themselves. Voters decide ***whether*** to vote for one candidate or another but they decide ***how much*** of what kinds of food, clothing, shelter, etc., to purchase.

In short, political decisions tend to be categorical, while economic decisions tend to be incremental. Voting is a package deal: You may agree with candidate ***A*** on economic policy, candidate ***B*** on foreign policy and candidate ***C*** on environmental issues but, in the end, when you enter the voting booth you have to vote for one candidate's whole package of policies on the economy, foreign policy, and the environment. Moreover, you don't get to change your mind until the next election. It is not like buying one brand of bread today and a different brand tomorrow if you change your mind.

Incremental decisions can be more fine-tuned than deciding which candidate's whole package of principles and practices comes closest to meeting your own desires. Incremental decision-making also means that not every increment of even very desirable things is necessarily desirable, given that there are other things that the money could be spent on, after having acquired a given amount of a particular good or service. For example, although it might be worthwhile spending considerable money to live in a nice home, buying a second home in the country may or may not be worth spending money that could be used instead to send a child to college or to buy an annuity for later retirement years.

One consequence of incremental decision-making is that additional increments of many desirable things remain unpurchased because they are almost— but not quite— worth the sacrifices required to get them. From a political standpoint, this means that there are always numerous desirable things that government officials can offer to provide to voters who want them— either free of charge or at reduced, government-subsidized prices— even when these voters do not want these increments enough to sacrifice their own money to pay for them. Ultimately, of course, the public can end up paying as taxpayers for increments that they would not have chosen to pay for as consumers. The real winners in this process are the politicians whose apparent generosity and compassion gain them political support.

Politics has sometimes been called "the art of the possible." But that implies a level of constraint that simply does not exist in democratic politics. As a noted economist has pointed out, "no voting system could prevent the California electorate from simultaneously demanding low electricity prices and no new generating plants while using ever increasing amounts of electricity." This is just one of many ways in which the impossible can win elections. Beliefs can trump facts in politics, and have repeatedly trumped facts throughout history. "Demagoguery beats data," as former Congressman Dick Armey put it. But the production and distribution of false beliefs is not solely a result of the skills of demagogues. There are certain kinds of beliefs that tend to be accepted without much evidence or even in defiance of evidence.

No political message has proven to be more welcome, in countries around the world, in both democratic and undemocratic nations, and among peoples of every race and culture, than the message that your problems are not your fault, but the fault of others— and it is they who must change, not you. Moreover, it is they who must pay the consequences if they do not change, but not you. Not only particular political candidates but, in some countries, whole revolutionary movements, have risen to power on the wings of that message.

Politicians

While politicians can be expected to pay far more attention to political decisions than the average voter will, the nature of that attention is also likely to be different. Elected officials' top priority is usually getting re-elected, and their time horizon seldom extends beyond the next election. Laws and policies that will produce politically beneficial effects before the next election are usually preferred to policies that will produce even better results some time after the next election. Indeed, policies that will produce good results before the next election may be preferred even if they can be expected to produce bad results afterwards.

Thinking beyond the immediate consequences of a law or policy is a task which neither voters nor politicians have much incentive to undertake. When most voters do not think beyond stage one, many elected officials have no incentive to weigh what the consequences will be in later stages— and considerable incentives to avoid getting beyond what their constituents think and understand, for fear that rival politicians can drive a wedge between them and their constituents by catering to short-run public perceptions.

The very way that issues are conceived tends to be different in politics from the way they are conceived in economics. Political thinking tends to conceive of policies, institutions, or programs in terms of their ***hoped-for results***— "drug prevention" programs, "gun control" laws, "environmental protection" policies, "public interest" law firms, "profit-making" businesses, and so forth. But for purposes of economic analysis, what matters is not what goals are being sought but what incentives and constraints are being created in pursuit of those goals.

We know, for example, that many— if not most— "profit-making" enterprises do not in fact make profits, as shown by the high percentage of new businesses that fail and go out of business within a few years after getting started. Similarly, it is an open question whether drug prevention programs actually prevent or even reduce drug usage, whether public interest law firms actually benefit the public, or whether gun control laws actually control guns. No economist is likely to be surprised when rent control laws, for example, fail to control rent, so that cities with such laws often end up with higher rents than cities without them[1]— New York and San Francisco being classic examples. But such outcomes may be very surprising to people who think in terms of political rhetoric focussed on desirable goals— and who do not think beyond stage one.

The point here is not simply that various policies may fail to achieve their purposes. The more fundamental point is that we need to know the ***actual characteristics*** of the processes set in motion— and the incentives and constraints inherent in such characteristics— rather than judging these processes by their goals. Many of the much discussed "unintended consequences" of policies and programs would have been foreseeable from the outset if these processes had been analyzed in terms of the incentives and constraints they created, instead of in terms of the desirability of the goals they proclaimed. Once we start thinking in terms of the chain of events set in motion by particular policies— and following the chain of events beyond stage one— the world begins to look very different.

In trying to understand the effect of politics on economics, we need to consider not only officials' responses to the various pressures they receive from different sources, but also the way that the media and the voting public

---

1 See my ***Basic Economics***, third edition, pages 40-48.

see economic issues. Both the media and the voters are prone to what might be called one-stage thinking.

ONE-STAGE THINKING

When I was an undergraduate studying economics under Professor Arthur Smithies of Harvard, he asked me in class one day what policy I favored on a particular issue of the times. Since I had strong feelings on that issue, I proceeded to answer him with enthusiasm, explaining what beneficial consequences I expected from the policy I advocated.

"And then what will happen?" he asked.

The question caught me off guard. However, as I thought about it, it became clear that the situation I described would lead to other economic consequences, which I then began to consider and to spell out.

"And what will happen after that?" Professor Smithies asked.

As I analyzed how the further economic reactions to the policy would unfold, I began to realize that these reactions would lead to consequences much less desirable than those at the first stage, and I began to waver somewhat.

"And *then* what will happen?" Smithies persisted.

By now I was beginning to see that the economic reverberations of the policy I advocated were likely to be pretty disastrous— and, in fact, much worse than the initial situation that it was designed to improve.

Simple as this little exercise might seem, it went further than most economic discussions about policies on a wide range of issues. Most thinking stops at stage one. In recent years, former economic advisers to Presidents of the United States— from both political parties— have commented publicly on how little thinking ahead about economic consequences went into decisions made at the highest level.[2] This is not to say that there was no thinking ahead about ***political*** consequences. Each of the presidents they served (Richard Nixon and Bill Clinton, respectively)

[2] Herbert Stein and Joseph Stiglitz.

was so successful politically that he was re-elected by a wider margin than the vote that first put him in office.

Short-run thinking is not confined to politicians but is often also found among the population at large. Nor is this peculiar to the United States or even to Western societies. When the government of Zimbabwe decreed drastic cutbacks in prices to deal with runaway inflation in June 2007, the citizens of Zimbabwe "greeted the price cuts with a euphoric— and short-lived— shopping spree," according to the ***New York Times***. But, just one month later, the ***Times*** reported, "Zimbabwe's economy is at a halt." This was spelled out:

> Bread, sugar and cornmeal, staples of every Zimbabwean's diet, have vanished... Meat is virtually nonexistent, even for members of the middle class who have money to buy it on the black market... Hospital patients are dying for lack of basic medical supplies.

That suppliers do not usually supply as much at a lower price as they do at a higher price is not a complicated economic principle, but it does require stopping to think, and especially to think beyond stage one. Price controls are essentially lies about supply and demand. In the case of Zimbabwe, the artificially low prices created the impression of an affordable abundance that was simply not there. As with other lies, political or otherwise, time may be required for the truth to come out, and it may be too late when it does.

"Do Something" Policies

In a market economy, millions of people in their various roles as consumers, employees, employers, investors, farmers, etc., are constantly adjusting to changing circumstances, whether these changes are due to technology or to mistaken decisions that set off changes in prices, wages, or rates of return on stocks and bonds. Sometimes these changes are benign, such as the dramatically declining prices of computers during an era when the capabilities of these computers have been increasing equally dramatically. Other changes are negative, as when financial markets adjusted to widespread defaults on risky mortgage loans in 2007 by forcing many borrowers and lenders of these loans into bankruptcy, and produced a tightening up on credit requirements for people who were trying to get new loans.

While a self-equilibrating system like a market economy confers benefits, its adjustments through changing prices, sales, employment, etc., can present difficulties for particular individuals and enterprises during the process of adjustment— and these difficulties present opportunities for political authorities to intervene, especially in response to demands that they "do something" to solve economic problems. Whether that undefined something will in fact make matters better or worse economically, in political terms the demand for action may be irresistible. Thus, in response to inflation in the United States, President Richard Nixon imposed the first peacetime wage and price controls in the history of the country in 1971, despite the advice of economists and despite Nixon's own knowledge of the adverse consequences of wage and price controls. Herbert Stein, chairman of Nixon's Council of Economic Advisers, in later years described some of these adverse consequences: "Cattle were being withheld from market, chickens were being drowned, and the foodstore shelves were being emptied." Such consequences became manifest some time after the elections, however.

The immediate ***political*** consequences, however, were overwhelmingly favorable, leading to widespread praise of the President in the media for taking action to deal with inflation, and ultimately to a landslide victory in Nixon's bid for re-election in 1972. In retrospect, the economic consequences of Nixon's wage and price controls have been widely recognized as negative but voters vote on the basis of how things look to them at the time, not how the consequences will be assessed later in retrospect. In short, "do something" policies are often a result of not thinking beyond stage one— and of politicians who respond to voter shortsightedness, even if the politicians themselves know better. As Herbert Stein noted, the wage and price controls "did not visibly affect the course of the inflation and were not expected by the White House to do so."

In his memoirs, Nixon said that his imposing wage and price controls "was politically necessary and immensely popular in the short run. But in the long run I believe that it was wrong. The piper must always be paid, and there was an unquestionably high price for tampering with the orthodox economic mechanisms." Looking back on the same events, Milton Friedman said: "The disastrous economic effects came ***after*** Nixon's landslide re-election in 1972, which the controls helped to bring about." Like other price controls in countries around the world and over thousands of years of history, Nixon's price controls led to a reduction in the amount of goods supplied while the lower prices led to an increase in the amount of goods demanded— producing shortages. These shortages were seldom blamed on Nixon at the time and the gasoline shortages that led to long lines at filling stations were blamed on oil companies by many in politics and in the media.

So politically successful was the demonizing of oil companies that neither of Nixon's next two successors— Presidents Gerald Ford and Jimmy Carter— dared to cancel price controls on oil, even after the other Nixon price controls had been lifted. As economist Herbert Stein, still on the White House staff during the Ford administration, said, "the main problem was probably political— fear of being accused of sacrificing homeowners and commuters for the profit of the oil companies." Later, President Carter began to loosen the oil price controls but, as late as 1979 there were recurrent gasoline shortages and long lines at filling stations, where motorists sometimes sat in their cars for an hour or more before reaching the pump, which in some cases ran out of gas by the time they got there. But, by this time, virtually no one traced the gasoline shortages back to the Nixon price controls years earlier, or to the demonization of oil companies, which kept oil price controls on, years after other price controls had been rescinded.

It was 1981— a decade after the Nixon price controls began— that the Reagan administration abolished the last of the price controls on oil, amid dire predictions from critics that gasoline prices would skyrocket. Instead, gasoline lines disappeared and, as supplies of oil increased, gasoline prices began declining, eventually reaching lower levels than under price controls.

Sometimes the temptation to "do something" reflects more than just a cynical calculation of political advantages. Often there is a belief that government intervention is necessary, even if the specific form of that intervention may have to be determined in a trial-and-error process. President Franklin D. Roosevelt articulated this approach during the Great Depression of the 1930s:

> The country needs and, unless I mistake its temper, the country demands bold, persistent experimentation. It is common sense to take a method and try it; if it fails, admit it frankly and try another. But above all, try something.

FDR did not mistake the temper of the country. He was the most successful politician in American history, being elected President an unprecedented four times. During his career and for decades thereafter, many saw his policies as responsible for getting the country out of the Great Depression. However, with the passing years and additional research and analysis, more and more economists and historians have seen his policies as needlessly prolonging the depression by generating a pervasive uncertainty as to what the government was going to do next, leaving both consumers and investors hesitating to part with their money. This in turn meant an inadequate demand for goods and for the labor to produce those goods.

FDR seems never to have considered that incessant experimentation, in and of itself, was a process which could have high costs for the economy, irrespective of the merits or demerits of particular experiments. Government experimentation is different from private experimentation which, for better or worse, affects only those who engage in it, and who have every incentive to stop when it becomes clear that the experiment is not working. But government experiments with the rules under which millions of other people must operate, and the prospect that the basic rules of the economy are likely to continue changing without notice at any time, is not a prospect that encourages long-term investment by businesses or even short-term spending by consumers. People tend to hang on to their money when they don't know what is likely to happen next.

Prior to the Great Depression of the 1930s, there was no tradition of federal government intervention to get the United States out of depressions. Roosevelt's predecessor, President Herbert Hoover, was the first President to take on that responsibility, and many of his interventions were later simply carried much further by FDR, despite a political myth that persisted for years that Hoover was a "do nothing" President. In much later years, even prominent former advisers of the Roosevelt administration admitted that FDR's New Deal was a further extension of what Hoover had been doing. Herbert Hoover was in fact the first President to decide to "do something" on a national scale to try to extricate the country from a depression, though there is no evidence that what he did made things any better and there is considerable reason to believe that they made things worse.

Earlier in the 1920s, a sharp decline in the economy had been largely ignored by President Calvin Coolidge— and the economy pulled out of its decline in a relatively short time, as it had pulled out of other such declines in the past. There was nothing inevitable about a stock market crash leading to a decade-long depression. Moreover, as Professor Peter Temin of M.I.T. has noted, the 1929 stock market crash was not unique:

> The stock market has gone up and down many times since then without producing a similar movement in income. The most obvious parallel was in the fall of 1987. The isomorphism was uncanny. The stock market fell almost exactly the same amount on almost exactly the same dates.

Another study referred to the October 19, 1987 decline as "by far the worst percentage decline day in the stock market's history." In 1987, however, President Ronald Reagan did not react as Presidents Hoover and Roosevelt had in the wake of the 1929 stock market crash. Instead, like Coolidge before him (whom he admired), Reagan let the economy recover on its own. Far from leading to a Great Depression, the recovery began one of the longest periods of sustained high employment, low inflation, and general prosperity in American history.[3] At the time, however, President Reagan was sharply criticized in the ***Washington Post*** for a "do-nothing, let-

---

[3] "For the past 20 years or more its economy has managed an enviable combination of steady growth and low inflation." "The Turning Point," ***The Economist***, September 22, 2007, p. 35.

the-problems-accumulate, Calvin Coolidge act of the 1980s" and was denounced in the *New York Times* for having "squandered the opportunity" to take action.

In short, there are many pressures on Presidents to "do something." Some (like Nixon) succumb to those pressures and others (like Reagan) just take the heat. It should be noted that Reagan was not eligible for re-election in 1987. Moreover, it is not just free market economists who regard government intervention in depressions as potentially harmful. Long before the Great Depression of the 1930s, it was none other than Karl Marx who referred to "crackbrained meddling by the authorities" that can "aggravate an existing crisis." There was not much in common between Ronald Reagan and Karl Marx but one of the things that both of them had done was to study economics.

Presidents are not the only elected officials under pressure to "do something." Nor are all the actions taken under such pressures due to cynical disregard of known economic consequences for political reasons, as with President Nixon. Inadequate knowledge of economics also plays a role, as well as an unwillingness to listen to economic advice. Well-known financier, philanthropist and government official William E. Simon commented on his sense of futility in testifying before Congress on numerous occasions:

> Most of these hearings were an abysmal waste to time. Nonetheless, I patiently complied with the Congressional invitations. I never neglected an opportunity to offer these gentlemen carefully documented evidence of their own historic irresponsibility.

In response to various economic problems in 2007, Professor N. Gregory Mankiw of Harvard, a former chairman of the Council of Economic Advisers, wrote:

> The question on the minds of many in Congress and in the White House is this: What they should be doing now to keep the economy on track? The right answer: absolutely nothing.

The feeling that the government should "do something" has seldom been based on a comparison of what actually happens when government does and when it does not "do something." Doing something almost always seems like such a good idea, to those who do not look beyond stage one, that they see no need to look back at history or to apply economics. The alternative to a "do something" approach is not to have the government always do absolutely nothing but, rather, to recognize that governments can only do something ***specific***— and that these specifics must be assessed in terms of their specific effects, both immediate and long-term, as well as the general effects of extended experimentation. Although Professor Mankiw urged politicians in Congress and the White House to do nothing, he also argued that the Federal Reserve System, with its professional economists, could do enough to prevent the economy from developing serious problems.

Many "do something" policies do in fact benefit particular industries, groups, regions or other segments of the national economy. But that is very different from saying that these policies produce a net benefit to the economy as a whole. For example, during the administration of President George W. Bush, policies to protect the American steel industry from the problems created by having to compete with lower-priced imported steel did in fact save the jobs of many American steelworkers and enhanced the profits of American steel companies. But the net result was a rise in steel prices within the United States, leading to rising prices of American products made of steel, making those products less competitive at home and in the world market. As a result, far more jobs were lost in American steel-using industries than were saved in the steel-producing industry, and the profit reduction in American steel-using industries was far greater than the profit increase in the steel-producing industry. The intervention seemed successful only to those who did not look beyond the immediate beneficiaries in stage one.

Sometimes it is not just that some people benefit at the expense of other people when future repercussions are not taken into account. Sometimes the very same people who are intended to be helped turn out to be harmed. For example, when the Americans with Disabilities Act was passed in 1992, the obvious goal was to benefit people who were physically or mentally impaired. Businesses and other institutions were mandated to make "reasonable accommodation" to those with disabilities, such as making businesses accessible to wheelchairs or taking other steps to enable employees with various disabilities to do their jobs more easily. But a study by two economists found that the employment of people with disabilities ***declined*** in the wake of this legislation. Employers simply responded to these extra costs imposed by the government by no longer being as willing to hire disabled workers in the first place.

The Long Run

Thinking beyond stage one is especially important when considering policies whose consequences unfold over a period of years. If the initial consequences are good, and the bad consequences come later— especially if later is after the next election— then it is always tempting for politicians to adopt such policies.

For example, if a given city or state contains a number of prosperous corporations, nothing is easier than to raise money to finance local government projects that will win votes for their political sponsors by raising the tax rates on these corporations. What are the corporations going to do? Pick up their factories, hotels, railroads, or office buildings and move somewhere else? Certainly not immediately, in stage one. Even if they could sell their local properties and go buy replacements somewhere else, this would take time and not all their experienced employees would be willing to move suddenly with them to another city or state.

Nevertheless, even under such restrictions on movement, the high taxes would begin to have some immediate effect. When businesses with branches in different locations face declining demand and have to choose which branches to close, those in high tax cities and states are especially likely to be chosen as the ones to shut down. There is also likely to be an increase in the rate at which businesses go out of business completely in high tax cities and states, as some struggling firms that might have been able to hold on longer, and perhaps ride out their problems, are unable to do so when heavy tax burdens are added to their other difficulties and become like the proverbial straw that breaks the camel's back.

Meanwhile, newly arising companies have options when deciding where to locate their factories or offices— and cities and states with high tax rates are likely to be avoided. Therefore, even if all existing and thriving corporations are unable to budge in the short run, the high-tax jurisdictions can begin the process of losing businesses, even in stage one. But the losses may not be on a scale that is large enough to be noticeable before the next election.

Then comes stage two. Usually the headquarters where a business' top brass work can be moved before the operating units that have larger numbers of employees and much equipment. Moreover, if the corporation has other operating units in other cities and states— or perhaps overseas— it can begin shifting some of its production to other locations, where taxes are not so high, even if it does not immediately abandon its factories or offices in the high-tax communities. This reduction in the amount of business done locally in the high-tax location will in turn begin to reduce the locally earned income on which taxes are paid by both the corporation and its local employees.

Stage three: As corporations grow over time, they can choose to locate their new operations where taxes are not so high, gradually transferring employees who are willing to move and replacing those who are not by hiring new people. Stage four: As more and more corporations desert the high-tax city or state, eventually the point can be reached where the total tax revenues collected from the remaining corporations under higher tax rates are less than what was collected under the lower tax rates of the past, when there were more businesses paying those taxes. By this time, however, years may have passed and the politicians responsible for setting this process in motion may well have moved on to higher office in state or national government.

More important, even those politicians who remain in office in the local area are unlikely to be blamed for declining tax revenues, lost employment, or cutbacks in government services and neglected infrastructure made necessary by an inadequate tax base. In short, those responsible for such economic declines will probably escape political consequences, unless either the voters or the media think beyond stage one and follow the sequence of events over a period of years— which seldom happens.[4]

New York City has been a classic example of this process. Once the headquarters of many of the biggest corporations in America, New York in the early twenty-first century was headquarters to just one of the 100 fastest growing companies in the country. With the highest tax rate of any American city, New York has been losing businesses and hundreds of thousands of jobs. Meanwhile, the city has been spending twice as much per capita as Los Angeles, and three times as much per capita as Chicago, on a wide variety of municipal programs. By and large, spend-and-tax policies have been successful politically, however negative their economic consequences.

Killing the goose that lays the golden egg is a viable political strategy, so long as the goose does not die before the next election and no one traces the politicians' fingerprints on the weapon. In a complex economy, there are always alternative explanations of local or regional decline that can be blamed, in order to deflect attention from policies that have led to economic decline.

One popular alternative is to blame jobs going overseas. But, whatever the reasons for the decline in ***existing*** jobs— which include technological

---

[4] There is another sense in which multiple stages must be taken into account, which may be easier to explain by analogy. Imagine that a dam can be emptied into a valley and that calculations show that this would fill the valley with water to a depth of 20 feet. If your home is located on an elevation 30 feet above the valley floor, it should be safe if the water is slowly released. But if the floodgates are simply flung wide open, a wave of water 40 feet high may roar across the valley, smashing your home and drowning everyone in it. After the water subsides, it will still end up just 20 feet deep, but that will not matter as far as the destruction of the home and people are concerned, even though both are now 10 feet above the level at which the water settles down. A Nobel Prizewinning economist has argued that economic policies suddenly imposed on various Third World countries by the International Monetary Fund have ignored the timing and sequence of reactions inside those countries, which may include irreparable damage to the social fabric as economic desperation creates mass riots that can topple governments and make foreign investors unwilling to put money into such an unstable country for years to come.

changes and changes in consumer preferences, in addition to jobs going overseas— existing jobs are always declining by the millions nationwide, even in a period of full employment. More than 17 million American workers lost their jobs between 1990 and 1995, and yet the unemployment rate was very low because ***new*** jobs were being created. However, the "rust belt" regions of the United States have lost jobs for reasons very much like the reasons that New York City has lost jobs. Even when very similar jobs are created in the American economy— Toyota hiring thousands of American workers to build automobiles while General Motors is laying off thousands— these jobs are usually ***not*** created in the places where a political or labor union environment is detrimental to business. It is not simply the lost jobs, but the obstacles to the creation of replacement jobs, that is at the heart of the problems of the "rust belt."

Political Incentives

When you have agents or surrogates looking out for your interests, in any aspect of life— political or otherwise— there is always the danger that these agents will look out for their own interests, which do not always coincide with yours. Corporate managements do not always put the stockholders' interest first, and agents for actors, athletes, or writers may sacrifice their clients' interests to their own. There is no reason to expect elected officials to be fundamentally different. But there are reasons to know what their particular incentives are— and what the economic realities are that they may overlook while pursuing their own political goals.

A bridge collapse in Minneapolis in 2007, with a number of fatalities among motorists who happened to be on the bridge at the time, led not only to nationwide shock over that particular disaster but also to widespread attention to the fact that many other bridges around the country were also at risk. Nor were bridges the only infrastructure whose maintenance and repair have tended to be neglected by elected officials. It has been common for roads and highways to develop potholes that are not repaired, even in places where money was being spent for building community centers, golf courses, and other amenities. Yet such choices were perfectly rational from the standpoint of the self-interest of elected officials, given the political incentives and constraints in stage one.

Repairing bridges, roadways, dams, or government buildings requires money that could be spent doing things with an immediate pay-off in favorable publicity for politicians. Building a new recreational facility, plaza, or other impressive structure creates opportunities for ribbon-cutting ceremonies that will be covered by the media, keeping a politician's name and image before the public in a favorable light, thereby enhancing that politician's re-election prospects. But there are no ribbon-cutting ceremonies for filling in potholes or keeping a bridge or school in good repair. Unless there is some obvious defect, both immediately visible and important to a large segment of the voting public, there is little or no political pay-off for doing such things. Moreover, delayed maintenance is in most cases unlikely to cause any serious problem before the next election, even if it leads to disasters in the long run, during some future administration.

Such incentives and responses are not peculiar to the United States or to modern times. In the eighteenth century, Adam Smith noted how in France some "work of splendour and magnificence" was more likely to be built by a "proud minister of an ostentatious court" than were "a great number of little works," even when the latter have "extreme utility." He said that in France, "the great roads, the great communications which are likely to be the subjects of conversation at the court and in the capital, are attended to, and all the rest neglected."

Not only do politicians tend to think no further than stage one, the laws and policies they create tend to proceed as if other people do not think beyond stage one. Thus a government agency set up to safeguard the pensions of workers in private companies has been used by airlines facing bankruptcy to transfer their pension obligations to the taxpayers. Why would these airlines (and other companies) have taken on pension obligations that they did not have the money to meet? Because they could avoid a strike by putting such benefits into a union contract that they signed, knowing that, if necessary, they could in later years shift those obligations to the government. They thought beyond stage one, even if those who supported this government program did not.

To analyze the market does not preclude the existence of non-market activities or prejudge their effectiveness, any more than the study of automotive engineering precludes the existence or prejudges the effectiveness of alternative modes of transportation. What economic analysis of markets does is utilize a body of knowledge, analysis, and experience that has accumulated and developed over a period of centuries to systematically examine the consequences of various economic actions and policies. The fact that these consequences can determine the poverty or prosperity of millions of citizens in a given country— and billions of people worldwide— is what makes it important to understand economics.

The real question is not which policy or system would work best ideally, but which has in fact produced better results with far from ideal human beings. Even with the more modest task of evaluating different policies within a given system, the real question is not which policy sounds more plausible, or which would work best if people behaved ideally, but which policy in fact turns out to produce better results with actual people, behaving as they actually do. This latter question will be addressed in different contexts in the chapters that follow.

Chapter 2

Free and Unfree Labor

A student asked his history professor: "Where did slavery come from?" "You're asking the wrong question," the professor replied. "The real question is: Where did freedom come from?"

Slavery is one of the oldest and most universal of all human institutions. Slavery has existed among peoples around the world, as far back as recorded history goes— and archaeological explorations suggest that it existed before human beings learned to write. ***No one knows when slavery began.*** It is the idea of freedom for the great masses of ordinary people that is relatively new, as history is measured— and this idea is by no means universally accepted around the world, even today. Slavery was stamped out over most of the world during the course of the nineteenth century, but it still survives here and there in the twenty-first century. Moreover, there have been, and still are, other kinds of unfree labor besides slavery.

One of the many freedoms we take for granted today is the right to choose what kind of work we will and will not do. Yet, for many centuries, there was no such choice for most people in most countries. If you were the son of a shoemaker, then your job would be to make shoes. And if you were the daughter of a farmer, there were a whole range of chores that you would perform while growing up and a still larger range of domestic responsibilities waiting for you after marriage. The difference between "free" and "unfree" labor in such times was whether or not you were paid for your work or were forced to do it without financial compensation.

Forced labors might be temporary and range from drudgery in the fields of the nobility or serving under those same nobles in their military campaigns, after which you were allowed to return to your own farming or to your other work. People who were less fortunate were full-time and lifelong serfs or slaves, with this status also being inherited by their children.

While free labor has become the norm in much of the world today, compulsory labor still survives, even in free democratic countries, in such forms as military drafts and compulsory jury duty. Outright slavery still exists in a few other countries, such as Mauritania, Sudan, and Nigeria. In remote parts of India, family members still remain in bondage over the generations because of debts contracted by some ancestor before they were born— a situation sometimes called debt peonage and sometimes called simply slavery in one of its variations.

Despite the sharp dichotomy between free and unfree labor in principle, in practice those who are free may nevertheless have many restrictions imposed on them by laws and policies, such as requirements to get an occupational license or belong to a labor union in order to work in some occupations, when in fact either union memberships or the necessary licenses may be arbitrarily limited in numbers. The wholly voluntary agreement between employer and employee in a free market exists as a model but not always as a reality. The employer's freedom to hire whoever will work for him is heavily circumscribed by child labor laws, anti-discrimination laws, and other regulations and policies, as well as by labor union contracts.

At the other end of the spectrum, even some slaves have had options, especially urban slaves, many of whom chose their own employers and simply shared their earnings with slaveowners who let them exercise this option. This practice existed as far back as ancient Greece, where some slaves lived and worked away from their owners and simply paid the owners some share of their earnings.

FREE LABOR

The advantages of a free labor market benefit not only the worker but also the economy. Since pay is usually based on productivity and workers tend to seek higher-paying jobs, this whole process tends to place people where they can contribute the most to the production of goods and services that other people want. Arbitrary restrictions on who can work where tend to sacrifice not only the interests of those who are denied jobs but also the interests of consumers, who are denied an opportunity to get the goods and services they want in the abundance they would like and at as low a price as possible. Nevertheless, most people would prefer not to see little children working in coal mines, as they once did, or in factories alongside powerful and dangerous machines. Virtually everyone would also prefer not to have anyone who wants to perform surgery be authorized to do so, with or without the benefit of medical training. Some occupations, such as burglar, are banned outright.

In one way or another, for good reasons or bad, there are many restrictions on free labor and on those who employ free labor. Among these restrictions are occupational licensing laws, job security laws, and minimum wage laws. It should also be noted that much of what is called "labor" is in fact capital.

Human Capital

Most people in modern industrial societies are called workers or labor. However, people represent not only labor but also capital investments. Schooling, job experience, reading, experience gained tinkering with cars or computers, as well as by absorbing the knowledge and experience of parents and peers, all contribute to the development of the skills, insights, and capabilities on the job that economists call human capital. Nor is the distinction between human labor and human capital just a set of abstract concepts without consequences.

The ability to labor is usually greatest in early adulthood, when people are in their physical prime. Back in the days when many workers did in fact contribute little more than their physical exertions, a middle-aged manual laborer was typically less employable than a young man in his twenties working in the same occupation but with more youthful vigor. Today, however, when most people who work for a living earn more as they grow older, this is much more consistent with their earning a return on their human capital, which tends to increase with age and experience. The human capital concept is also more consistent with narrowing income gaps between women and men, as physical strength counts for less and less in an economy where power increasingly comes from machines rather than human muscle, and an economy in which knowledge and high-tech skills count for more.

While the growing importance of human capital tends to create greater income equality between the sexes, it tends to create greater income ***inequality*** between those people who have been assiduous in acquiring knowledge and mastering skills and those who have not. In addition, like every other source of greater reward for work, it tends to create greater inequality between those who work and those who do not. American families in the bottom 20 percent of income earners supply only a fraction of the hours of work per year supplied by families in the top 20 percent. Both the rising incomes of more experienced workers and the growing inequality in incomes in free market societies show the influence of human capital.

While almost all jobs today provide both pay and experience, at one time it was common for inexperienced and uneducated young people to take jobs that paid them nothing. This was obviously an investment of their time and labor for the sake of acquiring human capital. Apprenticeship, with and without pay, has been a centuries-old institution in many parts of the world, and unpaid labor was not uncommon in the United States as late as the Great Depression of the 1930s, when people desperate for work took jobs without pay for the sake of gaining work experience that would improve their chances of getting paying jobs later, either with the same employer or with other employers who were hiring only experienced workers.

Back around the time of the First World War, a young black American named Paul Williams decided to become an architect— a virtually unheard of occupation for someone of his race at that time— and turned down the only paying job he was offered at an architectural firm, in order to go to work as an office boy without pay in a more prominent architectural firm, from which he expected to gain more valuable knowledge and experience.[1] He was clearly thinking beyond the initial stage of his career.

As the later stages of his development unfolded, Paul Williams went on to have a long and distinguished career as an architect, in which he designed everything from mansions for movie stars to banks, hotels, and churches, and participated in designing the theme building at the Los Angeles International Airport. Like people who invest money in stocks and bonds, he had invested his time and labor to acquire human capital that paid off during the course of his long professional career.

Another example, this time from the nineteenth century, was a poverty-stricken young man, dressed in ragged clothes, who applied for a job as sales clerk in a store in upstate New York. His name was Frank Winfield Woolworth, later destined to become head of a variety store chain that bore his name. But, as of 1873, he was just a very unpromising-looking prospect. Here was the scene:

> The shop owner fingers his waxed mustachio thoughtfully. The boy before him is clearly green, but he does seem sincere. Still, times were tough and at least twenty ***experienced*** candidates would soon be clamoring for this same job.
>
> And all in all, the boy is a sorry excuse for a potential salesman.
>
> But the owner sees something there.
>
> "Okay," he barks. "The job is yours. You start Monday!"
>
> Trying to control his elation, the young man asks: "What are you going to pay me, sir?"
>
> "Pay you!?" the owner exclaims. "You don't expect me to pay you, do you? Why, you should pay ***me*** for teaching you the business."

The terms might seem harsh— the first three months with no pay— and even exploitative. But who benefited most from this deal?[2]

---

[1] After he showed up for work, however, his employer decided to pay him a small salary, after all.

[2] While the employer had the prospect of more experienced job applicants, Woolworth's alternative was to remain on his father's farm. His brother described their routine of going out at 5:30 in the morning, barefoot even on cold mornings, to milk the cows: "We would stand on the ground upon which the cows had been lying to get a little warmth into our nearly frozen feet. No wonder we yearned to break away from the endless drudgery." Karen Plunkett-Powell, ***Remembering Woolworth's***, p. 26.

Woolworth was a conscientious worker, but he was also a country bumpkin who was so inept that his duties were at first confined to sweeping the floor, dusting the shelves, and doing other work that would not be considered too challenging for someone so lacking in sophistication or finesse. The other clerks in the store laughed at him, and it was a long time before anyone would risk letting him wait on customers. In short, he was being paid about what he was worth.

The three months of working for free— from seven in the morning until nine at night— that Woolworth invested paid off bigger than a lottery. After he became a paid employee, the knowledge and experience which he accumulated working in that store eventually enabled him to go out into the world to set up his own store— and, in the decades ahead, a whole chain of stores across the country, and then around the world, which made him one of the most fabulously wealthy men of his time.[3] In later years, he spoke with gratitude of the man who had hired him— and he made his former employer a partner in the F. W. Woolworth retail chain. He indeed ended up paying him for teaching him the business.

In more recent times, minimum wage laws and public disapproval of non-paying jobs have largely eliminated this particular way of acquiring human capital. However, many people continue to take lower-paying jobs than they could get elsewhere when they value the experience available to them in the less remunerative job and expect to cash in on it later on in their careers. They are thinking beyond stage one.

Some begin administrative careers as modestly paid officials in government regulatory agencies, in order to go on later to higher-paying jobs in the industries regulated by those agencies, where their inside knowledge would be valuable to these businesses in coping with numerous government rules and regulations. Some people with Ph.D.s in the sciences may choose to become post-doctoral fellows at prestigious universities, where they can work with world-class chemists or physicists, rather than

---

[3] The Woolworth Building in New York, once the tallest building in the world, may well still be the only skyscraper in the world whose construction was paid for in cash from the personal fortune of one man, F. W. Woolworth.

take a teaching post at a lesser institution where they would receive higher pay than they get from their fellowship. After they have learned from working with top people in their respective fields, their own enhanced reputations can then make them more marketable at higher-level institutions at higher pay.

Those who disdain low-paying jobs as "menial" or who refuse to accept "chump change" for entry-level work are usually not thinking beyond stage one. Not only isolated individuals like Paul Williams or F.W. Woolworth began in this way, so have great numbers of others who have developed human capital and collected the dividends later. Young people who begin by working at McDonald's seldom spend their careers at McDonald's. Just in the course of one year, McDonald's has more than a 100 percent turnover rate. What those who leave take with them is not only such basic experience as showing up for work regularly and on time, cooperating with others, and knowing how to conduct themselves in a business environment, but also a track record that enables them to move on to other and very different occupations at progressively higher levels in the years ahead. The experience and the track record from McDonald's are likely to be more valuable in the long run than the modest paychecks they earned serving hamburgers.

Put differently, whatever reduces opportunities for gainful employment for people with little or no experience has the effect of costing both them and the society far more than the lost jobs which have been dismissed as "menial" or as paying only "chump change." Nothing is easier than for third parties to take a lofty moral position that when minimum wage laws, for example, result in a reduction of low-paying jobs, it is nothing to regret, as some politicians and journalists have done. Having wage rates set by third parties' notions of workers' "essential needs" would be a radical departure from having wages set by supply and demand— and it is by no means clear how either the allocation of resources in the economy or the interests of the workers themselves would be better served in this way. These workers may well feel that their most "essential need" is a job. Reducing the number of jobs available by pricing inexperienced young workers out of the market solves no problem for these workers. The only clear beneficiaries would be those who acquire such arbitrary powers over their fellow human beings, and are thus able to feel both important and noble, while in fact leaving havoc in their wake.

Income

Most people of course work for the sake of earning an income— and while the earning of income might seem to be something simple and easy to understand, income statistics are full of pitfalls and fallacies. Underlying most fallacies about income are three key confusions:

1. Confusing income with wealth
2. Confusing statistical categories with human beings
3. Confusing the transient position of individuals in the current income stream with an enduring class

These are not difficult or esoteric distinctions. But they are distinctions that have to be made at the outset, in order to prevent discussions from becoming tangled up in undefined words and in slippery numbers that can easily be misunderstood.

The distinction between income and wealth is that income is a flow of money during a given year, while wealth is an accumulation of money— or of assets valued in money— over a number of years. A person of modest income can accumulate considerable wealth over a period of years, both from the money saved and from the interest, dividends or other increases in the value of the initial investments. People in their seventies average several times the wealth of people in their twenties, for example. Conversely, people with high incomes can sometimes end up with very little accumulation of wealth, when they spend so much that they have little or nothing left when they are no longer able to earn high incomes for one reason or another. Simple as all this may seem, politicians and journalists often refer to people with high current incomes as "rich" and people with low current incomes as "poor." Moreover, discussions of what tax rates are appropriate for "the rich" are almost invariably discussions of *income* taxes, not taxes on accumulated wealth, though one is rich only when one has accumulated wealth, not just because one has a high current income.

The distinction between abstract statistical categories and flesh-and-blood human beings is likewise not difficult to make but it is a distinction that many do not bother to make. Moreover, the failure to make that distinction produces much confusion and many fallacies. It is, for example, often said that the income gap between those in the top income brackets and those in the bottom brackets is widening over time. This may be quite true in the sense that the average income in the top bracket is increasing faster than the average income in the bottom bracket. But the economic fate of these abstract statistical categories can be— and often is— the direct ***opposite*** of the fate of flesh-and-blood human beings.

Between 1996 and 2005, for example, income tax data show that the share of the nation's income going to taxpayers within the income bracket of the top one percent of income recipients increased. But, at the same time, the average income of taxpayers who were in the top one percent in 1996 actually went ***down*** by 2005. While it might seem at first that both sets of data cannot be true at the same time, what enables them to be true is that large numbers of individuals ***move*** from one income bracket to another. The average income of taxpayers who were in the bottom 20 percent in 1996 ***rose*** 91 percent by 2005, while the average income of taxpayers who were in the top one percent in 1996 ***fell*** by 26 percent over the same span of time. Obviously, changes of this magnitude move many people from one income bracket to another, so that the growing income disparities between these brackets do not coincide with growing income disparities between actual flesh-and-blood individuals.

The common practice of referring to what is happening to the incomes of "the rich" and "the poor" over time produces many fallacies, not only because of the confusion between income and wealth, but more fundamentally because the same individuals can be in both categories— "rich" and "poor"— at different stages of their lives. A study at the University of Michigan showed that more than three-quarters of all the people who were actively in the labor force, and who were in the bottom 20 percent of income earners in 1975, were also in the ***top*** 40 percent of income earners at some point over the next 16 years. The turnover of individuals has been especially high in the highest income brackets. Internal Revenue Service data on the 400 highest income tax payers show that between 1992 and 2000, only one-fourth were in that category more than one year, and only 13 percent were among the top 400 more than two years. In other words, most of the people who were in the top 400 in income were in that category just one year. Between 1992 and 2000, there were thousands of people in the top 400, because of the high turnover during that period.

Crime as an Occupation

Perhaps the freest of all occupations is that of the career criminal, who simply ignores the restrictions that the law attempts to impose. Probably few, if any, people go through their entire lives without violating some law, but while many crimes may be committed by people in a moment of passion or a moment when temptations overcome both morality and logic, the person whose whole livelihood depends on the continuing commission of crimes is a very different phenomenon. Various studies over the years have shown that a very small percentage of the population commits a very large percentage of all crimes. Moreover, this has been true in country after country, as noted by one of the leading scholars on crime, James Q. Wilson:

> In studies both here and abroad it has been established that about 6 percent of the boys of a given age will commit half or more of all the serious crime produced by all boys of that age. Allowing for measurement errors, it is remarkable how consistent this formula is— 6 percent causes 50 percent. It is roughly true in places as different as Philadelphia; London; Racine; and Orange County, California.

Very similar patterns have been found for adult criminals.

Criminals are not a random sample of the population at large. They are typically younger on average than the general population, disproportionately male and, at least among those caught and convicted, have lower than average IQs. Nor can we assume that criminals as a whole have much higher IQs than those who are caught, since most of the serious crime committed is accounted for by those who pass through the criminal justice system, and there is not enough additional serious crime unaccounted for to indicate a large number of additional criminals. However, the career criminal cannot simply be dismissed as irrational, because there is too much evidence from too many countries that he is indeed quite rational. It is easy enough to say that "crime does not pay," but the real question is: Does not pay whom— and compared to what? It is doubtful whether Bill Gates could have done nearly as well financially as he has by becoming a burglar or even a hit man for organized crime, but those who do pursue these criminal occupations are unlikely to have had the same alternatives available that Bill Gates had because of his particular talents and circumstances.

Given the low educational and IQ levels of many who become career criminals, crime may well be their best-paying option. Given the short time horizons of many of those who make crime their occupation— especially young people and people from lower social classes— such things as selling illegal drugs may seem lucrative in stage one, whether or not it leads to prison in stage two or perhaps never living to see stage two. Crime is one of those occupations, like sports and entertainment, in which a relatively few at the top achieve very high incomes, while most of those who enter the occupation receive very low incomes. For example, many ordinary young sellers of drugs on the street live at home with their mothers, often in public housing projects— clearly not an indication of affluence— while the lavish lifestyles of drug kingpins attract many young people into this occupation, in hopes of rising to that level.

Again, the rationality of the choices being made depends on the alternatives available. Someone with a bad record in school, and perhaps an arrest record, is likely to have very limited options in the legitimate job market. Even someone with a clean record may be prevented from earning some much-needed money by child labor laws or by minimum wage laws that set a pay scale higher than an inexperienced teenager would be worth. But crime is an occupation that is always open to everyone.

The rationality of the career criminal is demonstrated in many ways, including variations in the amount and kinds of crime committed as the costs of committing those particular crimes vary. These costs include not only the legal penalties but also the dangers faced by criminals from their potential victims. For example, burglary rates tend to be affected by the proportion of homeowners who have guns in their homes. The rate of burglary is not only much higher in Britain than in the United States— nearly twice as high— British burglars are far less likely than American burglars to "case" the premises before entering, in order to make sure that no one is home. Even if someone is at home in Britain, there is far less danger that the person at home will have a firearm, given the far more strict British gun control laws. Moreover, people convicted of burglary are treated more leniently in Britain, seldom going to jail.

British and American burglars are both behaving rationally, given the respective circumstances in which they operate and consequently the different dangers which they face. While only 13 percent of burglaries in the United States occur while the home is occupied, more than 40 percent of the burglaries in Britain, the Netherlands, and Canada occur while the home is occupied. These latter three countries have much lower incidences of gun ownership than the United States, due to more severe gun control laws. After the Atlanta suburb of Kennesaw passed an ordinance requiring heads of households to keep a firearm in their homes, residential burglaries there dropped by 89 percent.

Another major cost to a criminal career is the danger of incurring legal penalties, usually imprisonment. Here criminal activity in general has tended to vary over time inversely with the risk of imprisonment— which includes the risk of detection, conviction, and sentencing. In the United States, various legal reforms of the 1960s had the net effect of reducing the likelihood that anyone committing a given crime would actually spend time behind bars as a result. Crime rates skyrocketed. The murder rate, for example, was twice as high in 1974 as in 1961, and between 1960 and 1976 an average citizen's chance of becoming a victim of some major violent crime tripled.

Data from other countries show similar trends. On a graph showing the rate of crime in Australia from 1964 to 1999 and the rate of imprisonment per 1,000 crimes committed over that same span, the two lines are virtually mirror-images of one another, with the rate of crime going up when the rate of imprisonment went down, and vice versa. The graphs for England and

Wales, New Zealand, and the United States are very similar. In the United States, the crime rate peaked in the 1980s and began falling as the rate of incarceration rose. In England and Wales, the crime rate peaked in the early 1990s— which is when the rate of imprisonment hit bottom— and then began a substantial decline as the rate of imprisonment rose. In New Zealand, the high point in crime was reached in the early 1990s while the low point in incarceration was reached about 1985 and then began to rise again, with the crime rate falling with a lag of a few years.

Another example of the rationality of criminals is their response to the unusual American institution of the private bail bondsman, a system used by only one other country, the Philippines, once an American colony. In the United States, indicted criminals can pay a bail bondsman to post a bond in their behalf to guarantee their appearance in court on their trial date, so that they can stay out of jail pending trial. Typically, the charge is about ten percent of the total bail posted, all of which is returned to the bail bondsman when the client shows up for trial as scheduled.

When the client fails to show up, however, the bail bondsman forfeits the bail unless he can find the client and turn him over to the court within a short specified time. The bail bondsmen— sometimes called "bounty hunters"— are authorized to go capture those who do not show up in court. The rationality of the criminal is shown by the fact that the rate of court appearances is higher when a bail bondsman is used than when criminal defendants are released pending trial in other ways. Because a bail bondsman has a vested interest in a particular individual, he is more likely than the police to focus on capturing him and is less likely to be inhibited in his methods of doing so. Criminals, being aware of this, are quite rational to show up for trial.

The same rationality among criminals is shown in other ways and in other countries. In pre-World War II Britain, for example, when both criminals and the police rarely carried firearms, even an accomplice to a firearms murder was subject to hanging. Therefore criminals planning a robbery together would frisk one another, to make sure no one was carrying a gun that could get all the others hanged if there was a killing and they were caught. That was a very rational thing to do under the circumstances.

While the amount and nature of crimes have varied with the likelihood of punishment, this is not to say that crime rates are unaffected by cultural or other differences among countries. There are serious cultural differences which are no doubt reflected in the ***absolute*** levels of crime among countries, though the similarity in ***trends*** already noted is very striking. As one example of substantial differences between countries in the absolute levels of crime, despite similarities in trends, in the nineteenth century guns were freely available in both London and New York City, and yet the murder rate in New York was several times what it was in London.

Early in the twentieth century, severe gun control laws were passed in New York State, years before such laws were imposed in England— and yet New York City continued to have several times as high a murder rate as London, as it has for two centuries. Clearly it was not such laws, or the absence of such laws, which made the difference. Eventually, Britain's gun control laws were tightened far more than those in the United States, especially after the Second World War. However, because New York's murder rate continued to be far higher than that in London, and that in the United States far higher than that in Britain, this differential was often attributed to differences in gun control laws, even though large differences in murder rates existed long before either country had gun control laws, and persisted even when the United States had gun control laws before Britain did.

While there are undoubtedly many complex factors behind the absolute crime rates in any country, the trends strongly suggest that ***changes*** in crime rates reflect rational reactions to changes by criminals in the costs they pay, both in punishment inflicted by the law enforcement system and the risks of being harmed by their intended victims. The asymmetrical effects of gun control laws on criminals and law-abiding citizens have been reflected in the fact that, as gun-control laws tightened in late twentieth century Britain, rates of murder and armed robbery increased, which is consistent with the fact that such criminal activities became safer when there was more assurance that potential victims were unarmed.

With criminal economic activities, as with legal economic activities, behavior differs when there is free competition in a given field as compared to monopolistic control of that field. With both legal and illegal activities, there tends to be more production with competition than with monopoly. That is, the incentives and constraints tend to lead to more crime being committed when the criminals are individual independent operators than when they are part of an organized crime syndicate. For example, a small-time criminal may find it expedient to kill some local store owner for the small amount of money in the store's cash register, if only to keep the store owner from identifying him, even though this might make no sense to organized crime.

Public outrage at such a murder could result in more law enforcement activity in the area, reducing the profitability of the crime syndicate's business in illegal drugs, prostitution, and other activities by making local customers more hesitant to engage in such activities when there was an unusually large police presence in their neighborhoods. This could easily cost the crime syndicate far more money than there was in the store owner's cash register.[4] Such repercussions can be largely ignored by individual criminals operating independently, since the killer of the store owner may lose little from the increased law enforcement, compared to what criminals as a whole are losing in that area. However, when the criminals in a given area are more likely to belong to a crime syndicate, their activities are restrained by organized crime leaders who have to take wider repercussions into account.

In other words, the monopolistic firm has incentives to produce less than competitive firms would have produced in the same industry, just as with legal economic activity. In this case, that means producing less crime.

---

[4] As with a conventional legal business, a crime syndicate will not produce beyond the point where the incremental gain in revenue is exceeded by the incremental cost. In this case, the incremental costs include the loss of revenue when there is increased law enforcement activity in response to a killing of an innocent civilian, as compared to the public's lesser concern when mobsters kill each other.

When there is strong organized crime control of a given neighborhood, even independent criminals operating in that neighborhood have to take into account whether some of the things that they would do otherwise might displease organized crime leaders and bring retribution.[5] In some cases, independent criminals may have to split their earnings with the syndicate for permission to operate, thereby reducing the rewards of crime and the incentives for being an independent career criminal.

One of the more dramatic examples of the restraining effects of a crime syndicate occurred in New York City in the 1930s, when crusading federal prosecutor Thomas E. Dewey was cracking down dramatically on organized crime, costing the crime syndicates considerable money and sending many of their members to prison. Crime boss Dutch Schultz thought that Dewey should be killed but other crime syndicate leaders decided that this would provoke too much public outrage— and consequently increased law enforcement activity that would discourage patrons of their prostitution, gambling, and other illegal activities, further reducing incomes from these enterprises. When Dutch Schultz announced that he was going to kill Dewey anyway, the syndicate had Schultz assassinated instead. They were well aware that the killing of a mobster would provoke far less public reaction than the assassination of a popular law enforcement official.

Decades later, there was a report of a desire of some crime leaders to assassinate Rudolph Giuliani when he was a federal prosecutor who sent many mobsters to prison in the 1980s. But, if so, no one repeated the mistake of Dutch Schultz. As the *New York Times* reported:

> For one thing, assassinating a prosecutor would go against decades of tradition. American Mafia leaders have generally treated their organizations as businesses primarily concerned with making money. Killing law enforcement officials, in this view, would only draw unwanted scrutiny.

---

[5] Many years ago, I lived in a New York neighborhood where organized crime leaders lived. That neighborhood was so safe that, when my wife happened to be awake in the middle of the night while I was asleep, she did not hesitate to walk several blocks to an all-night newsstand to buy a morning paper. The fact that a newsstand was open in the middle of the night suggests that many other people in that neighborhood also felt safe going there at that time.

The same reasoning that would lead us to prefer competitive producers, when what is being produced is what people want, would lead us to prefer monopolistic producers— organized crime— when what is being produced is an activity that most people do not want. Ideally, we would prefer that no crime at all be produced but, since the ideal is seldom realized, a more realistic goal is the optimum quantity of crime. Both law enforcement and organized crime tend to reduce the total amount of crime. Even if it were possible to reduce all crime to zero by providing vastly more resources to law enforcement agencies, that would not necessarily be economically optimal. While most citizens would probably welcome more government expenditures on crime control if that in fact reduced felonies, no one would be likely to be willing to spend half the country's income— that is, reduce the standard of living in half— to prevent occasional shoplifting.

UNFREE LABOR

Involuntary labor can range from jury duty to military draftees to inmates of forced labor camps to outright chattel slavery, in which people are bought and sold like cattle.

The power of American courts to force citizens to serve on juries has even been used to send out law enforcement officers to seize customers at random in shopping centers, taking them directly to court to fill in as jurors, when there have been inadequate numbers of jurors on hand to conduct trials. While this is an extreme example, it demonstrates the government's power to compel involuntary labor. According to a news item in the ***Wall Street Journal***:

> Michael Kanz was pushing a grocery cart toward the checkout lane at the Wal-Mart Supercenter here when a woman wearing a gun walked up and told him to follow her orders— or face the consequences.
>
> It wasn't a mugging, but a jury summons to report to court within an hour. And it's a perfectly legal way some judges have in recent years been getting jurors at the last minute.

The various categories of involuntary labor differ not only in duration but also in severity. Jurors do not usually serve as long as military draftees, and inmates of forced labor camps may serve for years but not necessarily for a lifetime, as slaves usually did. The severity of treatment also varies, being more severe for draftees than for jurors, and often more severe for inmates of government-run forced labor camps than for privately owned slaves, whose long-term productivity would be jeopardized by very severe treatment. But, because people in forced labor camps are not owned by anyone, their long-term productivity matters less— if at all— to the decision-makers directly in charge of them, who have no incentive to think beyond stage one.

Productivity of Involuntary Labor

In some forced labor camps, especially those run by the Nazis and the Japanese during World War II, the inmates were often simply worked literally to death. The same was true of most Chinese indentured servants sent to Cuba in the nineteenth century. In both cases, as well as in the Soviet Gulags of the twentieth century, total control and an absence of individual ownership meant that the long-run productivity of these workers meant nothing to those in charge of them, who had no incentive to think beyond stage one. It was much the same story in North Africa in the sixteenth and seventeenth centuries, when at least a million Europeans were enslaved along the Barbary Coast. The worst treated were the galley slaves owned by the governments of that region to row their warships. Slaves who died on board or who collapsed from the heavy work and brutal treatment were simply thrown overboard at sea to lighten the vessels. The years of potential labor left in a galley slave who collapsed meant nothing to those in charge of the galley, who had no incentive to think beyond stage one.

Only where privately owned slaves were very cheap and easily replaced were they likely to be worked at a literally killing pace or subjected to dangerous working conditions. Where they were expensive and not easily replaced, as in the American antebellum South, the need to preserve the existing slaves often led their owners to hire Irish immigrants to do work considered too dangerous for slaves. During Frederick Law Olmsted's celebrated travels through the antebellum South, he was puzzled to see black slaves throwing 500-pound bales of cotton down an incline to Irish workers who were at the bottom, catching these bales and loading them onto a boat. When Olmsted asked about this surprising racial division of labor, he was told that slaves "are worth too much to be risked here; if the Paddies are knocked overboard, or get their backs broke, nobody loses anything!"

It was likewise common to use the Irish for other work considered too dangerous for slaves, such as draining swamps that might be malarial, building levees that might collapse on the workmen, building railroads, or tending steam boilers that might blow up.

How does involuntary labor in general affect the allocation of scarce resources which have alternative uses— and therefore the economic well-being of the country as a whole? Because involuntary labor, by definition, does not have to be paid a price reflecting the value of the alternative uses of the workers' time and capabilities, such labor is often used for work that is less valuable than alternative uses. A chemist may be drafted into the army and then used as a clerk handling clothing supplies in the quartermaster corps. But, in an all-volunteer army, it would be cheaper for the military authorities to hire a civilian to perform such clerical duties than to pay enough to attract chemists or other highly skilled people to do this routine work.

If military personnel were used for such work in a volunteer army, these would more likely be individuals whose civilian skill levels were low enough that the army could attract them at considerably lower pay than would be required to attract people like chemists. Such financial considerations taken into account by military authorities would reflect more fundamental underlying realities from the standpoint of the economy as a whole: Involuntary labor is a less efficient way to allocate scarce resources which have alternative uses.

People summoned to jury duty may have great amounts of their time wasted waiting around to be told whether they will in fact be seated as jurors for pending cases on a given day or ordered to keep coming back on subsequent days until their tour of jury duty expired. Moreover, what they are paid is usually far below what they earn in their regular occupations. More fundamentally, they may sit on cases whose importance to the larger society may be less than the value of what they would be contributing otherwise in their regular lines of work. Such considerations tend to lead people in higher paid professions to seek to avoid jury duty by utilizing whatever exemptions or excuses may be available, while retirees or people in lower-level occupations may find jury duty less of a burden, and perhaps more interesting than alternative uses of their time.

As with the service of military draftees, the cost of involuntary labor to decision-making authorities understates its cost to the economy as a whole, and thereby results in misallocation of scarce resources. In the case of juries, the lesser likelihood of people from higher occupations ending up serving as jurors can also reduce the quality of jury decisions, to the detriment of justice. With the cost of justice, as with the cost of crime, the cost to the government is too often confused with the cost to society. In both cases, government officials are preoccupied with minimizing the cost to the government, which grossly understates the cost to society at large.

Forced Labor Camps

One of the largest and longest lasting systems of involuntary labor in the twentieth century was that of the forced labor camps— the Gulags— in the Soviet Union. As of 1949, for example, there were well over 2 million prisoners in Soviet forced labor camps. Because of turnover, due both to releases and incarceration of new prisoners, as well as substantial numbers of deaths within the Gulags, the total number of forced laborers over a period of decades was many times that.

Both inhumanity and inefficiency were hallmarks of these camps. Deaths averaged more than 50,000 prisoners per month in the particularly bad year of 1942, from a combination of overwork, malnutrition, mistreatment and harsh climatic conditions with inadequate clothing. During the war years as a whole, more than 2 million people died in Soviet prison camps. Despite the long hours of work and inadequate food, clothing, housing, and medical care that contributed to staggering death rates, the forced labor of the inmates still did not cover the costs of the Gulags. Shortly after Stalin's death, the head of the Soviet secret police— hardly a humanitarian— began closing the camps down for economic reasons. Those who ran the Gulags had unbridled power over the inmates but did not own them or their output as property, so they had no incentives to be efficient. As a Soviet official described it:

> As a rule, the plans are unrealistic; the requests for workers exceed that required for the plan severalfold, but the Gulag grants these requests, that is, in other words, the branch administrations do not value their workforce; they believe that, since the Gulag is right there with a ready reserve of workers, they can be wasteful with the workforce, to use it at any time and in any way they wish.

Because of the sheer size and scope of the Gulag system, it made huge contributions to various parts of the Soviet economy, but usually at far higher costs than those of comparable enterprises in the general economy. In its heyday, forced labor in the Soviet Union produced one-fourth of all the country's timber, 40 percent of its cobalt, 60 percent of its gold and 76 percent of its tin. Forced labor also produced coal, oil, and gas, and built many canals and even apartment buildings in Moscow, among many other economic activities. But just the purely economic costs— quite aside from the staggering human costs— were typically higher than the cost of doing the same things outside the Gulags. For example, the cost of producing bricks in a facility with forced labor was more than double the cost of producing them in a nearby Soviet brick factory. In addition, the Gulags were "notoriously reckless in their use of natural resources," according to a scholar at the Russian Academy of Sciences in Moscow. All of this was consistent with the incentives and constraints facing them, however much it violated both economic and humanitarian principles.

With the opening of the government's secret archives in the last years of the Soviet Union, the extent of the inefficiencies of forced labor were more fully revealed. The building of railroads was an example:

> By 1938 the length of railroads on which construction had started but had been suspended was approaching 5,000 km (not counting railroads that had been completed but were unused or partly used because they

were unneeded). Meanwhile, the total increase in the USSR's railroad system between 1933 and 1939 amounted to a mere 4,500 km. A considerable portion of the "dead railroads" was built at the cost of many prisoners' lives.

Slavery

Slavery has existed on every inhabited continent and among people of every race for thousands of years. The very word "slave" derives from the word for Slav, not only in the English language but also in some other European languages and in Arabic. That is because so many Slavs were enslaved for centuries before the first African was brought to the Western Hemisphere in bondage. More than a million Europeans from various countries were enslaved and taken to North Africa's Barbary Coast alone from 1500 to 1800. That is more than the number of Africans brought in bondage to the United States and to the 13 American colonies from which it was formed. Nor was the Barbary Coast unique in having European slaves, who were common in the Ottoman Empire, as well as in Europe itself in earlier centuries. Slavery was equally common among Asians who enslaved other Asians, as Polynesians enslaved other Polynesians and as the indigenous peoples of the Western Hemisphere enslaved other indigenous peoples of the Western Hemisphere.

The roles played by slaves have covered an enormous spectrum. Some were used as human sacrifices by the Aztecs of Central America or in Indonesia or in parts of Africa, among other places. In the Roman Empire, some slaves were forced to fight each other to the death as gladiators, for the entertainment of crowds in the Coliseum. After Europeans took over the Western Hemisphere, most African slaves brought there were used for routine manual labor, such as growing sugar cane in tropical countries or cotton in the American antebellum South. Yet, in various parts of the world and in various periods of history, slave roles have ranged all the way up to that of imperial viceroys and commanders of armies in the Ottoman Empire.

As a general pattern, the more highly skilled, the more intellectually demanding, and the more responsible the roles filled by slaves, the less they were treated with the brutality and contempt inflicted on slaves doing arduous manual labor. In short, although freedom and slavery are a stark contrast in principle, in practice there were degrees of slavery. In countries around the world, slaves who were domestic servants tended to be treated better than those who were field hands, manual laborers, or in earlier centuries, galley slaves. Those in higher level occupations tended to be less and less treated as slaves, while for some at the highest levels their bondage was nominal.

Slaves used as divers in the Carolina swamps, for example, had to exercise skill and discretion, and were accordingly treated differently from plantation slaves, being rewarded with both financial incentives and with greater personal freedom on and off the job. Similarly with slaves in lumbering operations or the processing of tobacco, which likewise required skill and discretion. In one remarkable case, a slave was made captain of a river boat in the antebellum South, with a crew of both black and white sailors under his command. These more responsible jobs often also offered more opportunities for escape, which in turn meant that severe treatment of such slaves would have been counterproductive, and was therefore much less common than on plantations where slaves performed routine manual labor.

Urban slaves in general were also treated less harshly for the same reason and Frederick Douglass described the typical urban slave in the antebellum South as "almost a free citizen." But being ***almost*** free was not the same as being free. Some, like Douglass himself, decided to become fully free citizens by escaping. While permanent escape from a slave plantation was very rare— perhaps two percent of the slaves made good their escapes without being recaptured— escapes by urban slaves were far more often permanently successful. Slaveowners who thought beyond stage one had to take into account the increased possibilities of escape. Obviously, the increased value of the work of urban slaves had to be great enough to cover these additional costs and risks.

These modifications of slavery implicitly recognized the inefficiencies of pure unmitigated force. For routine work that was easily monitored, such as growing sugar cane or cotton in the Western Hemisphere, or rowing as galley slaves in earlier times, slavery could extract the necessary efforts under the threat of the lash. But for anything requiring judgment, initiative, and talent, other incentives must be invoked, simply because it is hard for someone else to know how much potential for judgment, initiative, or talent any given individual has. Economic and other rewards cause the individual to reveal those qualities in exchange for being treated less like a slave and rewarded in other ways. The implications of this reach beyond slavery, for concessions to slaves are a clear demonstration of the limitations of what can be accomplished by power alone, whether under slavery, totalitarianism or other institutions.[6]

Where slave populations were large enough to have a serious potential for social disruption and danger to the lives of the free population, the need to minimize such dangers limited the extent to which the slave population could be educated for higher roles, since such education could also facilitate organized disruptions, individual escapes, and coordinated uprisings among the enslaved people. Therefore educating slaves was forbidden by law throughout the Western Hemisphere in post-Columbian times. From an economic standpoint, this meant that, in addition to inefficiencies in using people of a given capability, slavery also limited the capabilities that could be developed among people of a given potential. Put differently, freedom has not only personal and political benefits, but economic benefits as well.

Markets for Involuntary Labor

The wasteful use of unowned involuntary labor can be contrasted with the more careful allocation of involuntary labor that is owned and sold, since

---

[6] Modern dictators with similar arbitrary powers, including the power of life and death, over millions of people have sometimes ignored these limitations on what could be accomplished by power alone, to the detriment of their countries and sometimes to themselves. For example, Stalin's draconian edicts paralyzed economic innovation among the managers of Soviet enterprises, who found the rewards of successful innovation no compensation for the risk of imprisonment or death if an innovation failed, for Stalin could treat failure the same as treason. This extreme caution about taking on the risks of innovation became an ingrained habit that outlived Stalin. A later Soviet premier, Leonid Brezhnev, said that Soviet managers shied away from innovation "as the devil shies away from incense." Joint Economic Committee, Congress of the United States, ***Soviet Economy in a New Perspective***, 1976, p. 437.

both buyer and seller in free market economies have financial incentives to weigh the productivity of the labor in alternative uses. Moreover, the desire of those held involuntarily to be free imposes costs to keeping them in bondage, and these costs must be deducted from whatever gains their owners receive from their involuntary labor.

Slaves are not the only involuntary labor that is bought and sold. The services of German mercenaries, such as those who were used by the British in their attempt to suppress the American revolution, were sold or rented collectively by heads of the various German principalities of the time, who treated these soldiers as if they were property. Serfs were bought and sold as part of the land traded among medieval European landowners. Prison labor has been used by both government organizations and private individuals in the United States, well into the twentieth century.

Much of the white population of seventeenth-century colonial America— more than half in colonies south of New England— arrived as indentured servants, sometimes having contracted individually to work a specified number of years for those who had paid their passage across the Atlantic, and more often having indentured themselves to the owners of the ships that brought them to America, so that the captains of these ships then auctioned them off after reaching land, much as slaves were auctioned. Another variation on these arrangements was that the passengers would pay as much of the fare as they could and would then depend on family or friends to pay the rest when they arrived in America— failing which, they would then be auctioned off with other indentured servants to cover the unpaid portion of their fare.

Indentured labor was common in the Caribbean as well as in the American colonies and continued to be an important source of labor from India and China to various parts of the world, well into the nineteenth century. In the quarter century beginning in 1849, approximately 90,000 Chinese indentured laborers were shipped from China to Peru alone. Another 125,000 were shipped from China to Cuba during the period from 1847 to 1874. Most of the Chinese shipped to these countries never saw

China again and the brutal conditions of their labor in Cuba were such that most died before completing the eight years of their labor contracts.

Things were not much better in Peru, where guards were posted to prevent suicide among the Chinese shovelling bird manure into sacks for export as fertilizer, under conditions of stifling heat and stench. Suicides were common, beginning in the holding pens back in Macao, where some of these prisoners were seen "dripping with blood" as a result of punishments meted out to them. The suicides continued during the months-long voyages across the Pacific. Many of these Chinese had been tricked, drugged, or otherwise forced into these indentures— as had also been true of many seventeenth-century Britons, including children, who were brought to the Western Hemisphere involuntarily.

Indentured laborers and other forms of contract labor were usually a result of initially free choices, however, even if their subsequent assignments to individual purchasers or to particular tasks were no longer a matter of individual free choice on their part. The Portuguese trade in indentured— often coerced— labor from China was, fortunately, exceptional. Many, if not most, of the millions of emigrants from India to various parts of the world in the nineteenth century left as indentured laborers under contract. The fact that they not only completed these contracts but often renewed their contracts, either immediately or after returning to India for a sojourn, suggests that their treatment, though usually far from ideal, was not under such desperate conditions as to lead to suicides on a large scale or even to abandoning the role of indentured laborer.

Most of the elements of choice open to most indentured workers were lacking in the markets for slaves, where the choices were entirely in the hands of the buyers and sellers. This did not mean that the choices made by slave traders and slave owners were unconstrained expressions of personal whims, because they were constrained by economic considerations in general and by supply and demand in particular.

Costs of Enslavement

Costs are crucially involved in the very choice of whom to enslave in the first place. It is obviously more costly to try to enslave people who have the army and navy of a major nation around them— costly not only in terms of the money and lives expended trying to capture such people, but costly also in the risk of provoking retaliatory military action against the country that launched the slave raids. Broadly speaking, such costs defined those whom it was economically feasible to enslave and those whose costs of capture were prohibitively expensive. From the demand side, there must also be a sufficiently valued use for slaves to cover the costs of even moderately costly enslavement.

In some times and places, slaves were a by-product of military actions undertaken for other purposes. In ancient times, especially, captured enemy soldiers could be killed, sold back to their country for ransom, sold in slave markets elsewhere, or kept as slaves for use by those who captured them. Here it is not feasible to calculate the separate cost of capturing such slaves, since the costs of military operations were paid for other reasons and had other objectives and consequences. However, campaigns specifically undertaken to capture and enslave other people were more clearly constrained by costs. Moreover, these costs did not remain constant over time. Where small, scattered, tribal societies evolved into larger and more powerful states, the peoples within such societies became less and less likely to be targets of enslavement, as the costs of slave raids rose.

Since some societies evolved in this way and others did not, or evolved more slowly for one reason or another, those peoples likely to be enslaved changed over the centuries. In ancient times, when Britain was a primitive island, fragmented into tribal regions, Julius Caesar raided Britain and brought British slaves back to Rome but, in later centuries, after Britain had a government, an army and a navy, it would be too costly a place to raid for the sake of capturing slaves. However, many parts of the world were more difficult to consolidate into large states, sometimes because of geographic factors creating isolation in mountainous regions or on small islands spread across a vast sea. These more vulnerable regions remained major sources of slaves, whether in Europe, Asia, Africa, the Polynesian islands or the Western Hemisphere.

One such area was the Balkans, which is why its Slavic inhabitants were enslaved on a large scale, long before Africans were brought to the Western Hemisphere and called by the name "slave" derived from their Slavic predecessors in bondage. People were enslaved where the cost of enslaving them was less. For centuries that usually meant that Europeans enslaved other Europeans, Asians enslaved other Asians, Africans enslaved other Africans, and the indigenous peoples of the Western Hemisphere enslaved other indigenous peoples of the Western Hemisphere. Only in relatively recent centuries, as local sources of supply of slaves dried up with the consolidation of nation-states, and as growing wealth enabled people to be enslaved at greater distances and transported far away, did Africa become the principal source of supply of slaves for Europeans who transported them across the Atlantic.

Slave Prices

Even slaves destined for lowly manual labor were not simply labor but also represented human capital. Thus a slave in the American antebellum South cost about thirty times what a slave cost on the coast of Africa, and not all of that was due to transportation costs or even to an allowance for those who died en route. At a minimum, a slave in the United States had to be able to understand the English language. He also had to understand a new work routine, new work implements, and a living pattern different from those in Africa. The whole process of making these adjustments and acquiring various forms of human capital was known as "seasoning" and it often took place in the Caribbean before slaves were sold on the American mainland. Subsequent generations of slave descendants, raised in the new setting, would likewise command higher prices than someone new from Africa, for the same reasons.

In addition to this more or less general human capital, some slaves possessed such specific skills as carpentry or animal husbandry, and these commanded a still higher price. In the Ottoman Empire, eunuchs were in great demand to work in the harems of the wealthy and, because most of the slaves who were castrated died as a result, the price of the survivors had to cover all the costs incurred capturing and transporting those who did not survive, so eunuchs were the highest priced slaves of all. Slave prices also varied with the distance from the source, so that slaves in the United States— the most distant of the Western Hemisphere societies holding slaves from Africa— had higher prices than those in Brazil, which was closest to Africa.

One consequence of this difference in prices was that the slave population in Brazil never reproduced itself, but was replenished with new arrivals from Africa, while the slave population in the American South began reproducing themselves and increasing in size as early as colonial times. That was because Brazilian slaveowners found it cheaper to get new slaves from Africa than to raise a new generation from the existing slave population. Thus, in Brazil, there was not only an overwhelmingly male slave population, but also a separation of the sexes, and such slave women as became pregnant were not given as much time off, or sufficiently lighter work, to enable them to ensure the survival of their offspring. In the American South, where the cost of slaves was higher, it paid the slaveowners to have slaves live in families and to lighten the chores of pregnant women to the extent necessary for them to bear and raise the next generation, who represented capital assets to the slaveowners. The American South therefore became one of the few slave societies in the Western Hemisphere where the slave population reproduced itself at a level sufficient to replace existing generations.

The magnitude of the difference made by these different prices, and the different treatment resulting from them, may be indicated by the fact that over the years Brazil imported several times more slaves from Africa than the United States did, but the resident slave population in the United States was larger than that in Brazil. Even a small group of islands like the West Indies imported more slaves than the United States, despite the fact that the resident slave population in the United States was the largest in the hemisphere. Another example of the effect of economic incentives was in the treatment of slaves on plantations where the slaveowner was in residence, as distinguished from their treatment on plantations run by an overseer serving an absentee owner.

Incentives and Constraints

Overseers tended to be paid by immediate results, such as the output of sugar in the tropics or cotton in the American South. Therefore the overseer had little incentive to think beyond stage one. Special care for pregnant women or the spending of plantation resources on the raising of children who were not yet old enough to produce enough output to cover their upkeep was therefore not something that overseers serving absentee owners had an incentive to do. Even for able-bodied men, the overseer serving an absentee owner had incentives to work them at a pace that would maximize output during his tenure, even if this wore them out at an early age and left them less productive in later life. It was the same story when it came to maintenance and repairs on the plantation or the care of animals or the soil.

In all these ways, plantations with resident owners tended to operate more efficiently in long-run terms— with the people, the animals, the soil, and the structures and equipment better maintained, even if that meant somewhat less current output than if everything were sacrificed for the sake of immediate production. Most plantations in the American South had resident owners, who could see to it that overseers did not sacrifice the owners' long-run interests to the overseers' immediate interest in getting paid for maximum output and getting a reputation for "results" that would serve as an overseer's capital asset in finding his next job. In the West Indies, however, it was more common for the plantation owners to live in Britain, leaving resident overseers a far freer hand in making decisions. One consequence was that the infant mortality rate among slave women in the West Indies was some multiple of what it was among slave women in the American South.

Slaves and Wealth

In many parts of the world, slaves were bought for their ability to produce wealth that could be appropriated by the slaveowners. Elsewhere, however, especially in parts of the Middle East, slaveowners often had large numbers of slaves as a sign of the wealth they already possessed. These slaves served as personal servants, concubines, entertainers, or providers of other amenities— and were consumers, rather than producers, of wealth. In other kinds of societies, such as those of the Western Hemisphere, where slaves were primarily used as producers of wealth, just how much wealth was actually produced by slavery as an economic system has been a matter of controversy among scholars.

That the slaveowners gained wealth in the Western Hemisphere seems clear but whether the whole society gained wealth, on net balance over the long run, is less clear. In Brazil and the United States, which had the two largest slave populations in the hemisphere, the regions of these countries where slavery was concentrated— northern Brazil and the southern United States— remained noticeably poorer during the era of slavery and for generations thereafter. The side effects of slavery were not negligible, especially in the United States, where the staggering economic and human costs of the Civil War seemed to fit Abraham Lincoln's premonition that the war might continue "until all the wealth piled by the bondman's two hundred and fifty years of unrequited toil shall be sunk, and until every drop of blood drawn with the lash, shall be paid by another drawn with the sword."

The Economics of Freedom

A given individual's value as a free worker was likely to be greater than that same person's value as a slave, because of the constraints inherent in keeping someone in bondage. Whole categories of work were usually off-limits to Western Hemisphere slaves, such as work requiring extensive travel alone, or work requiring the use of firearms, or the handling of large sums of money— all of which could facilitate escape. Education was also both an instrument and an incitement to freedom. Hence its ban for slaves throughout the Western Hemisphere. This, however, then limited still further the kind and quality of work that could be performed by slaves, even when the individuals were perfectly capable of performing these same functions as free workers.

It is a common principle in economics that assets tend to move through the market to their highest valued uses, since that is where the bidding for them will be highest. Accordingly, the economic value of a slave would be greatest to the slave himself, even aside from the value of freedom, as such. While others could own the economic value of a slave, only that individual could own his higher economic value as a free worker. Therefore an ideal free market would lead to slaves buying their own freedom, since they would have an incentive to outbid others on economic grounds alone, even aside from their desire for freedom.

Some slaves have in fact purchased their freedom in many places and times, whether in ancient Rome or centuries later in the Western Hemisphere. Even where slaves have had no money, or inadequate amounts of money, ways have been found to arrange self-purchase on credit, to be repaid on the instalment plan after achieving freedom. In those societies which gave legal recognition to property owned by slaves— the ***peculium***, as it was called in ancient Rome— slaves might in some circumstances earn and save enough over the years to purchase their own freedom for cash.

In other times and places, various individuals or organizations might advance the money to purchase freedom. During the centuries when Europeans were being enslaved on a large scale in the Islamic countries of North Africa and the Middle East, the Catholic Church established institutions to use the money collected in its individual churches for redeeming Christian captives and maintained emissaries in the countries where they were being held, in order to facilitate such transactions. North African pirates who raided the Mediterranean coasts of Europe to capture and enslave the inhabitants would sometimes return in a day or so to sell these captives back to their families. Otherwise, they could be ransomed later— at a higher price— after they had become slaves in North Africa. In the Western Hemisphere, brotherhoods of ex-slaves would sometimes advance the money required to purchase the freedom of someone who would later pay them back.

The practical institutional difficulties of purchasing freedom were not the only reasons why this procedure was not more widely used, which could have eroded the whole system of slavery. Where the political authorities did not want a large population of ex-slaves of a different race living among the free population, legal restrictions impeded manumission by purchase or grant. Such restrictions became increasingly severe in the American antebellum South during the decades leading up to the Civil War. Thus blacks who had acquired freedom, by purchase or otherwise, often owned other members of their own family as a legal formality, simply because the costs and difficulties of getting them official freedom papers were so great. Some Southern whites who did not believe in slavery, such as the Quakers, likewise often owned slaves as a legal formality, while it was an open secret that those slaves lived the lives of free people.

In short, the very need to pass laws to keep slavery from self-destructing piecemeal was further evidence of its economic deficiencies, quite aside from its violations of moral and humanitarian principles.

Chapter 3

The Economics of Medical Care

The high cost of medical care has been a recurrent theme in countries around the world. In the United States, medical expenses absorb about one-sixth of the total annual output of the economy. Medical care is one of many goods and services that can be provided in a wide variety of ways. At one time, it was common for sick people simply to pay doctors and buy medicine individually with their own money. Today, both the medicines and the medical care are often paid for by third parties through either political or market institutions— that is, either by insurance companies or government agencies, or both, with or without some portion being paid by the individual patient. Only 13 percent of Americans' medical care costs are paid for directly out of pocket, with 35 percent being paid by private health insurance, 17 percent by Medicare, and the rest from various other sources.

In some cases, medicines and medical care have both been provided by government at no charge to the patient in Canada and some other countries, as they once were in China under Mao Zedong and in the Soviet Union under Stalin. Other countries have had, and some continue to have, various mixtures of government payment and private payment, with varying elements of voluntary choice by patients and physicians.

Since governments get the resources used for medical care by taking those resources from the general population through taxation, there is no net reduction in the cost of maintaining health or curing sicknesses simply because the money is routed through political institutions and government bureaucracies, rather than being paid directly by patients to doctors. Clearly, however, the widespread popularity of government-financed medical care systems means that many people expect some net benefit from this process.

One reason is that governments typically do not simply pay whatever medical costs happen to be, as determined by supply and demand. Governments impose price controls, in order to try to keep the costs of medical care from absorbing so much of their budgets as to seriously restrict other government functions. Government-paid medical care is thus often an exercise in price control, and it creates situations that have been common for centuries in response to price controls on many other goods and services.

PRICE CONTROLS ON MEDICAL CARE

One of the reasons for the political popularity of price controls in general is that part of their costs are concealed— or, at least, are not visible initially when such laws are passed. Price controls are therefore particularly appealing to those who do not think beyond stage one— which can easily be a majority of the voters. Artificially lower prices, created by government order rather than by supply and demand, encourage more use of goods or services, while discouraging the production of those same goods and services. Increased consumption and reduced production mean a shortage. The consequences are both quantitative and qualitative.

Qualitative Consequences

Even the visible shortages that follow price controls do not tell the whole story. ***Quality*** deterioration often accompanies reduced production under price control, whether what is being produced is food, housing, or numerous other goods and services whose prices have been kept artificially low by government fiat. Quality declines because the incentives to maintaining quality are lessened by price control. Sellers in general maintain the quality of their products or services for fear of losing customers otherwise. But, when price controls create a situation where the amount demanded is greater than the amount supplied— a shortage— fear of losing customers is no longer as strong an incentive. For example, landlords typically reduce painting and repairs when there is rent control, because there is no need to fear vacancies when there are more tenants looking for apartments than there are apartments available.

Nowhere has quality deterioration been more apparent— or more dangerous— than with price controls on medical care. One way in which the quality of medical care deteriorates is in the amount of time that a doctor spends with a patient. This was most dramatically demonstrated back in the days of the Soviet Union, which had the most completely government-controlled medical system:

> At the neighborhood clinics where 80% of all patients are treated, the norms call for physicians to see eight patients an hour. That is 7.5 minutes per visit, and Soviet studies show that five minutes of each visit is spent on paper work, a task complicated by chronic short supplies of preprinted forms and the absence of computers.
>
> "Our heads spin from rushing," say Pavel, the silver-haired chief of traumatology at a Moscow clinic, who, like some other Russians interviewed for this article, won't give his last name. A dozen patients with splints and slings sit in a dark corridor awaiting their turn at a 1950s-vintage fluoroscope. "We wind up seeing the same patients several times over," the doctor goes on, "when one thorough examination could have solved the problem if we had the time."

Although the Soviet Union was an extreme example, similar policies have tended to produce similar results in other countries. Under government-paid medical care in Japan, patients also have shorter and more numerous visits than patients in the United States. Under a Korean medical care system copied from Japan, a study found that "even injections of drugs were often split in half to make two visits necessary," because "the doctor can charge for two office visits and two injection fees." After Canada's Quebec province created its own government health plan back in the 1970s, telephone consultations went down, office visits went up and the time per visit went down. In other words, medical conditions which neither the doctor nor the patient previously thought serious enough to require an office visit, before price controls, now took up more time by both the patient (in travel time) and the doctor (in the office), thereby reducing the time available to people who had more serious conditions.

In general, where the doctor is paid per patient visit, then a series of treatments that might have taken five visits to the doctor's office can now take ten shorter visits— or more. Therefore political leaders can proclaim that price controls have succeeded because the cost per visit is now lower than it was in a free market, even though the total costs of treating a given illness have not declined and— typically— have risen. Skyrocketing costs, far beyond anything projected at the outset, have marked government-controlled medical care systems in France, Britain, Canada and elsewhere. Responses to such runaway costs have included abbreviated doctors' visits and hospital stays cut short.

The costs in Britain's government-run medical system have increased sharply, both absolutely and as a percentage of the country's rising Gross Domestic Product. The National Health Service in Britain absorbed just under four percent of the country's GDP in 1960 and rose over the years until it absorbed seven percent of a larger GDP by 2000. Nevertheless, the number of doctors per capita in Britain was just half as many as in Germany, where half the hospital beds were still in private hands, despite a large role for government financing there.

Quality deterioration has many aspects. According to the British magazine ***The Economist***, "patients in other rich countries can get prompt treatment with state-of-the-art medical technologies in clean rather than dirty wards." Apparently not in Britain, where quality deterioration is part of the hidden cost that does not show up in statistics. Britain's Healthcare Commission "painted a bleak picture of teeming wards where overworked nurses didn't even help patients to the bathroom," according to the ***Christian Science Monitor***, which also noted that the country's Health Secretary "was forced to apologize in Parliament this week after it emerged that at least 90 patients in southeast England died as a result of infections picked up in the hospital."

Britain has one of the oldest government-run medical care systems in the world, so it is far beyond stage one in the emergence over time of the qualitative problems associated with price controls in other contexts. Its medical care bureaucracy has also had time to become more bureaucratic, including job protection for hospital staff members to the point where it is hard to force any employee to do the work properly— in a situation where not doing the job right can entail pain, infection or death to patients. The British newspaper the ***Daily Mail*** reported on some of the reasons behind the widely complained of lack of cleanliness in British hospitals:

> Unlike the 'modern matron,' her old-style predecessor exercised control over every nurse, cleaner and porter and she knew every patient under her care— because she understood that it *was* her care they were under and for which she was accountable.
>
> She ran her wards like a military exercise. Today, that is impossible because nurses find that approach anachronistic and unacceptable. The result is sloppiness, a culture of excuses, gross dereliction of managerial duty and patient infection.

Another British newspaper, the ***Evening Standard***, reported on the manager of the emergency treatment department in a London hospital:

> She spent only one fifth of her time with her patients.
>
> Cleaning and maintenance took up most of her energy, to very little effect. Despite all the meetings, she had no authority over her cleaner. If a patient vomited in the waiting room, she had to clean it up because the cleaner refused to touch it.

Among the other common characteristics of bureaucracy that are especially harmful in a medical setting are ever growing numbers of meetings and ever growing paperwork requirements, leaving patients waiting while their doctors and nurses perform bureaucratic chores and rituals. Another symptom of bureaucracy is pompous language, the country's Chief Medical Officer citing as a factor in the dangerous dirtiness of British hospitals a "paucity of hand hygiene agents"— that is, not enough soap and water. Such bureaucratic behavior is ***not*** simply irrational. Paperwork, meetings, the hiring of more bureaucrats and the appointment of committees and task forces all provide protective cover for the authorities if critics accuse them of not knowing about problems or not doing anything about them. While such things help protect the careers of medical care bureaucrats, the time and resources they use up tend to reduce the care of patients.

The United States is at the other end of the spectrum in terms of government control of medical care. Some fault medical care in the United States for an average American life expectancy that is exceeded in a number of other countries. However, ***medical care is not the same as health care***, even though the two are often equated. Many things that shorten human life—including homicide, drug overdoses and obesity— are more a result of individual choices rather than the state of medical care. There is relatively little that doctors can do about such things, which tend to be worse in the United States than in some other Western countries.

When international comparisons of ***medical*** care, as such, are made the United States usually ranks higher than countries with government-run medical systems on such things as waiting times to see primary care physicians, waiting times to see specialists or have surgery, and cancer survival rates. A study by the Organisation for Economic Co-operation and Development found that 23 percent of the patients having elective surgery in 2001 in Australia waited more than 4 months for that surgery. So did 26 percent of the patients in New Zealand, 27 percent of patients in Canada, and 38 percent of the patients in Britain. In the United States, only 5 percent of patients had to wait that long. The conclusion:

> Waiting lists for elective surgery generally tend to be found in countries which combine public health insurance, with zero or low patient cost sharing and constraints on surgical capacity. Public health insurance and zero cost sharing remove the financial barriers to access to surgery. Constraints on capacity prevent supply from matching demand. Under such circumstances, non-price rationing, in the form of waiting times for elective surgery, takes over from price rationing as a means of equilibrating demand and supply.

Elective surgery, incidentally, was not limited to cosmetic procedures but included cataract surgery, hip replacements and coronary artery bypass surgery. Moreover, although a four month waiting period was used by the OECD as a benchmark for collecting statistics, in Britain 3,592 patients waited more than six months for a colonoscopy and 55,376 waited more than six months for an audiology diagnosis, according to a report in the ***British Medical Journal*** in 2007. In Canada, according to a provincial government website, 90 percent of Ontario patients needing hip replacements waited 336 days. In Britain, the wait is a year. As for technology, a 2007 study by the Organisation for Economic Co-operation and Development (OECD) showed that the number of CT scanners per million population was 7.5 in Britain, 11.2 in Canada, and 32.2 in the United States. For Magnetic Resonance Imaging (MRI) units, there was an average of 5.4 MRIs per million population in Britain, 5.5 per million population in Canada and 26.6 per million population in the United States.

Quantitative Consequences

Just as artificially low housing prices have led many people to seek their own separate housing units who would not ordinarily do so, if they had to pay the full costs in a free market, so artificially less expensive— in some countries, free— medical care has led many people with minor medical problems to absorb far more of doctors' time and expensive medicines and treatments than they would if they had to pay the costs themselves. France is an example:

> In every healthy Frenchman hides a sick one dying to be diagnosed, goes a wry French saying. The trouble is that doctors are encouraged to give patients what they want— scans, blood tests, antibiotics, sick leave— for fear of losing their custom and thus earning less. If they don't overload prescriptions to counter every conceivable germ and depressive tendency, patients may shop around until they find a doctor who does.

This is not peculiar to the French people or to medical care. More of anything tends to be demanded at a lower price— and especially when it is free. In Canada as well, a news story pointed out: "Since the system sets no limits on demand, patients seek as much care as they can get, driving up costs." In Britain, a twelve-year-old girl received a breast implant, paid for by the National Health Service. Excessive prescriptions were reported as "routine" under China's government-provided medical care and patients there "leave the dispensary with bags, rather than bottles, full of pills."

China has subsequently moved away from government-provided medical care.

In Britain, the over-use of the government-run National Health Service extends beyond the British population, because the free medical treatment it provides attracts immigrants from around the world. These immigrants impose not only financial costs but also the biological costs of the diseases they bring, which can spread to the British population at large.

Doctors, as well as patients, have incentives to use medical treatments more extensively when the government pays the bills. Many diseases can be treated in a variety of ways, and how often the most expansive— and expensive— treatments will be used can be affected by who is paying. In October 2002, for example, the FBI seized the records of a Redding, California, cardiologist who was accused of doing far more open heart surgeries than were called for by medical criteria, as a means of receiving more income from government payments. One patient who was told by this cardiologist that he needed triple bypass surgery was told by every other cardiologist he consulted that he needed no such thing.

The normal weighing of costs against benefits, which causes more urgent things to be done ahead of less important things when prices ration scarce resources, is less effective when costs are paid by someone other than the actual decision-makers. This can lead to less important things receiving medical attention while urgent things get neglected. When patients pay for their own medical treatments, they are more apt to establish priorities, so that someone with a fractured leg is far more likely to go to a doctor than someone with a minor headache. But, when both are treated free of charge to the patient, then people with minor ailments may take up so much of doctors' time and medical resources that those with more serious medical conditions must be forced to wait.

When prices no longer ration, then something else has to ration, since the underlying scarcity does not go away just because the government controls prices or provides things free of charge to the users. One of the alternative ways of rationing is by waiting. While this is common with price controls on many things, waiting for medical care is a more serious problem. In 2001, more than 10,000 people in Britain had waited more than 15 months for surgery. In Canada, a 2004 study showed the median waiting time from receiving an appointment with a specialist to actually being treated was 15 weeks for ophthalmology and 24 weeks for orthopaedic surgery. This does not include the waiting time between being referred to a specialist by a general practitioner and actually getting an appointment with that specialist, these additional waiting times varying by province from 7 weeks in Manitoba to 12 weeks in Prince Edward Island.

Waiting for medical care is particularly costly in human terms, not only because of the needless pain and debilitation that may be suffered while waiting, but also because the underlying malady may be getting worse when the waiting is not simply a matter of hours spent in a hospital's reception room but many months spent on a waiting list before being able to get treatment. People can die from conditions that were initially not very serious, but which grow progressively worse while they are on waiting lists to receive medical care. A celebrated example in Britain involved a woman whose cancer surgery was repeatedly postponed until it had to be cancelled, because the cancer had become inoperable in the course of all the delays. To call this quality deterioration is, if anything, an understatement.

Economic losses sustained by patients may also be considerable when the disease or disability prevents them from working. These costs do not appear among the statistics on the costs of medical care which are used when comparing such costs among different countries. But if an American who gets an operation three weeks after being diagnosed by a primary care physician pays $2,000 more than a Canadian who gets the same operation fifteen weeks after being diagnosed by a primary care physician, then the question of whose full costs are higher depends on whether the lost pay is greater or less than about $167 a week,[1] which is below the average rate of pay in either country. This does not assume that either the American or the

[1] This represents the $2,000 paid by the American worker, spread out over the 12 weeks of additional delay that the Canadian worker has before being treated for the same medical condition. The Canadian worker saves the $2,000 but loses an extra 12 weeks of pay, which will add up to more than $2,000 if the Canadian worker earns more than $167 a week.

Canadian returns to work immediately after the operation, but only that the time lost after the operation is the same in both countries.

Medical treatment in the United States has significantly higher costs per capita than in other countries, when costs are defined to exclude such things as lost pay and other uncounted costs of long waiting times for treatment— notably pain, debilitation and death while waiting. *A* will always appear more efficient than ***B*** if enough of the costs of *A* are left out.

Black Markets

Another feature of price controls in general which applies with special poignancy to medical care is the black market, which flourished in China under government-supplied medical care:

> Rather than wait in long lines for indifferent treatment, affluent Chinese traditionally "go through the back door" for better service, asking friends to provide an introduction to a doctor or giving gifts or payments to physicians and nurses. This practice, although illegal, can ensure faster, better and friendlier treatment. Mid-level hospital administrators tend to benefit most from this arrangement, as they become engaged in the lucrative practice of providing access to doctors.

A study found similar illegal payments in Japan, where "a $1,000 to $3,000 'gift' to the attending physician is common at top Tokyo hospitals." Official statistics do not capture these illegal financial costs, much less the even more important human costs of hasty diagnosis and treatments in abbreviated visits to doctors' offices and the long time on waiting lists before even reaching a medical facility. Thus, in terms of publicly visible costs and benefits, a price-controlled medical system may be a political success. For years, the Soviet Union boasted of having the largest number of doctors and hospital beds of any country in the world— all the while concealing the fact that it also had rising rates of infant mortality and a declining life expectancy in its population as a whole, facts which came out only in its last years under Mikhail Gorbachev's policy of ***glasnost*** or openness.

Opting Out

The unrecorded human costs of price-controlled medical care are indirectly indicated by those who opt out. These include patients, doctors, and medical facilities. Patients in countries with government-controlled medical prices have left the overcrowded government sector to seek private treatment at their own expense, either at home or in other countries. It is common for Canadians to go to the United States for medical treatment, but rare for Americans to go to Canada for such treatment. Doctors have also opted out in various ways. Some have gone into private practice, despite laws which make it illegal for them to do so if they treat any patients at all who are enrolled in government plans. Some Health Maintenance Organizations in the United States opt out by no longer accepting certain categories of patients for whom the government's reimbursement is deemed inadequate to cover their costs.

Some doctors have opted out of vaccinating patients because the reimbursement they receive from government or from insurance companies is considered inadequate. This can have a special impact on the vaccination of babies because infants are especially in need of vaccinations and because the benefits extend over a longer span of time than with older patients. According to the ***New York Times***:

> The nation's pediatricians, the foot soldiers in the campaign to vaccinate America's children, are starting to revolt.
>
> The soaring cost and rising number of new vaccines, doctors say, make it increasingly difficult for them to buy the shots they give their patients. They also complain that insurers often do not reimburse them enough, so they can lose money on every dose they deliver.
>
> As a result, some pediatricians are not offering the newest and most costly vaccines. And some public health experts say that if the situation worsens, it could lead to a breakdown in the nation's immunization program, with a rise in otherwise preventable diseases.

Sometimes the opting out occurs earlier, when fewer people enter medical school after the rewards of being a doctor are reduced. More than one-third of the doctors in Britain, for example, were not trained in British medical schools but have been imported from many other countries, including Third World countries where the training may not be up to the standards of British medical schools.

Paying less and getting less—whether less is defined quantitatively or qualitatively— is not necessarily a bargain, least of all in the case of medical care.

THIRD-PARTY PAYMENTS

Third-party payments are at the heart of much confusion about the cost of medical treatment— and are also a major factor in the ***increased*** cost of that treatment. In government-run medical systems, the public pays in taxes for its medical care, either wholly or in part, with a share being paid directly by the individual patient. Political slogans about "bringing down the cost of medical care" are almost invariably about programs or policies directed toward lowering the price paid directly by the patient. But the fact that only part of the costs are reimbursed by direct out-of-pocket payments from individual patients to doctors, hospitals, or pharmacies in no way indicates that the total cost of the particular medical treatment is any lower than before. When the public pays part of its medical costs in taxes that the government uses to subsidize medical treatment, or in premiums paid to health insurance companies, none of that lowers the total cost in the slightest.

To the extent that the direct payments by patients are lower than they would be if they had to cover the full costs, medical treatments tend to be sought more often— and that alone is enough to cause the total cost of medical care to ***rise***, not fall. Whether these lower payments are due to price control or to supplementary payments by insurance companies or the government, the net result is that lower prices tend to cause more of any goods or services to be demanded, including medical treatment. To the extent that third-party payments require a bureaucracy to administer these payments— whether a government bureaucracy or a private insurance company bureaucracy— the people in those bureaucracies have to be paid, adding still more to the cost of medical care.

Finally, there are costs of medical care not counted in any economic statistics comparing costs in different countries with different medical payment systems. These are the costs in pain, debilitation, and premature deaths, as well as costs in lost income while unable to work for medical reasons. All these costs tend to be greater in countries with government-run medical systems, which almost invariably have longer waiting times between diagnosis and treatment, and especially for treatment that requires a referral from a primary care physician to a specialist. To compare "the costs of medical care" in countries with such systems to the costs in countries with privately financed medical care is to compare apples and oranges. Even within a predominantly private medical care system, such as that in the United States, many payments for medical care are made by third-party payers, whether insurance companies or the government.

The particular system of private third-party payments for medical care in the United States, with health insurance provided by employers, was a fortuitous consequence of tax laws and wage controls during the Second World War— and had nothing to do with any special qualifications of employers to deal with medical care issues. Because employers were prevented by wage controls from raising pay rates to attract more workers during the labor shortages brought on by those controls, they resorted to increased "fringe benefits" to achieve the same results and these benefits were not taxed, so that their value to the workers exceeded their costs to the employers. Before the war, in 1940 only 10 percent of Americans had private health insurance but, a decade later, half did.

Given the situation in which employers could pay workers something worth more to the workers than the cost to the employers, it is hardly surprising that the proportion of the population covered by private insurance plans— many, if not most, provided by employers— continued to increase, just as other "fringe benefits" grew to be such a substantial part of total worker compensation that the word "fringe" disappeared over time.

Even in the absence of the price-control factor, having medicines or medical care paid for by third parties changes the way individuals use medical care. Despite a tendency to regard medical care as a more or less fixed "need," the amount that is demanded can vary greatly according to who is paying. For example, the use of tax-free medical savings accounts in the United States has tended to increase sharply in December, since unexpended money in those accounts is not carried over to the next year. One chain of eyeglass stores reported that its sales were 25 percent higher in December than in any other month "as people scoop up a second or third pair of fashionable frames." As one such customer, who already had eight or nine pairs of glasses, put it, "They go out of style after a while."

Even if it is medically necessary for a given person to wear glasses, is keeping up with fashions also medically necessary? More to the point, would this same customer have bought eight or nine pairs of glasses with her own money? If not, then medical savings accounts have led to a misallocation of resources to buy things that are not worth what they cost, but which are purchased anyway because the government is helping to pay for them by exempting from taxes the income that goes into medical savings accounts. Eye glasses are not the only goods or services that can be charged to these accounts. Condoms, birth control pills, and massages have also been paid out of medical savings accounts. So long as a physician signs off on the expenditure, it is legal— and the physician has no strong incentives to hold back on the spending of someone else's money.

Free market prices, paid by the customer, do not simply convey more or less inevitable costs. They restrain costs by providing incentives for the individual to use a given good or service only to the extent that its incremental value to that individual is greater than its incremental costs. But, when third parties cover all or part of these costs, then additional increments continue to be used beyond that point. Often a given medical problem can be treated in more than one way. For example, an arthritic knee may be treated by taking medication, having therapeutic exercises, or undergoing surgery. Eyesight problems can be treated not only with glasses of varying degrees of fashion, but also with the use of contact lenses, eye exercises, or laser surgery. Choices among these and other treatments depend not only on how serious the medical problem is, but also on how much each of these treatments costs— and who pays those costs. When third parties pay, the more expensive treatments become more likely than when the individual pays.

Because medical care is so often discussed in politics and in media as if there is a more or less fixed amount of "need" and the only question is how to pay for it, much attention has been focused on those who do not have any form of health insurance. But these financial arrangements are not ends in themselves. The real question is: How much medical care is available, whether or not particular individuals have health insurance?

The most poverty-stricken person living on the streets in the United States will be treated in an emergency room, with or without health insurance. Abandoned babies are likewise treated without regard to their ability to pay. No doubt those with insurance, and still more so those with wealth of their own, can get more comfortable accommodations with more amenities in a hospital and can afford more elective or even cosmetic, medical procedures. But to discuss people without health insurance as if they were also without access to medical care is very misleading. The availability of medical care, regardless of health insurance, in fact reduces the incentives to become insured.

Some uninsured people have low incomes but others with incomes sufficient to purchase health insurance simply choose to use their money for other things, especially when they are young and feel less at risk of medical problems. Forty percent of uninsured Americans are under the age of 25 and more than 60 percent are under the age of 35. Fewer than 10 percent of people over 55 are uninsured, despite the widespread political use of an image of old people who have to choose between food and medical care. That may be the political image of the uninsured, but it is hardly the reality.

Third-party payments for medical care transfer the decision-making ability to determine how much medical care, and of what kind, each individual will receive. Given that economic resources of all sorts are scarce— that is, insufficient to provide everyone with enough to satisfy all desires— rationing is going to have to take place, whether for medical goods and services or for anything else, and whether those decisions are made by each person individually or by a government agency collectively for the population at large. But the location of that decision-making power can change the decision itself, with consequences that can be very different from what they would have been if the decision were made elsewhere.

We have already seen what can happen— quantitatively and qualitatively— when the government simply provides or subsidizes medical treatment and leaves individuals free to determine what they want. Skyrocketing costs have forced either restrictions on individual choice or have rationed those choices with waiting times— whether hours of waiting in a doctor's office or months of waiting for surgical or other procedures. Other options include having government officials approve or disapprove particular medical treatment for particular conditions.

In Britain, for example, medical care officials determine who can and cannot receive certain expensive treatments, based on those officials' judgment or on formulas or guidelines about how much quality of life is likely to be achieved and for how many years. Thus an eighty-year-old man is unlikely to be approved for receiving a heart transplant. While some medical choices and trade-offs may be obvious, many others are more complicated. Here, as elsewhere, the most important decision can be: Who makes the decision?

MEDICAL MALPRACTICE INSURANCE

One of the major sources of the high costs of American medical care is malpractice insurance for doctors and hospitals. The average cost of this insurance for individual doctors ranges from about $14,000 a year in California to nearly $40,000 a year in West Virginia. In particular specialties, such as obstetrics and neurosurgery, the cost of malpractice insurance can exceed $200,000 a year in some places. These costs of course get passed on to patients, the government, or whoever is paying for medical treatments. Even so, these are not the only financial costs created by medical malpractice lawsuits, nor are financial costs the only costs or necessarily the most important costs. One-stage thinking has much to do with these costs.

The threat of lawsuits can impose costs on obstetricians which raise their insurance premiums high enough to cause many of these doctors to stop delivering babies, or to stop delivering them in places where high jury awards on dubious evidence make it uneconomic to continue practicing obstetrics. The net result of this can be that pregnant women in those places are at more risk than before because now there may be no doctor available in the vicinity to deliver their baby when the time comes. Nor are obstetricians the only doctors who flee from places where it is easy to file lawsuits and win large damage awards. Pennsylvania, for example, lost one-third of its surgeons between 1995 and 2002.

Ideally, juries would award malpractice damages only when the probability that malpractice had actually taken place was sufficiently clear, and the award only at a level sufficient to compensate real damages and deter such malpractice in the future. In reality, an injured, deformed, or brain-damaged baby and an eloquent lawyer can lead to jury awards in the millions of dollars, even when it is by no means clear that the doctor who delivered that baby was in any way at fault. A large study conducted jointly by the American College of Obstetricians and Gynecologists and the American Academy of Pediatrics— released in 2003 and reviewed and approved by leading medical authorities in and out of government, as well as from as far away as Australia and New Zealand— concluded that "the vast majority of brain damage and cerebral palsy among these infants originates in factors largely or completely ***outside*** the control of delivery-room personnel."

According to ***The Economist***, "few clinicians think that babies get cerebral palsy because the obstetrician failed to deliver them by caesarean section." Yet "fear of being sued prompts doctors to perform unnecessary C-sections— a risky and invasive procedure." Nevertheless, "a five-fold increase in C-sections in rich countries in the past three decades has brought no decrease in the incidence of cerebral palsy." Seventy-six percent of American obstetricians have been sued at least once. The rationale for medical malpractice lawsuits is to force doctors to be more careful and thereby reduce risks to patients. The actual consequences, however, include unnecessary medical procedures, such as delivering babies by Caesarean section, as well as ordering medically unnecessary tests that doctors feel are financially necessary to protect themselves against lawsuits.

There may also be additional risks to patients when substantial numbers of doctors leave an area where malpractice lawsuits are easy to file and win. Doctors usually win lawsuits that go to trial but the pressure to settle out of court is substantial, since the average damage award in jury trials is $4.7 million. Given the size of the damage awards and the resulting escalating costs of malpractice insurance, it is hardly surprising that defensive medicine has become widespread among obstetricians. A study of obstetricians in Pennsylvania found that "54% frequently called for tests, like sonograms, they felt were unnecessary and 38% often admitted to invasive procedures, like biopsies, that were not called for." Such "defensive medicine" may not make patients any safer and in some cases, such as Caesarean sections and biopsies, can create additional risks. It is not merely the damages awarded in medical malpractice cases that add to the costs of medical care but also the greatly increased costs of defensive medical procedures.

It costs a jury nothing to "send a message" warning doctors to be more careful, and the particular doctor in the case at hand probably has insurance from a company that can pay a few million dollars easily out of its billions of dollars in assets. Only if the jurors think beyond stage one will they take into account the increased cost of medical treatment brought on by their awards and the future non-financial costs to pregnant women unable to find obstetricians in their area at the time of delivery and the lifelong costs to babies who may incur more or worse injuries or disabilities as a result. This is especially likely to be the end result in states where juries hand out multimillion-dollar awards readily, such as Nevada:

> Kimberly Maugaotega of Las Vegas is 13 weeks pregnant and hasn't seen an obstetrician. When she learned she was expecting, the 33-year-old mother of two called the doctor who delivered her second child but was told he wasn't taking any new pregnant patients. Dr. Shelby Wilbourn plans to leave Nevada because of soaring medical-malpractice insurance rates there. Ms. Maugaotega says she called 28 obstetricians but couldn't find one who would take her.

While the direct costs of malpractice lawsuits have been estimated as less than one percent of the total cost of medical care in the United States, the indirect costs include expensive tests and procedures, as well as the additional medical risks to patients that some of these tests and procedures pose. Perhaps the biggest costs are those imposed on patients who cannot find a doctor available because the ease of filing malpractice lawsuits in particular places has led doctors to relocate. These costs are literally incalculable.

There is of course genuine malpractice, genuinely deserving of lawsuits and large damage awards. However, the ease of filing and winning lawsuits on the basis of shaky or speculative evidence, or on the testimony of "hired gun" experts who have financial incentives to back up what is said by the lawyer who hired them, has made the connection between malpractice lawsuits and genuine malpractice tenuous. As in so many cases, political "solutions" to the malpractice problem can create new problems. One popular political solution has been to put upper limits on the amount of awards for "pain and suffering." But if the carelessness or incompetence of some physician or surgeon has in fact caused someone to be in pain for the rest of his or her life, a quarter of a million dollar cap, as in California, is completely inadequate as compensation and inadequate as a deterrent. The fundamental problem is not with the amounts of money awarded, as such, but with the fact that there may be no adequate basis for any award at all.

With laws and policies on medical malpractice, as with other laws and policies, what is most important from a political perspective may be the goals and rationales of those laws and policies. But, from the standpoint of economic analysis, what is most important are the incentives and constraints created by laws and policies, and the consequences that follow from those incentives and constraints— not only in stage one but beyond.

PHARMACEUTICAL DRUGS

The high prices of pharmaceutical drugs have been a contentious issue, though they are a relatively small part of total spending on medical care in the United States— about ten percent, according to data from the Centers for Medicare and Medicaid Services. The costs behind these prices are not only high, but unusual, in the predominance of research costs over the cost of actually manufacturing the medications themselves.

While the process of creating a new pharmaceutical drug involves science, it also involves trial and error, often taking years. In the pharmaceutical drug industry, creating a new medicine to cure a particular disease can involve many failures before finally developing a drug that is simultaneously effective, affordable, and without major adverse side-effects for most people. In 2003, an official of the drug producer Pfizer said: "Last year we made over 5,000 compounds. Only half a dozen of them will make it to clinical trials." How many of those half dozen would prove to be successful in the clinical trials and then make it through the approval process of the Food and Drug Administration (FDA) only the future would tell.

If the pharmaceutical company has spent years working on many different chemical compounds before finally coming up with one that meets all the criteria— and gets the approval of the Food and Drug Administration as well— then its profits on that successful drug have to cover all its costs on the many unsuccessful ones. Otherwise there will not be sufficient earnings to repay all the individuals, pension funds, and other investors whose money they use to finance the creation of new drugs.

Since the creation of a single new drug typically costs hundreds of millions of dollars,[2] keeping enough investors willing to continue supplying such huge sums of money is essential to keeping the discovery of new drugs going.

Those who do not think beyond stage one see the situation in wholly different terms. Rather than examine what happens before and after a new drug is created, they essentially treat existing drugs as having been created

---

[2] "It can take fifteen years and hundreds of millions of dollars to go from finding a bacterial target to putting a drug into production." James Surowiecki, "No Profit, No Cure," *The New Yorker*, November 5, 2001, p. 46. "Estimates range from around $250 million per drug to more than $800 million." "Drug Prices: A Much-Needed Primer," *Wall Street Journal*, July 22, 2002, p. A15.

somehow and focus on how these drugs are priced, what profits they earn, and how those prices can be brought down. Since the cost of manufacturing a pharmaceutical drug is often a small fraction of its total costs, or of the price paid by the consumer, there are ample opportunities for politicians, journalists, and others to decry the "unconscionable," "outrageous" or "obscene" profits made by charging two dollars a pill when the ingredients in the pill may cost only a quarter.

By ingredients they mean physical ingredients, which are usually inexpensive, rather than the knowledge ingredient which is usually astronomically expensive because of years of research, with much trial and error, including many costly and failed attempts to create effective new medicines.

The same misconception of costs can appear in another form when politicians, journalists, etc., contrast the high price charged for a pharmaceutical drug by the company that created it versus the much lower price of a "generic equivalent" produced by another company, which simply uses the same formula, free of charge, after the patent has expired. The second company's costs are just the low costs of manufacturing the drug, so that they may be able to make a profit selling a generic equivalent for a fraction of what the company that created the drug charged. In the case of a pill whose ingredients cost a quarter, the generic manufacturer may be able to make a profit charging thirty-five cents for the same pill, causing the brand-name manufacturer who created the drug to be accused of unconscionably exploiting people who are ill and desperate by charging a much higher price before the patent expired.

The combination of very high fixed costs for developing a new drug and very low incremental costs of producing it leads to other economic consequences that are easy to misunderstand or misrepresent by those who do not think beyond stage one. For example, Canadians pay much lower prices for American pharmaceutical drugs than Americans do. When a government agency in Canada buys vast quantities of medicines for its comprehensive, government-run medical care system, and offers an American pharmaceutical company a price which covers the incremental costs of manufacturing a particular drug, but not the vast costs of developing that drug in the first place, the pharmaceutical company's alternatives are (1) to lose millions of dollars in sales by not accepting the offer or (2) earn whatever money it can by accepting the offer, since the past costs have already been paid and are irrelevant to current decision-making. As economists say, "sunk costs are sunk."

Seldom is a given medicine the only one that can be used in treating a given disease, so a drug company's ability to hold out against Canadian or other governments is very limited, when those governments can buy someone else's medications if they do not get the price they want from a particular pharmaceutical company. Moreover, in countries with government-controlled comprehensive medical care systems, there may be little or no market for a given medicine from the small, or non-existent, private sector.

Those who do not think beyond stage one focus on the money that can be "saved" by allowing Canadians to re-export back to the United States the American drugs they have bought at lower prices than Americans pay, thereby reducing the costs of medical care for the American government, individuals and medical organizations. Not only would there be direct savings by individuals and organizations importing American medicines from Canada, the pharmaceutical drug companies would then be under pressure to lower the prices they charge in the United States as well, after losing sales because of competition from the sales of their own medicines being imported back from Canada. None of this, however, deals with the crucial question for those who do think beyond stage one: Since the fixed costs have to be paid by somebody, if the development of new medicines is to continue, how can evasions of such payments of fixed costs fail to reduce the rate of investment and discovery of new medicines?

Even in the United States, there are large buyers of pharmaceutical drugs such as health maintenance organizations and the federal government, who can likewise present a pharmaceutical company with a take-it-or-leave-it offer at a price that allows the company to make some money over and above manufacturing costs, but not nearly enough to cover the high fixed costs required to develop new drugs. Policies or legislation prescribing the substitution of generic pharmaceutical drugs for similar or identical brand-name drugs can often reduce the cost to hospitals or health-insurance systems. Some demand that all drugs be generic, ending the high prices and presumably unconscionable profits of the brand-name drug producers. But here we must beware of the fallacy of composition. What is true for some is not necessarily something that can be made true for all. The overlooked factor is that generic drug producers are essentially getting a free ride on the costs and experience built up at great expense by producers of brand-name drugs.

Since it usually takes a decade or more to develop a new pharmaceutical drug, this situation is virtually ideal for political demagoguery. A politician can gain instant popularity by advocating any of a number of ways of forcing down the price of medications immediately, and it could be at least ten years later before people begin noticing a decline or disappearance of new pharmaceutical drugs to deal with deadly diseases that still ravage millions of people. But, by this time, our popular politician could be elected president, serve two terms in the White House, and be living in retirement as a revered figure. As noted in Chapter 1, killing the goose that lays the golden egg can be a viable political strategy.

It should also be noted that "generic equivalents" may not all be equivalent for all people. Some patients report adverse side effects from generic equivalents that they did not have from the original brand of the medicine. Generic equivalents do not have to be chemically identical, as a health reporter noted:

> By law, generics must have the same active ingredient and the same action as the brand-name version, which allows them to piggyback on the original safety and efficacy trials. But generics do have different inactive ingredients, which can affect how they are absorbed into the body. Generics can produce blood levels as much as 20% below or 25% above that of the original drug and still be considered "bioequivalent," according to Food and Drug Administration guidelines.

Leaving aside the question whether an ingredient is truly inactive if it affects the rate at which the active ingredient is absorbed by the body, there is also a question whether a lesser known firm— perhaps in a Third World country— copying a medication developed by an internationally known pharmaceutical company, has the same incentives to maintain production quality standards as the original producer of the drug, for whom billions of dollars' worth of international brand name reputation is at stake, not just for this particular drug but for all its many other drugs, present and future.

Price Controls

While past costs are irrelevant to present decision-making— they are history but they are not economics— those past costs do matter when pharmaceutical companies decide whether, or to what extent, to invest in developing more new drugs. If those past costs have not been covered, future costs may not be as readily incurred to create future drugs to cure or prevent such scourges as Alzheimer's, AIDS, or cancer. Despite such weighty economic considerations— for the society, as well as for the company— in political terms the pharmaceutical drug industry is virtually ideal for imposing price controls. As noted in Chapter 1, price controls can be very popular in the short run, with their bad effects usually coming some time after the next election.

Since pharmaceutical drugs can easily take a decade or more to be created, even if price controls caused all research and development of new drugs to come to a halt immediately, it would be long after the next election before people began to notice that no new medications were being created to deal with the ravages of still deadly diseases. These are virtually ideal political conditions for killing the goose that lays the golden egg. The short-run result would be visibly lower drug prices, making millions of voters happier, and the long-run consequences would be postponed until several elections later, by which time even those suffering needlessly from illnesses that new medications could have cured or prevented may see no connection between their own suffering and political decisions made years earlier.

The effects of such political incentives can be seen in many countries around the world. The United States is the only major industrial nation without price controls on pharmaceutical drugs. In other words, politicians in other countries have already sacrificed the long-run medical benefits of pharmaceutical drug research and reaped the immediate political benefits, leaving their countries to depend on the American pharmaceutical industry to supply a wholly disproportionate share of the new medications in the world. If a similar policy is followed by the United States, the resulting drying up of American pharmaceutical research would affect not only the American population, but also the populations of other countries that have been able to rely on the creation of new drugs in the United States and being able to buy these drugs by paying prices that cover only the manufacturing costs, while Americans pay prices that cover the far larger costs of developing such drugs.

As was pointed out by a Commissioner of the Food and Drug Administration, "the U.S. is paying the lion's share of the cost of developing drugs." Americans pay in two different ways. As ***BusinessWeek*** magazine pointed out, "it's not just that the higher prices Americans pay for drugs fund half of the industry's research efforts. U.S. taxpayers also support most of the world's government-funded basic biomedical research— as much as 80%, by some estimates."

One of the irrelevant distractions in many discussions of the costs of creating new medications is that much of the drug companies' research is a continuation of more fundamental scientific research done in academic institutions and government agencies such as the National Institutes of Health. However, in every aspect of our lives, we all stand on the shoulders of giants, and all those giants were not in the past. The costs incurred in turning scientific discoveries into new medications are no less real and no less important because other individuals and organizations incurred other costs earlier. Nor does the fact that the taxpayers' money was used mean that the best way to make decisions about pharmaceutical drugs is to take those decisions out of the marketplace and have them made by politicians. Yet this non sequitur is what seems to be implied by those who think that the prior costs of scientific discoveries change the economic requirements for producing new medicines.

While advocates of price controls on pharmaceutical drugs refer to this as "bringing down the cost" of these drugs, it is in fact simply refusing to pay those costs— and ignoring the consequences of that refusal, especially when those consequences occur after stage one. Europe has already gone that route:

> Already, Europeans are fretting that their relatively low prices are killing their pharmaceutical industry. In 1990, European and U.S. companies each held about a one-third share of the world drug market. Now, Europe's share is down to 21%, while the U.S.'s has jumped to 50%. European companies have increasingly moved their R&D operations to the U.S., and they make 60% of their profits in the American market, analysts estimate.

In short, European policies that Americans are being urged to emulate are what drove much European research and development out of Europe to the United States. If the United States does now follow the European policies, this can shut down much of the world's research and development of new pharmaceutical drugs. It could mean killing off the biggest goose that is laying most of the world's golden eggs when it comes to producing new medications to fight painful, debilitating and fatal diseases.

Advertising

However easy it may be for outside observers to dismiss advertising as an expense that accomplishes nothing for society and only increases the advertiser's profits, that is in fact not the case. The most wonderful drug ever created will help no one's medical condition unless it becomes known. Advertising does that. Nor is making the drug known something that can be done once and for all, and advertising discontinued thereafter, without consequences.

After the patent for the drug Ceclor expired and its producer, Eli Lilly & Co., cut back on the promotion of it when generic substitutes began to be marketed by other companies, prescriptions for this drug fell to one-fifth of the former level. The generic producers had little or no incentive to advertise, since no one of them would have a large enough share of the increased sales to recover the advertising expenditures. As far as the practical effect on patients is concerned, advertising can save lives, just as creation of a new medication can.

There is another aspect to advertising that is seldom understood. When a medication is approved by the Food and Drug Administration for one use and other uses are later discovered for it, the FDA can forbid the pharmaceutical company from advertising the other uses unless and until it has gone through the long and costly process of meeting FDA requirements for that new use. Depending on whether the anticipated additional sales would cover these additional costs— which can run into many millions of dollars— the company may or may not try to get the approval needed to permit advertising uses which medical science has already shown to be beneficial. A classic example is aspirin, which has long been approved as a medication for headaches but may be even more valuable in other uses which, until recent years, were not permitted to be advertised. During the period of the ban on advertising aspirin's benefits to those with heart problems, a study concluded:

> There is substantial medical evidence that taking a daily dose of aspirin can reduce the risk of heart attack in middle-aged males. . . by almost 50 percent. Indeed, the results are so well known that there exists a pamphlet, ***Amazing Aspirin***, available for 89¢ at the checkout stand of grocery stores, which discusses this benefit at great length. What is surprising is that neither the package for the aspirin itself nor any advertising for it indicates this valuable use. Why does Bayer largely forgo the possibility of the increased sales from providing this information to consumers?
>
> On March 2, 1988, at a meeting in the offices of FDA Commissioner Frank Young, all companies making aspirin were told that they could not advertise the benefits of the product in reducing risks for first heart attacks. If they did, the FDA would bring legal action.

As a consequence, "the ban on aspirin advertising undoubtedly causes tens of thousands of needless deaths per year," the study concluded. Obviously, the Food and Drug Administration's ban on advertising medication for purposes that the FDA has not approved is designed to promote safety. But the purpose of the ban does not change the consequences. Fortunately, in this case, the FDA eventually relented and allowed aspirin companies to advertise the use of their product to reduce deaths from heart attacks. However, the deaths of those who might have saved their lives by taking aspirin, if they had known about its benefits for those suffering heart attacks, was a high price paid for the delay.

More fundamentally, when thousands of lives can be saved by advertising, are those lives any less important than a similar number of lives saved by the development of an entirely new medication? What research does for the scientific community— provide information they might otherwise not know— is what advertising does for doctors and patients. Moreover, because physicians are the ones who prescribe pharmaceutical drugs, they are a more knowledgeable audience than the audiences for many other kinds of advertising, and are therefore harder to deceive or to impress with mere puffery. Moreover, a drug company which attempted to deceive doctors about a particular drug would be risking an enormously costly loss of confidence in that company by doctors who prescribe a wide range of medicines, and who in the aggregate could therefore steer billions of dollars in sales away from the deceiving company and toward its rivals.

Like other advertising, the advertising of pharmaceutical drugs is often thought of as adding to the costs which the consumer must pay for, driving up the price of the product. That would be true if advertising had no effect on sales and sales had no effect on economies of scale in production. But the obvious purpose of advertising is precisely to have an effect on sales— and there are huge economies of scale when there are high fixed costs, running into hundreds of millions of dollars, for producing a pharmaceutical drug and very low costs of actually manufacturing the drug. The larger the number of sales over which the huge fixed costs are spread, the lower those fixed costs are per unit of medication. Pharmaceutical drugs are a classic example of economies of scale. Yet many in politics and in the media speak as if it is axiomatic that advertising drives up the cost of medications.

Often the animus against advertising by pharmaceutical companies extends to the common practice of these companies to give free samples of new medications to doctors, who are able to pass them on to their patients without charge. Since the pharmaceutical companies' purpose is obviously to gain faster and wider acceptance of their medications, this is often regarded by critics as somehow inimical to the public— as if this were a zero-sum transaction, in which someone must lose when someone else gains. But patients would not go to doctors and doctors would not prescribe medications, nor the pharmaceutical company produce them, unless everyone involved benefitted from this process. The pharmaceutical company has a special interest in how fast its new drugs are accepted because it has a limited number of years before its patent runs out and rival companies can then take away much of their market with cheaper generic equivalents.

The idea that there is something morally wrong about pharmaceutical companies giving doctors free samples, in order to benefit their business, is so deeply ingrained that Stanford, Yale and the University of Pennsylvania have prohibited the doctors in their medical schools from accepting such free samples. This symbolic gesture costs university administrators nothing but can cost patients both money and information about new medications for their conditions. Nationwide, the retail value of free samples provided by pharmaceutical companies has been estimated at $16 billion annually. Some have claimed that the cost of these free samples will drive up the cost of the medications sold by these pharmaceutical companies. But this is repeating the same fallacy that advertising must add to the cost of the goods advertised, ignoring economies of scale resulting from the advertising, of which free samples are just one form.

Government Approval of Drugs

It is illegal for a pharmaceutical company to begin selling a drug without prior approval by the Food and Drug Administration. The drug approval process attempts to reduce the risks of new and untried medicines before they are made available to the general public. In addition to being reasonably safe for most people, pharmaceutical drugs must also be shown to be effective for whatever medical conditions they are intended to treat. A medicine that is safe but ineffective is not only a fraud but a danger, as it may be used for diseases and conditions for which there are alternative treatments that are in fact effective, thereby depriving sick people of benefits that are already available, and perhaps costing them their lives. Yet the question of ***how safe*** and ***how effective***, and at what cost, must be considered as regards the years of tests and trials prescribed by the FDA's drug approval process.

The more years that the trials go on and the larger the number of people in the sample taking the drug, the more reliable the end results as to both safety and effectiveness— and the more sick people will be left to suffer and perhaps die while these processes go on. A new drug may be tested for effectiveness against a placebo or against the effectiveness of some other drug. The latter may be a better process in terms of the validity of the end results but one such trial involving more than 30,000 people added ***another eight years*** to the testing process. A lot of people can die in eight years— and yet absolute certainty is still not achievable by human beings, no matter how much testing goes on. Moreover, these deaths during the trial period are not necessarily recouped in lives saved later over the lifetime of the particular drug or treatment, which may be superseded by new drugs or treatments for the same diseases in few or many years, as the case may turn out to be.

The incentives and constraints facing government officials in charge of testing pharmaceutical drugs are asymmetrical. Ideally, these officials could weigh the costs and the benefits equally— for example, stopping the testing process at the point where the estimated number of lives lost while waiting longer for more drug tests to be completed would exceed the estimated number of lives saved by getting more data on the drug's safety. But neither the public, the media, nor the political leaders to whom health officials are ultimately responsible are likely to use that standard.

If a thousand children die from a new drug allowed into the market with less testing and ten thousand children would die while more testing was going on, the public outcry over the deaths of those thousand children would bring the wrath of the whole political system down on the heads of those officials who permitted the drug to be approved with "inadequate" testing. But if ten or a hundred times as many people die while prolonged testing goes on, there will be few, if any, news stories about those people in the media.

For one thing, the thousand deaths attributable to the drug approved by the FDA are far more likely to be provable deaths to identifiable individuals, whose stories can make headlines. That is not true, however, of the deaths of ten thousand unidentifiable individuals whose inability to get a life-saving drug shows up only in death-rate statistics comparing what happens where the drug is available and what happens where it is not available. But statistics are never as dramatic as television interviews with distraught widows or bereaved mothers of those have who died from the side effects of a drug.

These asymmetrical incentives and constraints have led American health officials to ban life-saving drugs that have been in use for years, if not decades, in Europe— with few, if any, ill effects— because these drugs have not yet gone through the long and costly process necessary to get approval under American laws and policies. Even if the effectiveness and relative safety of these drugs have been reported in scientific studies published in leading medical journals, that is not accepted as a substitute for the prescribed FDA approval process. Desperately ill people have been known to either have the unapproved medications smuggled into the country or, if they can afford it, go outside the United States themselves to get them. Sometimes safety precautions can be carried to the point where they are fatal.

A former Commissioner of the Food and Drug Administration noted the institutional incentives and constraints:

> In all our FDA history, we are unable to find a single instance where a Congressional committee investigated the failure of FDA to approve a new drug. But the times when hearings have been held to criticize our approval of a new drug have been so frequent that we have not been able to count them. The message to FDA staff could not be clearer.

The United States is by no means unique in either the presence or the degree of delay in approving new pharmaceutical drugs. Both Canada and the countries of the European Union take longer.

A more fundamental question is: How much risk is too much— and who should decide? Vioxx, one of the well-known drugs for treating arthritis, was withdrawn from the market by its producer, Merck & Co., after tests showed that people who took Vioxx for more than 18 months had twice as many heart attacks or strokes as those who had taken a placebo. While twice as many sounds large, this doubling was from 0.75 percent who suffered heart attacks or strokes without taking Vioxx to 1.5 percent of those who took Vioxx for more than 18 months. Meanwhile, those who took Vioxx for less than 18 months "had no increased cardiovascular risk," according to a report in the ***Wall Street Journal.***

The real issue here is not Vioxx but risk, benefits, and alternative medications. Arthritis can be both painful and crippling, and only doctors and medical scientists are likely to know what alternative treatments are available or how effective they are compared to Vioxx. Moreover, whether arthritis is a minor problem or a severe handicap can vary from patient to patient. The risk that may matter most to the producer of Vioxx may be the risk of lawsuits. But, as far as the risk to patients is concerned, each patient knows how big a problem that particular patient's arthritis is, and the patient's doctor knows what alternative treatments are available and what their risks are, since nothing is perfectly safe. But a legal system that makes it easy to sue can deprive patients of a choice to assume a given risk for a given benefit, even if that risk is less than other risks that people are free to take, just for the sake of recreation, such as white-water rafting, sky-diving or mountain-climbing.

ORGAN TRANSPLANTS

The most stringent of all price controls is permitting no price at all to be charged. That is the legal situation in the United States and in various other countries, when it comes to people who donate one of their own organs to be transplanted into the body of someone else whose liver, kidneys, or other organs are badly malfunctioning. It is illegal in these countries to charge for donating one's organs, though it is legal in some other countries such as Iran or Pakistan. Here again, we can begin by looking at the effects of price control in general, and then see how that applies in a particular case, such as organ transplants.

The most common effect of laws limiting how high prices will be permitted to go is to reduce the quantity supplied. In the case of organ transplants, the number of Americans on waiting lists vastly exceeds the number of organs available, so that an absolute majority of those people die while waiting to get a new liver, kidney or other organ. While 25,076 organ transplants were performed in the United States in 2003, the number of patients on official waiting lists for organs was more than three times that—specifically 89,012. Both the number of kidney transplants and the number of people on waiting lists have doubled in a period of 15 years, so the gap between the two has been widening. More than 50,000 Americans were on waiting lists for kidneys, while only about 12,000 kidneys were available to be transplanted. Similar patterns are found in other countries. According to the British *Journal of Medical Ethics*, in Western Europe 40,000 people were on waiting lists for kidney transplants but only 10,000 kidneys were available— and nobody knows "how many people fail to make it onto the waiting lists and so disappear from the statistics." Meanwhile, there are an estimated 700,000 patients on dialysis worldwide.

The benefits of organ transplants extend beyond the saving of thousands of lives to a restoration of a level of health and vigor that many have not enjoyed for years:

> A successful transplant can provide a patient with a feeling of virtual rebirth and allow a return to a full and productive life. In that regard, organ transplantation stands out as one of the most significant medical advances of the past few decades.

Conversely, delays in getting a transplant can cost the patient suffering and debilitation, and entail large medical costs for such things as kidney dialysis or other expensive treatments for other malfunctioning organs, as well as causing a general physical deterioration that increases the dangers of a transplant operation, if and when an organ eventually does become available. Over the years, waiting times for organ transplants have grown. Between 1988 and 1997, waiting times for heart transplants in the United States nearly doubled. Between 1988 and 1995, median waiting times in the United States for a kidney transplant increased from just over a year to more than two and a half years— and by 2000, the waiting time exceeded three years.

Organs may be transplanted from either living people or from the bodies of people who have recently died. For kidneys, for example, more than twice as many transplants are from the dead as from the living. For liver transplants, the ratio of postmortem transplants is several times as high as transplants from living donors. Still, more than 6,000 organ transplants from living people were performed in the United States in 2006. Obviously, the cost of a transplant from a living person includes the organ donor's pain, risk, and lost time from work while recuperating, but obviously none of these costs apply when organs are transplanted postmortem. Just as people while alive can legally grant permission to transplant their organs after death free of charge, so they could charge for granting such permission if the law did not forbid that.

If organs were allowed to be sold by their donors, what would be the consequences? What are the consequences today, where organ sales are illegal? How much would an organ cost in a free market and how would organs be allocated in such a market, compared to how they are allocated today?

On the most basic economic principles, it should be expected that more organs would be supplied at some price than at no price. How high that price would have to be depends on the value of the organ to the potential donor, as well as the risks of the operation and the increased risk to a kidney donor, for example, if the one remaining kidney were to malfunction at some future time. For people who are paid while living for an organ to be transplanted after death, even a heart has no postmortem value to the donor, nor would the financial costs or medical risks of a transplant be a deterrent. Where parents or other family members are allowed to sell the organs of someone who died unexpectedly, there may be psychic costs for some upon realizing that a loved one's body is to be cut up or there may be psychic benefits in knowing that their loved one is passing on the gift of life to another human being. It is unnecessary for third parties to weigh the balance, since each individual is different and all can make their own decisions on such personal matters, as can living organ donors.

Current prices paid for organ transplants, in countries where paying is legal, provide only the most general and potentially misleading idea of what such prices would be in a free market. Given the many countries in which organ sales are illegal, that illegality restricts the world supply, causing prices to be higher than otherwise in those countries where such transplants are legal. Where organ transplant sales take place despite being illegal, the price paid must be higher than the free market price, as with all black markets, for the risks of the illegality to seller or broker must also be compensated, in order for this activity to continue. Perhaps the highest price of all for illegal organ transplants is the absence of the quality of medical care and organ screening that would be expected if the operation took place under normal and legal conditions. ***The Economist*** magazine, for example reports:

> Ailing, rich patients are buying kidneys from the poor and desperate in burgeoning black markets. One bigwig broker may soon stand trial in South Africa. . . Clandestine kidney-sellers get little medical follow-up, buyers often catch hepatitis or HIV, and both endure the consequences of slap-dash surgery.

It is necessary to distinguish the financial costs of organ transplants from the medical costs and risks— and to distinguish both these inherent costs of the transplanting and its aftermath from the costs created by its illegality. As things stand today, the price paid to organ donors is far less than the money collected by brokers who arrange these transplants. ***Forbes*** magazine estimated the markup of Internet organ transplant brokers as "between 60% and 400% over costs." These kinds of markups can seldom survive in an open and competitive market. A living donor in Iran, where organ sales are legal, "expects to get between $3,000 and $4,000 for one of his kidneys," according to ***The Economist***. On the other hand, the prices charged by an Internet broker in California are considerably higher, according to *Forbes*:

> His customers face certain death if their diseased organs aren't quickly swapped out. They find him on the Internet; his stated fee— $140,000 for a kidney and $290,000 for a heart, liver, or lung— includes hospital and surgeon charges, and flights and accommodation for a fellow traveler, such as a nurse or spouse.

Similar amounts were charged by another organ transplant broker in Taiwan, where two options were offered— "a liver transplant at the Shanghai International Transplant Center for $120,000 or an $80,000 version at a no-frills provincial hospital in Nanjing." This was before selling organ transplants was banned in China in 2007.

The international flight for two offered by the California organ broker is an expense made necessary by the illegality of paid organ transplants in the United States and the desire of patients to have someone such as a family member with them at a trying time. Moreover, the cost of the operation falls wholly on the patient only because its illegality means that insurance cannot cover it. Medical risks are also higher than if the operation were performed under normal conditions, according to a report in *The Economist*:

> As long as they receive decent after-care, kidney donors suffer only the tiniest increase in their own risk of dying of kidney disease. And transplants make economic sense: the cost of one kidney operation and a lifetime's supply of anti-rejection drugs equals that of three years' dialysis. Kidneys donated by a living person last for a median 22 years in another body; when they are taken from a fresh corpse, the figure is 14 years.

Since many, if not most, people who need an organ transplant are no longer young, 22 years or even 14 years may often be enough to allow them to live out a normal life span.

While it is reasonable to expect the supply of organs to be transplanted to increase if payments to donors would become legal, that still leaves the question of ***how much*** would the supply increase— and how much would it have to increase in order to make a dent in the huge backlog of people waiting for organ transplants. *The Economist* magazine estimates that it would take less than one percent of healthy Americans from ages 19 to 65 to part with one kidney to eliminate the waiting list on which thousands of patients die each year.

Currently the rationing of donated organs for transplanting is handled by bureaucracies set up for that purpose, applying such arbitrary rules as they choose, based on whatever notions of "fairness" they happen to have, and dispensing such special favors as they choose to whatever individuals they choose, such as Governor Robert Casey of Pennsylvania, who in 1993 received a heart and liver transplant ahead of others who had been on the waiting list much longer, or former baseball star Mickey Mantle, who received a liver transplant after a relatively brief time on a waiting list. Not surprisingly, these bureaucracies are opposed to free markets that would render them superfluous and deprive them of their power and importance.

Like other bureaucracies, organ transplant organizations tend to create restrictive rules and paperwork burdens in complying with those rules. In 2007, the American Society of Transplant Surgeons responded to proposed new restrictions by one of these bureaucracies, the United Network for Organ Sharing (UNOS) by saying: "Dictating the practice of medicine and surgery is not the role of [UNOS], let alone in the best interests of patients." A surgeon at the Yale medical school put it more bluntly: "You don't see my patient, and you don't see my donor, and you're going to tell me who I can and can't use?" But, so long as these organizations control a supply of desperately needed organs, they will have arbitrary powers, whether they have corresponding knowledge or not.

As for the cost of a transplant under legal circumstances and in a free market, a study by economists Gary Becker of the University of Chicago and Julio Jorge Elías of the State University of New York at Buffalo concludes that "monetary incentives could increase the supply of organs for transplant sufficiently to eliminate the large queues in the organ market, and it would do so while increasing the overall cost of transplant surgery by no more than about 12 percent."

Whether under legal or illegal circumstances, the full cost of an organ transplant includes not only the price paid for the organ itself— which has procurement costs, even when the organ is donated without charge— but also the cost of the operation and the subsequent medical costs for both the donor and the recipient after the operation, including continuing costs for medications for the recipient to protect the donated organ from being attacked by the recipient's immune system. This is a very expensive process but the cost of purchasing the organ itself in a legal transaction— estimated by Professors Becker and Elías at $15,200 for a kidney and $37,600 for a liver— is in the range of what people pay for automobiles, and would add only modestly to the total cost of the organ transplant process. Moreover, the cost of ***not*** making the transplant is not cheap: kidney dialysis costs more than $66,000 a year and cannot produce the same benefits as a kidney transplant, besides being an annually repeated cost, as distinguished from a one-time cost for a kidney transplant operation.

Professors Becker and Elías estimate the total cost of the whole organ transplant process at $210,000 for a kidney and $392,000 for a liver. While these are huge sums of money for an individual, they are in the range of what is ordinarily paid for a house in a moderately priced housing market. Since Medicare already covers the annual cost of kidney dialysis and financing can be arranged for buying homes, these are not insurmountable costs for most people and could be covered by insurance if organ purchases were legal. For those too poor to handle such costs through insurance, private or government agencies could take care of such individuals. In any case, the costs of the organ purchases would not be the main costs of the organ transplant process. It has been estimated by an organ transplant specialist that the savings from reductions in the use of kidney dialysis by the use of kidney transplants could on net balance "reduce government expenditures significantly."

In short, price controls— in this case, making sales of organs illegal at any price— have relatively little effect on the total cost of an organ transplant, but can have serious effects in reducing the number of organs available to be transplanted. Since there has long been a program of legal organ sales in Iran, the effect of legalizing the sale of organs is not just a matter of speculation. Eleven years after the legalization of organ sales in Iran, there was no longer a waiting list for kidney transplants.

Objections to the sale of organs center on the fact that poor people are more likely to sell an organ, including people "under desperate and trying circumstances," as a noted ethicist put it. But are their circumstances any *less* desperate when they are forbidden to seek one of the very few ways available to them to escape their desperation and better their lives? Since people on waiting lists for organ transplants are also in desperate circumstances, to have the options of both sets of people reduced, and their choices overridden, by people who are healthy and prosperous seems painfully ironic, as if the squeamishness of third parties should be decisive. Sometimes the argument is made that it is wrong to have a human organ reduced to the level of a "commodity," as if avoiding a word is worth losing a life. Moreover, a purchase from a stranger avoids the documented emotional pressures on both donor and recipient when they know each other.[3]

SUMMARY AND IMPLICATIONS

A number of confusions plague discussions of the economics of medical care. A confusion between prices and costs has allowed politicians in various countries to be able to claim to be able to bring down the cost of health care, when in fact they only bring down the individual patient's out-of-pocket costs paid to doctors, hospitals, and pharmacies. The costs themselves are not reduced in the slightest when additional money to pay for these costs is collected in taxes or insurance premiums and routed through either government or private bureaucracies. Since these bureaucracies and the people who work in them are not free, they ***add*** to the cost of providing medical treatment. Most proposals to bring down the cost of medical care

[3] See Sally Satel, "Desperately Seeking a Kidney," *New York Times Magazine*, December 16, 2007, p. 65.

pay little or no attention to the actual *cost* of creating pharmaceutical drugs, training medical students, or building and equipping hospitals.

To the extent that the government imposes some form of price control by refusing to pay doctors, hospitals, or pharmaceutical companies as much as they would receive through supply and demand in a free market, that does not lower the costs either. It simply means that the government refuses to pay all those costs— and such refusals to pay costs have a centuries-old track record of leading to a reduction in the amount supplied, whether what has been subject to price controls has been housing, gasoline, food, or other goods and services. Medical treatment has been no exception. The reduction in the supply of doctors, hospitals, or pharmaceutical drugs may be quantitative, qualitative, or both.

In Britain, with one of the oldest government-run health systems and therefore one which has long since gone past stage one, there have been such difficulties in getting enough British doctors that there have been large and chronic importations of foreign doctors, many from Third World countries whose qualifications standards are not always up to those in more affluent countries. British hospitals not only lack technologically advanced medical equipment that is more common in the United States, for example, but lack even elementary cleanliness, leading to deaths by infection for patients whose maladies before entering hospital care were not life-threatening. As for pharmaceutical drugs, countries which have succumbed to the politically attractive policy of keeping drug prices low by fiat, or by ineffective patent protection, have had much lower rates of discovery of major new medications than does the United States, which has been left to supply a disproportionate share of the world's major new medications.

Another confusion in discussions of medical care issues and policies is the confusion between ***medical*** care and ***health*** care. Dr. Dana Goldman, director of health economics at the RAND Corporation, has pointed out that a patient's medical care and health care are very different, noting that for a patient with diabetes, "the doctor is paid to check his feet, they're paid to check his eyes; they're not paid to make sure he goes out and exercises and really, that may be the most important thing."

Much has been made of mortality statistics which suggest that Americans' health is not as good as in some countries with government-run medical systems, as if medical care determines the state of people's health. But medical care has little effect on the homicide rate, on obesity or on deaths from drug overdoses that occur before any doctor sees the patient. Yet the identification of ***health*** care, as indicated by mortality rates, with ***medical*** care has become so automatic that a study which showed higher infant mortality rates among black Americans than among white Americans was instantly taken as showing that less prenatal care among pregnant black women was the reason. But American women of Filipino ancestry, Mexican ancestry, and of Central American and South American ancestries all had less prenatal care than white women— and *lower* infant mortality rates than white women. Indeed, Mexican Americans had less prenatal care than blacks and lower infant mortality rates than either blacks or whites.

The implicit assumption that mortality rates reflect the amount or quality of medical care is seldom subjected to any empirical test in media or political discussions comparing American medical care with medical care in other countries with more comprehensive government involvement in medical care. But the relevant comparison would be between mortality rates in different countries from health problems in which medical care makes a substantial difference, even if not the only difference. This would still not be a perfect comparison, since even here other differences between the populations in the countries being compared are factors as well. But it would be a much more relevant comparison than those that are usually made by the media and politicians. When the American College of Physicians calculated the death rate for "mortality amenable to health care" the United States was in the top three countries with low death rates of this sort out of 19 countries studied.

Various organized groups in a position to bargain for lower medical charges or lower drug prices— government agencies, health insurance companies, or large health maintenance organizations, for example— may receive preferential prices but the total costs do not go away and have to be paid by somebody. One consequence is a multi-tiered set of prices for the same medical treatment or the same medication, with the highest prices of all being paid by patients who do not have health insurance, do not belong to a health maintenance group, and are not covered by any government program. In short, misconceptions of the economic function of prices lead not only to price controls, with all their counterproductive consequences, but also to organized attempts by various institutions, laws, and policies to get most of the costs reflected in prices paid by somebody else. For society as a whole, there is no somebody else.

Chapter 4

The Economics of Housing

Shelter is one of the most basic requirements of human life and housing costs are a major item in most people's budgets. For those who own their own homes, the value of the house is often the largest item in their inventory of personal wealth. It is also one of the largest items in the cost of living. Whether housing costs are high or low can greatly affect what kind of standard of living individuals and families can afford with what is left over after paying for a place to live.

HOUSING PRICES

The old rule of thumb that housing should cost about one-fourth of one's income has become outdated for 28 million American families, who pay upwards of 30 percent of their incomes for housing. In some places, it is not uncommon for people to pay half their monthly income for the rent on their apartment or for their monthly home mortgage payment. Clearly that restricts what kind of standard of living they can afford with the other half.

The price of housing varies according to many things. One is the quality of the housing itself. Mansions generally cost more than bungalows, though there are places where a bungalow costs more than it would cost to buy a mansion in some other places. When we say that housing prices are higher in one community than in another, we implicitly mean housing of a given quality. Prices mean little if we are comparing apples and oranges—say, a villa on the beach versus a cabin in the woods.

Price Disparities

A study by the National Bureau of Economic Research in 2006 referred to "an ever-widening gap in the price of housing between the most expensive metropolitan areas or communities and the average ones." For example, during the same week, an impressive-looking four-bedroom, six-bath house with 4,370 square feet of space and "a screen-enclosed pool/spa," located adjacent to a golf course and country club, was advertised in the ***Wall Street Journal*** for $550,000, while a rather ordinary-looking house on an ordinary city street, with just 1,300 square feet of space and no pool, was advertised in the ***Palo Alto Weekly*** for $1,095,000. The first house was located in Leesburg, Florida, while the house costing nearly twice as much was located in Palo Alto, California, near Stanford University.

Meanwhile, a house with 6,000 square feet of space, including an indoor lap pool, and set on more than an acre of land in Elmira, New York, was advertised for $349,000. A number of less grandiose houses in Elmira were advertised for less than $100,000, even though most were larger and at least as attractive as the house in Palo Alto that was advertised for more than a million dollars. Such disparities were not peculiar to Palo Alto and Elmira. Similarly striking differences were found when comparing home prices in Houston, Texas, and San Jose, California:

> According to the real estate company Coldwell Banker, a standard four-bedroom, two-and-one-half bath home in a "typical middle management neighborhood" of relatively unregulated Houston cost $155,000 in 2006. That same home in San Jose cost more than $1.4 million.

Why were houses selling for nearly ten times as much in one community as in another? Clearly, it does not cost ten times as much to build a house in one place as in another. Construction costs seldom, if ever, vary by such magnitudes.

Realtors sometimes explain such disparities by saying that the three most important factors in housing prices are "location, location, and location." In a sense, that is true. But, in another sense, that explanation can be very misleading. The houses in Leesburg and Elmira had more attractive individual locations than the one in Palo Alto, in addition to being more attractive houses in themselves. Nevertheless, location is important in the sense that undoubtedly most houses in Palo Alto cost far more than most houses in Leesburg or Elmira. But that fact is not an explanation. In reality, it calls for an explanation itself.

Housing prices may be higher in one place than in another for any of a wide range of reasons. The growth of industry, income, or population may be greater in one place, leading to more competition for given amounts of housing or for land on which to build housing. In addition to these or other effects on the demand for housing, there are effects on the supply side of the equation. Restrictions on the use of land or on the building of housing can cause rising prices of homes and rising rents for apartments.

In the case of Palo Alto, the prices of homes nearly quadrupled in one decade— the 1970s— while the population actually declined slightly and several schools had to be closed, as the number of children enrolled fell by one-third. For California as a whole, that same decade saw its housing prices rise dramatically above those in the rest of the country, even though the rate of increase in income in California was *less* than that in the country as a whole. All this strongly suggests that the cause of rising housing prices in California was not from the demand side but from the supply side. The average home price on the San Francisco peninsula— the area including the city and stretching southward to Silicon Valley, 30 miles away— was $651,000 in 2005, more than three times the national average.

By and large, these prices more than three times the national average were not due to grander homes on the San Francisco peninsula, but to grander prices for ordinary homes, many of those in San Francisco itself being on very small lots because of the extremely high land prices there. In adjoining San Mateo County, where average home prices topped one million dollars in 2007, the average size of those houses was only 1,760 square feet. The states with the highest percentage of homes with four or more bedrooms— Utah, Maryland, Virginia, Colorado, and Minnesota— are not the states with the highest home prices.

In other words, there is no reason to believe that grander homes are the main reason for higher home prices in some states. In Palo Alto, not a single new house was built during the entire decade when home prices skyrocketed, so this was clearly a case of the very same houses costing some multiple of what they had cost before. Palo Alto was not unique. Moreover, the decade of the 1970s was the crucial time when housing prices skyrocketed in San Jose as well. Before that decade began, in 1969 the median price of a home in San Jose was 2.2 times the median family income in San Jose. Spending one-fourth of the median family income was enough to cover the median monthly mortgage payment and pay off the mortgage in 12 years. A decade later, in 1979, the median family home in San Jose cost 4 times the median family income in San Jose— and now it would take 40 percent of the median family income in San Jose to cover monthly mortgage payments and pay off the mortgage in 30 years. A decade after that, in 1989, the median family home in San Jose cost 5 times the median family income in the same city— and by 2005, it cost 7.5 times the median family income.

Much of California has had similar severe building restrictions and similarly high prices for both homes and apartments. Not surprisingly, rates of home ownership in California have remained significantly below home ownership rates in the country at large. As already noted, there are other parts of the country where housing prices are a fraction of what they are in California. Which of the possible causes of California's extraordinarily expensive housing are most responsible? And are those same factors at work in other places with skyrocketing housing costs like those in California?

Land Use Restrictions

An empirical study under the auspices of the National Bureau of Economic Research concluded that zoning laws "are highly correlated with high prices" of housing and that severe land use restrictions are confined to a relatively few places, many in coastal California, but also including midtown Manhattan and various other affluent enclaves scattered here and there around the country. In short, it is the land that is very expensive in these places, rather than the houses or apartments built on the land. In such places, the land often costs far more than the housing that is built on it.

In most of the country, "housing costs are quite close to the cost of new construction," the NBER study concluded, and these are areas where "land is quite cheap." As an example of how much the land adds to the cost of housing in various places, the NBER study estimated that the value of a quarter-acre lot adds about $140,000 to the price of a house in Chicago, over and above the cost of construction. In San Diego, a quarter-acre lot adds about $285,000 to the cost of the house itself, in New York City the same size lot adds about $350,000, and in San Francisco nearly $700,000. Among other things, this high price of land helps explain why many homes in San Francisco are built on less than a quarter-acre of land, often being modest-sized houses jammed close together, while selling for prices usually charged for luxury homes on spacious lots in other parts of the country.

Given the high man-made costs of various restrictions on land use, how and why do such restrictions occur? One reason is that many voters simply do not think beyond stage one— that is, they do not see the connection between land use restrictions and the various consequences which unfold over time. Another reason is that those who clearly ***do*** see the connection may not pay those costs themselves, and may instead gain financially from laws which cost others dearly. Those who already own their own homes will see the value of their homes rise as restrictions are put on the building of new homes. It is those who are already living in a given community who vote on its laws, while newcomers are the ones confronted with the higher housing prices that these restrictive laws create. Old settlers in the same communities often bought their homes when prices were lower and many of them have already paid off their mortgages.

A wide variety of devices are used to restrict the building of homes. In addition to outright prohibitions on building anything— so-called "open space" laws— there are planning commissions with arbitrary powers to limit building permits, or to make the issuance of such permits contingent on carrying out whatever designs or ancillary amenities the planning commission members choose to impose. Delays alone from repeated appearances before planning commissions in the course of trying to build even a modest-sized development can stretch out for years,[1] with these delays adding costs that can make a building project prohibitively expensive. Where a development is being financed by money borrowed from a bank or other financial institution, interest payments must continue to be made, even if the actual construction is stalled for months or years. Moreover, the mere knowledge of what a time-consuming process can be required to get planning commission approval may be a sufficient deterrent to prevent building projects from being undertaken, even if purely economic considerations would make such projects look promising in an area where housing is very scarce.

There are also "historical preservation" laws that allow all sorts of structures to be forbidden to be torn down, even when the historic nature of these structures is far less obvious than the usefulness of such laws in preventing development. In San Mateo County, California, for example, when an old racetrack with declining attendance was scheduled to be torn down and plans were under consideration to build housing and businesses on the site, a local group was quickly formed to object and demand that the race track be designated as a "historic" structure to be preserved. That group was headed by a woman who admitted that she had never set foot in that race track in all the years that both she and it had been in San Mateo County. Yet the demolition of the race track was held up for years in the

---

[1] A 2007 news story reported: "An earlier proposal approved by the city of Half Moon Bay was appealed to the California Coastal Commission in 1999, which is still conducting biological studies on the property to see where— or whether— housing would be appropriate." Julia Scott, "Trust to Purchase Contested Property," ***San Mateo County Times***, August 17, 2007, p. News 1. This project— eight years' delay and still counting— was by no means a record.

courts— after having been held up for years in the political arena.[2] "Historic preservation" is part of the arsenal of weapons available to stop development. When properly packaged politically and expressed in sufficiently lofty rhetoric, such policies attract much additional support from people who sincerely believe the rationale and do not think beyond stage one.

The preservation of agricultural land is another of the ways of restricting the building of homes or other development. Just as historical preservation restrictions do not have to prove that any structure is actually historic in any meaningful sense, so no one is required to prove that there is insufficient agricultural land before using the preservation of farmland as yet another reason to forbid building. The California Land Conservation Act offers huge reductions in property taxes to landowners who agree to keep their land agricultural. Other devices used to impede the building of homes include a refusal to connect new homes to the existing water system, on the grounds that there is insufficient water in the system— which may also be accompanied by a refusal to connect the existing water system to additional sources of water. Efforts to improve roads or highways may be resisted locally as another means of discouraging development. Efforts to improve a stretch of coastal highway in northern California known as "Devil's Slide," because of many fatal accidents there, have been thwarted repeatedly by local residents who do not want the community where they live to become more accessible to others.

The most severe land use restrictions are those which simply forbid the building of any housing at all in specified areas. Such laws are typically described politically in terms of their ostensible goals— "open space," for example— rather than in terms of what they actually do, which is ban the building of housing and other structures. When more than two-thirds of the land in San Mateo County, on the San Francisco peninsula, is legally off-limits to housing as "open space," it can hardly be surprising that the

---

2 Among the claims made was this: "We believe that the race track is an irreplaceable cultural and economic part of San Mateo." Dana Yates, "Track Battle Gets Another Day in Court," ***The Daily Journal*** (San Mateo), September 5, 2007, pp. 1 ff.

price of the remaining land is much higher than in places without such severe restrictions on land use. Nor is San Mateo County unique. Such housing ban ("open space") policies are common in communities on the San Francisco peninsula.

What all this means, from the standpoint of the economy as a whole, is that the allocation of land among its competing uses is not determined by the competing bids of potential users but is heavily influenced by tax policies, as well as by legal restrictions on the transfer of land to non-agricultural uses, and by the building bans known as "open space" policies. Once land has been subjected to these and other legal restrictions on its uses, its market value can decline drastically. At that point, some government agency or private non-profit conservationist organization can buy the land for a fraction of its value to alternative users who are seeking to use that land for housing. On the San Francisco peninsula, for example, the Peninsula Open Space Trust has purchased "17,000 acres of open space," in order to "ensure that prime Coastside real estate is not developed into mini-mansions, but preserved for farming," as the ***San Mateo County Times*** put it.

In short, under severe land use restrictions, prices no longer serve the function of allocating scarce resources among competing alternative users. Instead, third parties are able to override other people's desires or preferences with their own desires and preferences, not by competing with them on an equal plane in the market but by using politics to tilt the competition in their direction by passing laws to prohibit the choices of other people. This has been made possible not only by courts' erosions of Constitutionally guaranteed property rights but also by media disparagements of such things as "mini-mansions"— as if large homes are something negative— as part of a general slant of disparaging what some people want to do and being in favor of what other people want done.

Often posterity is invoked, as in this case, where one of the farmers benefitting from the official Midpeninsula Regional Open Space District's policy was quoted as saying: "I've got 10 grandkids and some of them would like to be here someday. We want to keep farming as long as we can." As in many other such cases, what some people want is stated as if it is automatically pre-emptive over what other people want— and as if their posterity's desires are pre-emptive over the desires of the posterity of other people with different desires and preferences.

Although California has a disproportionate number of places with severe land use restrictions and extremely high housing costs, such restrictions have produced similar results elsewhere. Moreover, history tells the same story as economics. Before such laws and policies spread through much of coastal California in the 1970s, housing prices in that state were very similar to what they were in the rest of the country. Afterwards, California prices for given housing became some multiple of what they were in places without such severe land use restrictions. Indeed, housing prices in coastal California became some multiple of housing prices in that same state's interior valleys, where such policies either did not exist or were far less severe. Particular places in other parts of the country with land use restrictions similar to those in coastal California have likewise had very high prices for homes and very high rents for apartments.

Nantucket, Massachusetts, became the first large community in the United States where the average price of a home exceeded a million dollars, and its land use restrictions are among the most severe anywhere. Loudoun County, Virginia, enacted laws in 2001 that restricted the building of homes to one house per 10 acres in some places, 20 acres in others and 50 acres in still others. According to the ***Washington Post***: "The board's actions yesterday wiped 83,158 potential homes from Loudoun's plans"— no doubt ensuring rising prices for existing homes. Outsiders who might have lived in those tens of thousands of additional homes of course had no vote in Loudoun County. In an earlier time, their interests would nevertheless have been represented in the marketplace because property rights would have been protected by the courts, so that homes and apartments could be built as property owners saw fit, without political authorities being able to place such severe restrictions.

Even if existing landowners in Loudoun County had no desire to build more homes or apartment buildings, housing demand from more than 80,000 people would provide ample incentives for developers to offer bids to buy land from those existing landowners. Obviously there would be more buyers— and therefore higher prices and more profits available for those existing landowners who were prepared to sell— when developers were free to determine how many houses they would build per acre than when such decisions are restricted by law. The crucial point here, however, is not the good or bad fortune of landowners or developers, but the fact that it is the demand of home-seekers— including apartment tenants— which enables developers to profit by supplying that demand. In other words, the real competition for land is between those who wish to buy homes and rent apartments in Loudoun County, on the one hand, versus those current Loudoun County voters who pass laws at no cost to themselves that impose great costs on others.

In short, there are two competing sets of people who wish to use the same resources in different ways. Ordinarily, property rights allow such competition to take place in the marketplace, while court-sanctioned abridgements of property rights allow the competition to take place through a political process in which only one set of competitors can vote. While property rights are often thought of as rights whose purpose and effect are to protect those fortunate enough to own substantial property, the larger purpose is to serve the economic interests of the whole society, including people who own no property. In the case of housing, property rights allow the interests of people who rent apartments to carry weight in economic competition because, although they own no housing and may have modest incomes, in the aggregate their purchasing power can exceed that of affluent residents in a community that wants to keep them out.

Intermediaries such as developers bid against the affluent residents on the basis of the money they anticipate making from building homes and renting apartments. In such a competition, mansions on large estates can be bid away and the land then broken up into smaller units, on which more modest homes and apartment buildings can be built. Even if many existing residents wish to maintain their community as it is, if individual property rights are respected by the courts, then those particular residents who find the developers' bids for their property to be attractive will sell— and the remaining residents will find the character of the community changing around them, whether they resist selling or not. At some point, the holdouts may decide to leave and seek to find the kind of community they like somewhere else. The alternative is to forestall this whole process before it can get under way by abridging individual property rights through collective action to pass land use restrictions under such names as "open space" laws, "environmental protection" policies, "smart growth," or whatever other phrases have political resonance.

Housing markets and markets for commercial properties are among the most dynamic markets, when they are not frozen by law. Many thriving urban communities in California are located in places that were orange groves within living memory. Theodore Roosevelt grew up in a home that was out in the suburbs, at a location which is today in midtown Manhattan, on the same street as Carnegie Hall. In communities across the country, the poor live in neighborhoods that were once the neighborhoods of the affluent and the rich— and in other communities "gentrification" has moved the affluent and the rich into neighborhoods once populated by the poor. Over the lifetime of given individuals, those individuals often occupy very different kinds of housing at different stages of their own development— a room in their parents' homes or in a college dormitory, their own small apartment upon entering the workforce, a larger apartment or a house after getting married and having children, and later perhaps a condominium in a retirement community after the children are grown and gone.

It is much the same story with commercial buildings. The original Waldorf-Astoria hotel was torn down to make way for the Empire State Building to be erected on the same site. Madison Square Garden has been torn down and a successor rebuilt a number of times and at a number of locations in the many years since it was first built at Madison Square on Fifth Avenue and 23rd Street. In short, whether with residential or commercial buildings, there has been no fixed, ideal configuration of structures. Instead, structures have adapted to the changing circumstances of individuals and of the economy and society. But those who are today ensconced in many upscale communities often seek to freeze the existing community as it is by law, using various political devices to block others from exercising the same freedom of choice that they exercised when they chose to live where they settled. Often this is done using noble phrases expressing concern for "preserving" something for "posterity." But what this amounts to is that the posterity of existing residents is to have a legal right to keep out the posterity of other people.

Many advocates of land-use restrictions claim that rising housing prices only show that their policies have made the protected communities more desirable, thereby causing increased demand. But demand by itself cannot explain skyrocketing housing prices, so long as the supply of land has not been restricted by government. By and large, it has not been the growth of either income or population which has caused housing prices to increase drastically. As a study of housing prices in various parts of the country concluded:

> In the absence of restrictions on land supply, homebuilders have proven themselves able to meet the demand for housing in the fastest-growing areas. San Jose grew by nearly 14 percent per year in the 1950s, yet housing remained affordable in 1959. During the 1990s, the Atlanta, Dallas-Ft. Worth, Houston, and Phoenix urban areas all grew by 900,000 people or more, while the Denver, Los Angeles, and Portland urban areas grew by only about 400,000, and San Jose grew by only about 100,000 people. The relatively unregulated regions also grew faster in percentage terms than the regulated ones. Yet the fast-growing regions all maintained or even increased their housing affordability, while the slower-growing regions either remained unaffordable or significantly lost affordability during the 1990s.

Although the population of Las Vegas almost tripled in the last two decades of the twentieth century, the real median housing price— that is, the money price corrected for inflation— did not change, as the supply of newly built housing kept up with the demand. There were few local land-use restrictions. However, 90 percent of the land in Nevada is owned by the federal government and, after environmentalist groups raised objections to the continued sale of federal lands to developers at the beginning of the twenty-first century, Las Vegas housing prices shot up as such prices have shot up under local land-use restrictions elsewhere. Although this restriction on the supply of land was federal rather than local, it was still the supply, not the demand, that was responsible for rising housing prices.

Affordable Housing

The often-expressed desire for a national government program to produce "affordable housing" has misconceived the reality. There is not a crisis of high housing prices across the nation, there is a severe housing price crisis in particular places where land use restrictions and other severely restrictive building regulations have driven housing prices up beyond what most people can readily afford. Historically, the government has not been the solution to the problem of "affordable housing" but a major part of the problem, especially when its restrictions drive the price of housing well above the cost of constructing new housing.

The virtual impossibility of producing much housing that ordinary people could afford under severe land use restrictions has led to various token amounts of affordable housing being created, either by government subsidies or by imposing legal requirements on private developers to build a certain percentage of their housing to be sold or rented at prices "below market," as a precondition for getting permits to build at all. The amount of "affordable housing" produced by either of these methods has of course been very limited by the unwillingness of taxpayers to pay for massive amounts of subsidies and by the fact that developers could recover their losses on "below market" housing only by increasing still more the rent and home sale prices to others, who obviously do not have unlimited resources either.

Laws and policies to force builders to sell or rent a certain percentage of their housing at prices "below market" are sometimes called "inclusionary zoning." Palo Alto pioneered in "inclusionary zoning" in 1973 and, by 2007, nearly one-third of the cities and counties in California had such policies. Under the headline "Affordable Housing Quotas Working," the ***San Mateo County Times*** quoted the head of a local non-profit housing group as declaring inclusionary housing policies to be "a solution that's actually working by putting roofs over people's heads." "Working," however, is in the eye of the beholder. When only 7 percent of Palo Alto's police are living in Palo Alto, this suggests that the amount of "affordable housing" created by "inclusionary zoning" comes nowhere close to solving the problem created by policies which make "inclusionary zoning" a cosmetic solution to a very real and very serious problem.

It is not uncommon in Palo Alto for the "below market" price of a condominium to be $300,000 or $400,000, which would not be below market in much of the rest of the country, and which is hardly something that could be afforded by people with low incomes. Full-sized houses "below market" would of course be even more expensive and beyond the reach of many people with middle-class incomes.

The vision of affordable housing as government-subsidized housing built specifically for people of modest or low incomes misconceives the nature of the housing market. Different parts of that market are not hermetically sealed off from one another. When new upscale houses are built for sale to affluent or wealthy buyers, these buyers usually vacate existing homes or apartments when they move into their new homes. As affluent and wealthy people move up into the latest and most luxurious housing, middle class people are able to move into the housing that has been vacated. Similarly, people of lower incomes move into the housing left vacant by the movement of the middle class into better housing. This chain reaction means that the increased supply of housing tends to reduce the price not only of the particular kind of housing that was built but reduces both home prices and apartment rents in general, since there has after all been an increase in the total supply of housing.

Such a chain reaction is not usually a protracted process because the owners of vacated housing, whether homes or apartments, have financial incentives to minimize the amount of time that the housing remains vacant, since unsold houses and unrented apartments do not bring in any money. Because of such chain reactions, homes and apartments occupied by working class people today were not necessarily built for working class people originally. Often this housing was built for people in higher income brackets who vacated it over the years as that housing aged and newer housing with more modern amenities was built. In the early twentieth century, for example, Harlem was the home of middle class white people, though two decades later it was the home of working class black people.

One of the incidental consequences of this circulation of housing among different classes of people over time is that an era of improved housing for all is often marked by laments that "the old neighborhood is going downhill." Not only does a given neighborhood age, as it does so it is often occupied by people of successively lower socioeconomic levels, often with less genteel lifestyles. Nevertheless, all classes of people may be living in better housing than they had before, despite the widespread laments. The various forms of land use restrictions attempt to bring this circulation of housing to a halt, for the benefit of existing residents of upscale communities.

Although many people see government intervention as necessary to produce "affordable housing," history as well as economics says otherwise. Prior to the advent of large-scale government involvement in the housing market, people tended to pay a ***smaller*** proportion of their incomes for housing, even though incomes in earlier times were lower. Back in 1901, Americans spent a smaller proportion of their income on housing than they did a century later—23 percent in 1901 versus 33 percent in 2002-03. New Yorkers paid 24 percent of their incomes for housing in 1901 and 38 percent in 2003, even though real income had quadrupled over that span of time. Even in California, home prices were much lower, and very similar to home prices elsewhere in the nation, before local building restrictions became severe in many parts of that state during the 1970s. Just as building new housing for the affluent tends to lower housing prices for all classes of people, so restricting housing tends to raise all housing prices, including the prices of housing that were once affordable.

In short, it does not take the government to produce affordable housing and, in fact, rapid escalation of housing prices has often followed increased government intervention, especially in the form of building restrictions.

Human Consequences

The kinds of people adversely affected by land use restrictions and the rise of housing prices to levels they could not afford include many people that every community employs, such as school teachers, nurses, and policemen. Such people are seldom paid enough to be able to live in the communities where they work, when those communities have skyrocketing housing costs. As already noted, in Palo Alto only 7 percent of that city's police force actually live in the city; nearly one-fourth live on the other side of the San Francisco Bay. A study published in *The Economist* magazine found that the average salary of a nurse would make a two-bedroom apartment affordable, with 30 percent of that salary going for rent, in Dallas, Boston, or Chicago, would almost make it affordable in Washington, but would be less than three-quarters of what would be needed to rent such an apartment in San Francisco. In New York, according to the *New York Times*, "the supply of apartments considered affordable to households with incomes like those earned by starting firefighters or police officers plunged by a whopping 205,000 in just three years, between 2002 and 2005."

Low-income people are especially hard hit. The black population in San Francisco, for example, declined from more than 79,000 to less than 61,000 between the 1990 and 2000 censuses, even though the city's total population grew by more than 50,000 people during that same span. Similarly, in adjacent San Mateo County, the black population fell from more than 35,000 to less than 25,000 during the same decade, even though the total population of this county also grew by about 50,000 people. All the while, people in such places continued to speak of a need for "diversity" and "affordable housing"— neither of which they have or are likely to have.

High housing prices in San Francisco have driven many people to relocate across the Bay in Oakland or in other parts of Alameda County. But, after a while, this increased demand drove housing prices up in Alameda County to levels that many people there could not afford, and so they moved farther inland, to Contra Costa County and beyond, to find housing within the range of their incomes. For example, a story in the ***San Francisco Chronicle*** in 2003 began:

> Each weekday at 4:30 a.m., Frank Montgomery rolls down the driveway of his brand new home to begin the 70-minute trek to work at a Sunol water filtration plant in Alameda County.

Far from being atypical, this commuter represented a growing trend. Data from the U.S. Bureau of the Census showed a 49 percent increase between the 1990 and 2000 censuses in the number of people commuting from seven outlying counties into the nine counties in and around the San Francisco Bay Area. "Many of them endure hours-long drives each way on congested highways," according to the ***San Francisco Chronicle***. How early people from these distant areas have to start may be indicated by a local newspaper account of commuters from the eastern part of Contra Costa County, whose traffic clogs the highways into the San Francisco Bay Area so much that the movement of that traffic turns "to molasses at 5:20 a.m., and it stays that way for four hours." California realtors call such long commutes "driving 'til you qualify" to buy a house you can afford, even if it means spending three hours a day on the highway.

The difference that distance makes in home prices can be shown by the fact that when the average home price in San Francisco in 2005 was $790,000, in adjacent Alameda County across the Bay it was $621,000 and in Contra Costa County, on the other side of Alameda County, the average home price was $575,000. Sales agents farther out in the valleys report that most of those who are looking for homes in newly built subdivisions there "are Bay Area residents thrilled by the idea of paying less than $300,000 for a 2,000-square-foot house." Even in California's central valley, however, a rapid growth in population, due to people displaced from in and around San Francisco, has produced a rapid growth in housing prices, though not to the levels found in coastal California. In just five years, the average price of a house out in Merced County— more than a hundred miles from San Francisco— rose from $96,000 to $166,000.

In the San Francisco Bay Area, the black population has moved outward over the decades, from the most expensive to the less expensive areas. One sign of the economic reasons for this population displacement is that, while the black populations of San Francisco and San Mateo County have declined significantly in just one decade— as has the black population of Los Angeles, Marin County, Monterey, and other coastal California communities— the black population of various inland communities has been increasing dramatically. From 1990 to 2006, the black population of San Francisco fell by 35 percent and fell by 33 percent in adjacent San Mateo County. Across the Bay in Alameda County, the decline was less— 16 percent— and in Contra Costa County, on the other side of Alameda County, there was an actual increase in the black population of 23 percent. In Solano County, on the other side of Contra Costa County, the increase was 28 percent, and in Napa County, still farther away, the increase in the black population was 104 percent over the same span of time.

Far away, out in the valleys, it is the white population which is expected to be overtaken soon by the various minorities moving in, and to become a minority themselves.

Rent Control

One solution to the problem of "affordable housing" that many find attractive is rent control. It shares both economic and political characteristics with other forms of price control. Its political advantage is that its goal is attractive, so that it gains the political support of those who think in terms of desirable goals, rather than in terms of the incentives and constraints created— or the consequences of such incentives and constraints. Those who do not think beyond stage one find rent control especially attractive because the good effects come immediately, while the bad effects come later— and persist for decades or even generations.

Among the consequences of price controls in general have been (1) a shortage, as the quantity demanded increases while the quantity supplied decreases, both in response to artificially lower prices, (2) a decline in quality, as the shortage makes it unnecessary for the sellers to maintain high quality in order to sell, and (3) a black market, when the difference between the legal price and the price people are willing to pay becomes large enough to compensate for the risks of breaking the law. These same consequences have recurred again and again, for all sorts of different goods and services whose prices have been held down by law, in countries around the world, over a period of centuries, and under governments ranging from monarchy to democracy to totalitarian dictatorship. It should hardly be surprising that similar things happen in the housing market when there is rent control.

Perhaps the most basic principle in economics is that people tend to buy more at a lower price than at a higher price. Rent control enables people to demand more housing than they would otherwise. In San Francisco, a study in 2001 showed that 49 percent of that city's rent-controlled apartments were occupied by just one person each. Similar patterns have been found under rent control in New York City and in Sweden. One reason, then, for a housing shortage under rent control laws is that more people occupy more housing space than they would in a competitive market, where they would have to bid against others whose needs for housing might be more urgent than theirs or who would have two incomes from which to bid for housing.

The other reason for a housing shortage is that less housing gets supplied at a lower price than at a higher price. Builders tend to reduce the amount of housing they build when their ability to recover their costs from the rents they charge is reduced. Where rent control laws are severe, there may be no new housing built at all, except for government-subsidized housing where the taxpayers make up the difference between the cost of supplying housing and the rents that can be charged under rent control. Therefore one of the consequences of rent control over time is an increase in the average age of housing, as the building of new housing declines or stops completely.

A study in San Francisco in 2001 found that more than three-quarters of its rent-controlled housing was more than half a century old and 44 percent of it was more than 70 years old. In Melbourne, Australia, not a single new building was built in the first nine years after World War II because rent control laws made it unprofitable to build any. In Massachusetts, a state law banning local rent control laws led to the building of residential housing in some communities for the first time in a quarter of a century.

Usually, rent control laws do not apply to office buildings, so there may be surplus office space, with high vacancy rates, in the same city where there is a housing shortage with virtually no vacancies available in rent-controlled apartment buildings. In some places, rent control laws do not apply to luxury housing, so there is a shift of resources from the building of ordinary housing for ordinary people to the building of luxury housing that only the very affluent or the wealthy can afford. A study of rent control in various countries in Europe concluded: "New investment in private unsubsidized rented housing is essentially nonexistent in all the European countries surveyed, except for luxury housing." Such shifts to luxury housing help explain one of the supreme paradoxes of rent control— that cities with rent control laws typically have ***higher*** rents than cities without such laws. New York, after decades of severe rent control laws, has had the highest apartment rents in the nation. In New York, vacant apartments that rent for $2,000 a month or more are freed from the rent regulations that apply to half the apartments in the city.

Not only does rent control reduce incentives to build new housing, it reduces incentives to maintain existing housing. Painting, repairs and other maintenance activities all cost money. In a competitive market, landlords have no choice but to spend that money, in order to attract tenants to keep the apartments filled. Under rent control, however, there are more applicants than apartments, so there is less need to maintain the appearance of the premises or the functioning of the equipment that keeps the heating system and other systems working. In short, existing housing tends to deteriorate faster, as a result of reduced maintenance under rent control, and replacements are built more slowly, if at all. Declining numbers of rental units available after rent control laws were passed have been observed in various American cities, as well as in Canada and overseas.

Laws that make both landlords and tenants worse off provide incentives for the two to operate outside the law, that is, to have black markets. Bribes to landlords or building superintendents to be put at the top of waiting lists have been one common form of black market activity under rent control. Other forms of illegal activity include landlords' abandonment of buildings after the services they are legally required to provide cost more than the rent they are legally allowed to collect. The New York City government has found itself in possession of literally thousands of abandoned buildings, as landlords have fled underground to escape ruinous losses. Many of these buildings have been boarded up, even though they are perfectly capable of providing much-needed housing, if maintained. The number of housing units in abandoned buildings in New York City is far more than enough to house all the homeless people sleeping on the city's streets.

Although rent control is often thought of as a way to protect the poor from unaffordable housing, only the poor who initially occupied the rent-controlled housing benefit. Those who are on the inside looking out— whether rich or poor— benefit when rent control begins. Later, others on the outside looking in benefit only to the extent that they are relatives or friends of the initial beneficiaries and have the rent-controlled housing passed on to them when the original occupiers leave or die. Some outsiders bribe the original occupiers to get the rent-controlled apartment. In any event, the actual connection between income and the benefits of rent control are tenuous. More than one-fourth of the households in rent-controlled apartments in San Francisco in 2001 had incomes of $100,000 or more.[3]

"Creative" Financing

One of the key factors in the housing market is the interest rate charged on mortgage loans. Since mortgage loans compete with other credit in the country's general financial markets, they tend to go up and down when the interest rates on other forms of credit go up and down, and all are influenced by the interest rate set by the Federal Reserve System, based on its assessment of conditions in the economy as a whole. This means that, like other interest rates, the interest rates on mortgage loans have varied widely over a long span of years— and sometimes within a relatively short span. For

[3] Incidentally, this was the first empirical study of rent control commissioned by the city of San Francisco. Since rent control began there in 1979, this means that for more than two decades these laws were enforced and extended with no serious attempt to gauge their actual economic and social consequences, as distinguished from their political popularity.

example, conventional 30-year mortgage loans charged about 8 percent interest in 1973, and that rose to about 18 percent by 1983, and then fell gradually, with small scale ups and downs, to about 6 percent by 2005.

In the housing market, a difference of just a percentage point or two in the interest rate can have a major effect on the cost of buying a house. To borrow $500,000 to buy a house when the interest rate is 6 percent would require a mortgage payment of nearly $3,000 a month with a 30-year mortgage. But, when the interest rate is 4 percent, the mortgage payment would be just under $2,400 a month. That is a difference of more than $7,000 per year in housing costs. Another way of looking at the same thing is that a monthly mortgage payment that would allow someone to buy a home costing $500,000 when the interest rate is 6 percent would allow that same person to buy a home costing $600,000 when the interest rate is 4 percent, making the same monthly mortgage payment.

Since how much an individual can afford to borrow in order to buy a house is affected by the interest rate, low interest rates tend to lead more people to have a demand for more houses, as distinguished from apartments, as well as more expensive housing.[4] This tends to lead to home prices being bid up to higher levels when interest rates are low. At the height of the housing boom in California, home prices in San Mateo County rose by an average of $2,000 a *day* during the month of March, 2005. Skyrocketing housing prices then tend to cause buyers to seek, and lenders to provide, creative ways of lowering monthly payments on mortgage loans.

One way to lower monthly mortgage payments is to have an interest-only loan— that is, to pay only the interest on the loan and nothing toward reducing the debt itself. However, this interest-only arrangement is usually limited to the first three to five years, after which higher mortgage payments are required, with the additional amounts now going toward repaying the

[4] Another side effect is to cause people to take out new loans to pay off existing loans made when interest rates were higher. Such refinancing shot up in the years from 2000 to 2004, then dropped sharply as the interest rates began to rise from their unusually low levels. Matthew Miller, "A Visual Essay: Post-Recessionary Employment Growth Related to the Housing Market," *Monthly Labor Review*, October 2006, p. 24.

mortgage loan. Such an arrangement enables a home to be bought by someone who expects to have rising income over time, so that larger mortgage payments can be afforded in later years.

Interest-only mortgage loans became especially popular during a period of unusually low interest rates at the beginning of the twenty-first century. These were usually adjustable-rate mortgages, which meant that as interest rates rose to more normal levels in the economy as a whole, the interest rate on the mortgage loan would rise correspondingly. Mortgage payments could therefore increase over time, even before it became necessary to make payments toward the principal on the loan, and doubly so after both higher interest rates took effect and payments toward the mortgage principal became due.

What made it tempting for many home buyers to enter into these risky financial arrangements was not just that this enabled them to get started on buying a home, at a time when their income was inadequate to afford high prices otherwise, but also that this was a way for them to build up equity in their home, even before beginning to pay off the mortgage loan. That was because home prices were rising sharply in many places, and especially in California. Thus a home buyer with an interest-only, adjustable rate mortgage on a house costing $600,000 might pay nothing toward the loan for five years and yet, if the house increased in value to $800,000 over those years, the buyers would have gained $200,000 in equity. What that means is that, even if it became impossible to make the larger mortgage payments due when the interest-only period expired, the home buyer could sell the house, repaying the $600,000 mortgage out of the proceeds of the sale price, and still have $200,000 left over as profit.[5]

---

[5] Another advantage of acquiring equity as home prices rise is that the mortgage can be refinanced, extracting some of that equity to spend immediately. For example, if the $600,000 home rose in value to $800,000, the buyer could take out a $200,000 loan, using the home as collateral, and spend half of it to reduce the mortgage to $500,000, thereby lowering the monthly mortgage payment, while still having $100,000 left to spend. From January 1999 to 2006, homeowners extracted more than $2.6 trillion in equity from their homes. Damon Darlin, "Mortgage Lesson No. 1: Home is Not a Piggy Bank," *New York Times*, November 4, 2006, pp. C1, C6.

All of this is based on an assumption of rising home prices. If home prices remain stable or fall, the home buyer might simply have to give up the house when the time arrived for larger mortgage payments, without a corresponding increase in the home buyer's income. All the mortgage payments made up to that point would in effect have been simply rent, with an option to buy, and any down payment made would be money lost— often a substantial amount of money whose loss could be ill-afforded by people whose modest incomes led them into using such a risky way of financing the purchase of a home in the first place.

Rapidly rising home prices in many places in the early twenty-first century led increasing numbers of people to try these "creative" and risky methods of purchasing a home. Fewer than 10 percent of new mortgages in the United States were interest-only mortgages in 2002 but that rose to 31 percent by 2005 as home prices rose. Such financial arrangements were especially prevalent where housing prices were especially high. The *New York Times* reported: "In most California cities, as well as in Denver, Washington, Phoenix and Seattle, interest-only loans represented 40 percent or more of all mortgages issued in 2005." In the San Francisco Bay Area, where home prices were rising especially sharply, interest-only mortgages went from being 11 percent of all new mortgages in 2002 to being 66 percent of all new mortgages in 2005.

After reducing interest rates to record lows at the beginning of the twenty-first century, the Federal Reserve System began successively raising these rates in 2004 and continued doing so until interest rates rose from one percent to 5.25 percent by 2006. Housing prices began leveling off and then declining, in the wake of higher interest rates, which reduced the demand for houses. At the same time, these higher interest rates raised the monthly payments on adjustable-rate mortgages, putting many home buyers who had resorted to risky loans in a precarious financial position, from which they could no longer extricate themselves by selling their homes for higher prices than they paid. In 2006, average home prices in the United States fell for the first time in more than a decade— and fell by record amounts. In September 2006, California led the nation in mortgage foreclosures, which doubled over the previous year in San Francisco and adjoining San Mateo County, and more than tripled in Alameda County across the Bay.

In 2007, the ***New York Times*** reported:

> The day of reckoning is near for millions of homeowners who financed their dream house by taking out an adjustable-rate mortgage.
>
> Rates are resetting higher, and in some cases, the monthly mortgage payments that were so affordable in 2004 or 2005 when the loan was signed will push homeowners to their limit or beyond. . .
>
> But know this: lenders do not want to get stuck with a property. They have to maintain it and then try to sell it on the open market, usually at a loss. Some industry analysts say that it costs a bank an average of $40,000 to foreclose on a loan.

Even so, in 2007 there was an 800 percent increase in the number of California homes whose deeds reverted to bank ownership. In short, rising rates of mortgage foreclosures indicated that both borrowers and lenders found themselves backed into a very bad corner. In June 2007, foreclosure notices nationwide were up 87 percent over the previous year. In the San Francisco Bay Area, foreclosures nearly tripled in one year. Financial institutions were hard hit by the defaults that preceded these foreclosures. Merrill Lynch lost $7.9 billion in mortgage-related transactions. As far away as Germany, the Deutsche Industriebank was bailed out as a result of "losses on U.S. subprime mortgages," the ***Wall Street Journal*** reported.

Another "creative" way of financing the purchase of a home has been to take out a mortgage with no down payment. As with interest-only mortgages, this reduces the initial cash outlay required. But, in this case, it means a larger mortgage debt for a house of a given price, and therefore larger monthly mortgage payments than if there had been a down payment. As a representative of a private research group that studies the California economy put it, "The only way some people are able to buy is to become more heavily indebted and put less down. That's a scary sign." As with other risky expedients for buying a home, this method of financing was especially resorted to in the high-priced California housing market— and particularly by first-time home buyers. Less than 5 percent of California mortgages were no-down-payment mortgages in 2000 but, by 2006, such mortgages were 21 percent of all California mortgages. Among first-time home buyers in California, such mortgages were 40 percent of all mortgages. What one housing expert called "some pretty funky financing" contributed to the later skyrocketing rates of foreclosure.

Among the political responses to the housing market decline were demands that the government "do something" to help people who took out risky loans. "Our heart goes out to these people," said the mayor of South San Francisco. "It's not fair. I think somehow they're coerced into these situations they can't get out of." One of his constituents who was paying 6.5 percent on an adjustable rate mortgage in 2004 was by 2007 paying 12 percent, with corresponding increases in monthly mortgage payments. In short, politicians began to cast themselves in the role of rescuers of people from risky deals that people got themselves into as a result of soaring housing prices created by local politicians' land use restrictions and the Federal Reserve System's low interest rate policies. But those who do not think beyond stage one were unlikely to connect the dots.

Apartments and Condominiums

Communities with expensive houses usually also have expensive apartment rents, since high land costs and high demand to live in a given community affect both. However, short-run trends can be very different, and even opposite, when it comes to the cost of buying a home versus the cost of renting an apartment.

Unusually low interest rates, such as prevailed in the first years of the twenty-first century, reduce the cost of buying a house but have little or no immediate effect on the cost of renting an apartment.[6] People who are weighing these alternative housing options would therefore tend to choose

---

[6] The long-run effect of low interest rates would be to reduce the cost of borrowing money to build apartment buildings, thereby increasing the supply and reducing rents. But constructing apartment buildings usually takes longer than building a house, so the tendency of a larger supply of apartments to reduce rent would be delayed, even if other things were equal. But other things are not equal because, when people are moving out of apartments into houses, there is less incentive to construct apartment buildings.

buying a house more often than otherwise during a period of unusually low interest rates. Thus apartment occupancy rates declined in many San Francisco Bay Area communities in the early twenty-first century, as low interest rates led many people to move into houses.

The shift of people from apartments to houses tended to reduce the demand for apartments, keeping apartment rents lower than otherwise while raising housing prices. Both remain higher than the national average in communities with severe building restrictions but the short-run ***movements*** of home prices and apartment rents still tended to be in opposite directions. Nationally, both home prices and apartment rents rose between 1996 and 2006, but the ***ratio*** of apartment rents to housing prices began falling, as home prices more than doubled while apartment rents rose by 48 percent.

During the home prices boom in various communities in the San Francisco Bay Area, average apartment rents in several communities on the San Francisco peninsula actually declined absolutely from their 2001 peak of more than $1,900 a month to a low of about $1,300 a month in 2005. Conversely, when home prices began falling in 2006, apartment rents began to rise in these communities for the first time since the dot-com bust, which had earlier put a damper on the rise of home prices. They also rose in San Jose and other Bay Area communities to more than $1,500 a month, as occupancy rates rose, "particularly near universities and job centers," according to the ***San Francisco Chronicle***.

In San Francisco itself, by August 2007 the average monthly rent for a one-bedroom apartment was about $1,980, for two-bedroom apartments $2,900, and for three-bedroom apartments $3,800. As with houses, high prices in San Francisco did not imply grand luxury. The ***San Francisco Chronicle*** reported a graduate student seeking a place to live, "visiting one exorbitantly priced hovel after another." Pretty talk about "open space" can lead to some very ugly economic realities overlooked by those who do not think beyond stage one. San Francisco was not unique. There was a 12 percent increase in rents in just one year in San Jose.

Condominium prices move more like the prices of houses but those who build condominiums take on more risk. As the *Wall Street Journal* reported:

> With single-family homes, "you put up a couple of model homes and build the rest as you get sales contracts." says James Haughey, director of research at Reed Construction Data in Norcross, Ga. "But you have to build the entire . . . building before you can sell a single condo."

A sudden change in the housing market while condominiums are in the process of being built, such as occurred in 2006, can leave the builders of condominiums further out on a limb financially when condominium sales drop. In the San Francisco Bay Area, some condominium builders resorted to auctions to sell their units quickly, with units initially priced at more than $400,000 being put on sale for bids starting at $250,000. Since those who build condominiums are usually expected to pay off the loans that financed the construction shortly after the construction is completed, the money is not there to do so if there are not enough condominiums sold within a relatively short span of time. This problem for builders then becomes a problem for lenders, who cannot collect the debts that are owed to them and foreclosures, which are often money-losing propositions for lenders even in good times, are an even bigger problem in a market where condominiums are not selling very fast.

During the housing boom, the amount of bank loans for the building of condominiums rose sharply, from less than $10 billion in 2003 to more than $20 billion in 2005 and more than $30 billion in 2006. But the sudden slump in the housing market in 2006 left many borrowers unable to repay their loans and many lenders taking huge losses as a result. Corus Bankshares of Chicago, one of the largest lenders to condominium builders, saw their "nonperforming assets" rise to nearly 400 times their previous level in just one year, from $620,000 to $242 million.

Just as markets for luxury houses, middle-class houses, and working-class houses are not hermetically sealed off from one another, so markets for houses, apartments and condominiums are not independent of one another.

The same physical unit in a building can be either an apartment or a condominium, or change its status from one to the other, as the general housing market changes. After the housing price drop of 2006, the ***Wall Street Journal*** reported in 2007:

> More people who stretched to buy homes have returned to the rental ranks, while others, limited by tightening credit, have delayed jumping into the ownership pool. At the same time, after years of existing apartment buildings being converted into condominiums, the trend is reversing; according to Real Capital Analytics, a New York-based research company, "reversions"— condo buildings that were turned back into rentals— outstripped condo conversions in the second quarter of 2007, the first time that has happened since the 1980s.

HOUSING "REFORMS"

For more than a century, political and social movements in various countries have promoted laws and policies which over-ride the choices made by tenants, landlords, builders, home buyers, and others involved in the private market for homes and apartments. Among the most common of these interventions have been "slum-clearance" programs. Other interventions include laws intended to prevent "urban sprawl," or to either promote or prevent the racial segregation of housing.

Slum Clearance

Whether called "slum clearance" in the nineteenth century or "urban renewal" in the twentieth century, government programs to demolish housing considered unsatisfactory by third party observers have displaced vast numbers of low-income tenants, often supposedly for their own good. However, all this activity, expense, and disruptions of lives are based on the crucial— and unsubstantiated— assumption that third parties who pay no costs know better what is good for low-income tenants than those tenants themselves do.

Slum clearance programs in the nineteenth century created no new housing and urban renewal programs in the twentieth century created fewer housing units than they destroyed, with rents on many of these new units being beyond the price range that the displaced tenants could afford. The net result was that both these programs restricted, rather than expanded, the options available to low-income tenants. However disagreeable the pre-existing housing may have looked to journalists or social reformers, the tenants who lived there would obviously have been living in better housing if they could have afforded it— consistent with their other goals and desires.

Even famed nineteenth-century crusading journalist Jacob Riis noted in passing that Jewish immigrants packed into crowded slums on New York's lower east side saved a substantial proportion of their incomes. Since the money that they saved could have been spent on better housing, they obviously had other goals besides maximizing the space, comfort, or amenities of the places where they lived. When slum clearance forced them to move into housing more pleasing to third-party observers, the costs of this upgrading had to be paid by the tenants, not the observers, and it would come at the expense of the tenants' other goals and desires. Among these other uses of their incomes was sending money to family members in Europe who were often suffering both economic deprivation and social persecution, including mob violence.

Most of the Jewish immigrants to America in the late nineteenth and early twentieth centuries came with their passage across the Atlantic paid by family members already living in the United States. In an earlier generation, the same was true of the Irish, who likewise lived in slums and yet came up with the money to pay to rescue their families in Ireland from the great famine there in the 1840s and to bring millions of them to America.

There is no question that early Jewish immigrants lived in over-crowded tenements, under conditions that most other Americans considered appalling at the time, and which we today would consider unbelievable. When the lower east side of Manhattan was a predominantly Jewish slum, it contained three times as many people per square mile as it did when it was a low-income ghetto for other groups a hundred years later. Half of the Jews in this nineteenth century ghetto slept three or four to a room, and nearly one-fourth slept five to a room. Moreover, mid-nineteenth century slums had toilets out in the yards and alleys behind the building. Only later in that century did running water come into the buildings themselves, to be ***shared*** by the tenants, who jointly had access to the same water faucets and toilets. In 1894, there were only 51 private toilets in nearly 4,000 tenements and only 306 persons out of more than a quarter of a million had bathtubs in their homes.

The people living in these slums were thinking beyond their immediate circumstances to a better future for themselves and their children in America. Their savings helped prepare for that future, which turned out to be far better than most people might have imagined at the time. What slum clearance did was force these and other slum tenants to use some of their hard-earned incomes to finance housing that left third-party observers feeling better, though these tenants could have moved into such more expensive housing before if they had considered it worth sacrificing other things to do so.

During the same era, Italian immigrants— mostly men— lived in housing that was at least as appalling in New York and in other cities in Europe and South America. Yet, by enduring miserable living conditions, and often skimping on their own food, these men were able to save, enabling them to send money back to Italy to maintain their families there until their savings reached the point where they could either return to Italy to make a better life for them there or else bring their families over to join them in America or wherever else they settled. In both cases, they and their families rose economically over the years. But that rise was not helped when social reformers, armed with the power of government, forced them to buy more or better housing than they wanted at the time. In a later era, it was different minority groups who were displaced by urban renewal. A landmark study of urban renewal programs in the 1950s found that two-thirds of the people displaced were either blacks or Puerto Ricans.

It is always possible to make people better off in one dimension, such as housing, at the cost of making them worse off in other dimensions that are not so visible to third-party observers. Where this must be done against their will, by imposing the power of government through slum-clearance programs, it is by no means clear that the supposed beneficiaries of these programs are better off on net balance. Would the slums never have been cleared otherwise? One way to test this proposition would be to consider another nineteenth-century poverty-stricken group living in substandard housing whom housing reformers overlooked at the time— the newly freed blacks in the South.

When the Civil War ended, blacks were still living in the same log cabins with dirt floors that they had lived in as slaves. Such amenities as window panes were nearly unknown among the former slaves at this point. Yet, without anyone crusading for better housing for Southern blacks, the ordinary pressures of the marketplace led to improvements in the housing that blacks lived in. This happened not only where blacks owned or rented their homes but also where they lived in housing supplied by white landowners for whom they worked as laborers or as sharecroppers. Competition for labor forced whites who were supplying the housing for blacks who worked for them to improve the housing that black families lived in, just as such competition led to rising incomes which enabled black families who bought or rented their own housing to pay for such upgraded housing themselves. Log cabins were replaced by frame houses, dirt floors were covered by planks and, by the turn of the century, glass window panes began to appear. The kind of housing which blacks had inhabited at the end of the Civil War had almost totally disappeared by the beginning of the twentieth century— without any slum clearance or other housing crusades.

Racial and Ethnic Segregation

The residential clustering or segregation of particular groups has been the rule, rather than the exception, in countries around the world and over the centuries. While this has been strikingly visible to the naked eye when the groups were different in appearance, as with blacks and whites in the

United States, the same phenomenon has been common where the differences could not be seen with the naked eye.

Sometimes groups cluster spontaneously; sometimes they are found clustered because they have been rejected by other groups, who don't want them living in their neighborhoods; and sometimes governing authorities assign them to separate living areas. The term "ghetto" originated centuries ago in Europe, to describe the neighborhoods where Jews were confined by the authorities, sometimes behind walls that were closed off at night. But Ibos from southern Nigeria were likewise confined to separate neighborhoods in northern Nigeria, even though inhabitants of both areas were black Africans whom others might have had difficulty telling apart. In earlier centuries, the Chinese minorities in Southeast Asia were often likewise confined to neighborhoods prescribed by the ruling authorities, rather than being allowed to live at random among the indigenous populations or among their European overlords.

Residential clustering also occurs where people are legally free to live wherever they wish. In late-twentieth century Brazil, where racial distinctions were broken down into "browns," "blacks" and "whites," the browns and blacks were more residentially separate from one another than the browns were from the whites. Similarly, in late-twentieth century America, it was found that "51.6 percent of the population of Southern European origin would have to be redistributed in order to achieve full integration with the Northern European population."

The term "segregation" has often been used to describe both spontaneous residential group clustering and residential separation imposed by authorities. In its strict sense, the term is used to refer to the latter. Sometimes group clustering is due to an inability of a particular group to find acceptance— or perhaps even toleration— in communities of other groups. But social clustering occurs even within a given racial or ethnic enclave. There are also combinations. For example, for most of the twentieth century, blacks in Manhattan were largely confined to Harlem because they were not welcome in other neighborhoods. However, even within Harlem, there were further clusterings of people voluntarily, according to their incomes, education, and times of arrival from the South, the more fortunate blacks living on the outer regions of Harlem and leading the expansion of that community into surrounding white neighborhoods. It was much the same story on New York's lower east side during the European immigrant era, when Polish, Hungarian, and Romanian Jews lived clustered separately within the larger Jewish enclave.

Many lament racial or ethnic residential clustering and see it as a "problem" to be "solved." However, affinities of culture, kinship, and language have led many people to prefer to live within their own groups, even when opportunities were available to live elsewhere. The immigrant generation, still speaking a foreign language, has tended to cling to neighborhoods where they could communicate and interact in familiar ways with others from the same country, even after they had moved up economically and could afford to move on to more prosperous neighborhoods inhabited by the native-born population. Second and later generations, who tended to be more acculturated, could more readily move out of ethnic enclaves and into the mainstream of the larger society— which was correspondingly less resistant to their moving into the new neighborhoods.

Changes within a given group over time can change the degree of acceptance or resistance, as the costs of associating with them change. Back in the nineteenth century, the Irish were unwelcome as neighbors— and this was not merely a matter of "perceptions," "stereotypes," or other wholly subjective factors. Cholera was unknown in American cities before the massive influx of Irish immigrants, beginning in the 1840s, when a cholera epidemic struck Boston, almost exclusively in Irish neighborhoods. The same disease struck disproportionately in Irish neighborhoods in New York. Tuberculosis and alcoholism also plagued Irish communities in various cities. Irish neighborhoods were also tough neighborhoods. In New York, the predominantly Irish Sixth Ward was known as "the bloody ould Sixth," another predominantly Irish neighborhood was known as "Hell's Kitchen," and still another as "San Juan Hill" because the battles there were reminiscent of the battle of San Juan Hill in the Spanish-American war.

Irish neighborhoods in other cities had similar names for similar reasons. The resistance to the Irish moving into other neighborhoods was not simply a matter of inexplicable "perceptions" or "stereotypes." However, as the Irish themselves changed over the generations, attitudes toward them also changed, as reflected in their greater acceptance in housing, as well as in employment, where the stock phrase, "No Irish Need Apply" faded away over time.

All housing segregation has not been spontaneous. Baltimore passed a housing racial segregation law in 1911. It was one of a number of municipal governments to make racial segregation in housing a policy in the twentieth century, in response to massive migrations of Southern blacks into Northern cities, bringing with them rates of crime and violence far higher than among blacks who had lived in those cities for generations. The federal government likewise promoted racial segregation. The Federal Housing Administration refused to make government-insured housing loans unless the housing was racially segregated, on into the late 1940s. The fact that the government later reversed this policy and began to place blacks in neighborhoods that were previously all white does not mean that government, as such, is necessarily for or against racial segregation. It all depends on the attitudes and the politics of the times. Moreover, the economics of housing segregation differs from the politics of it.

Where black ghettoes expand into previously all-white neighborhoods through the operations of the marketplace, such expansion has tended to be led by better-educated and higher-income individuals and families already living on the periphery of the ghetto. These are the kinds of people likely to encounter less resistance than lower-income, more poorly educated, and more violent people from farther inside the ghetto. But, where racial integration is promoted by government, those blacks inserted into white communities via housing projects or individually subsidized housing vouchers tend to be those with lower incomes, poorer education, and higher crime rates.

Either kind of ghetto expansion can encounter resistance. But the resistance to the government programs has tended to be much more vehement. Nor can this resistance all be attributed to racism. Indeed, some black middle-class communities have bitterly resisted the transplanting into their midst of the kind of people they had sought to escape by moving out of the ghetto.

SUMMARY AND IMPLICATIONS

The economics of housing is very different from the politics of housing. In the politics of housing, issues can be framed in terms of the desirability of various goals, such as "affordable housing" or "open space." The economics of housing can only make us aware of the costs of our goals—and that these costs are inescapable, whether or not we acknowledge their existence or assess their magnitude. For example, one study of California found that "planning laws saved 3.4 percent of the state from development at a cost to home-buyers of $136-170 billion per year." The question is not simply whether saving that small a proportion of the land is worth that high a cost. A more fundamental question is whether political goals shall be judged by how attractive they sound or by how much must be sacrificed to achieve them.

Politics offers attractive solutions but economics can offer only trade-offs. For example, when laws are proposed to restrict the height of apartment buildings in a community, politics presents the issue in terms of whether we prefer tall buildings or buildings of more modest height in our town. Economics asks what you are prepared to trade off in order to keep the height of buildings below some specified level.

In places where land costs can equal or exceed the cost of the apartment buildings themselves, the difference between allowing ten-story buildings to be built and allowing a maximum of five stories may be that rents will be much higher in the shorter buildings because land costs are now twice as high per apartment. Nor are money costs the only costs. With twice as many shorter buildings now required to house the same number of people, the community must spread outward, since it cannot spread upward, and that means more commuting and more highway fatalities. The question then is not simply whether you prefer shorter buildings but *how much* do you prefer shorter buildings and what price are you prepared to pay to mandate height restrictions in your community. A doubling of rents and three additional highway fatalities per year? A tripling of rents and ten additional highway fatalities per year?

Economics cannot answer such questions. It can only make you aware of a need to ask them. Economics was christened "the dismal science" because it dealt with inescapable constraints and painful trade-offs, instead of more pleasant, unbounded visions and their accompanying inspiring rhetoric, which many find so attractive in politics and in the media. Moreover, economics follows the unfolding consequences of decisions over time, not just what happens in stage one, which may indeed seem to fulfill the hopes that inspired these decisions. Nowhere are the consequences more long-lasting than in housing, where a community can have an aging and shrinking supply of apartment buildings, with accompanying housing shortages, for decades or even generations, after passing rent control laws which have a track record of leading to such consequences in countries around the world.

The passage of time insulates many political decisions from public awareness of their real consequences. Only a small fraction of New Yorkers today are old enough to remember what the housing situation was there before rent control laws were introduced during World War II. Only a dwindling number of Californians are old enough to remember when that state's housing prices were very much like housing prices in the rest of the country, instead of being some multiple of what people pay elsewhere for a home or an apartment. These and other consequences of particular political decisions in the past are today just "facts of life" that new generations have grown up with as something as natural as the weather or other circumstances of their existence which are beyond their control.

The vast numbers of frustrated California motorists who endure long commutes to and from work on congested highways are unlikely to see any connection between their daily frustrations and attractive-sounding policies about "open space" or "farmland preservation." Nor are economists who point out that connection likely to be as popular with them as politicians who are ready to offer solutions to rescue these motorists from their current problems, using the same kind of one-stage thinking that created those problems in the first place.

Chapter 5

Risky Business

The American Statistical Association offered at their annual meeting a T-shirt bearing the motto: "Uncertainty: One Thing You Can Always Count On."

Nothing is more certain than risk. The insurance business is just one of the ways of dealing with risk. Having government agencies come to the aid of disaster victims is another. Mutual aid societies helped victims of social or natural disasters long before there were government agencies charged with this task. Individuals have spread their own risks in various ways and families have sought to safeguard their members for centuries—longer than any other institution has taken on the task of cushioning people against the inescapable risks of life.

Whatever social mechanisms are used to deal with risk generally seek to do two crucial things: (1) reduce the magnitude of the risk and (2) transfer that risk to whoever can bear it at the lowest cost. Where the transfer of risk is accompanied by a net reduction of risk, this process makes it mutually beneficial for the person initially at risk to pay someone else to share the risk or to carry the risk completely, since the risk costs less to those to whom it is transferred. This in turn means that society as a whole benefits from having its risks minimized and the resources put aside for dealing with risks reduced, making those resources available for other uses.

Why would the same risk cost less to some than to others? Because an aggregation of risks often costs less than the sum total of the individual risks carried individually. A life insurance company with a million policy-holders has more likelihood of knowing when the average policy-holder will die than any given policy-holder has of knowing when he or she will die. In times past, when ships sank more often, a ship owner who owned one ship outright had a greater risk of a catastrophic loss from sinking than someone who owned ten percent of ten ships or one percent of a hundred ships. Although the total investment might be the same in all these cases, the likelihood of a catastrophic loss was less when the number of ships was greater, even though the likelihood of a sinking was greater among a hundred ships than with one.

Merely providing information or assessments of risk is a valuable service, for which credit-rating services are paid, whether these are companies like TRW that provide businesses with information on the credit history of individual consumers, or companies like Moody's or Standard & Poor's which rate the relative risks of bonds issued by businesses themselves, states, or nations, so that investors can be guided accordingly in choosing where to invest and at what interest rates to compensate for differences in risk.

When trade associations of insurance companies test automobiles for safety in crash tests, that likewise creates benefits for the companies in these associations, by allowing them to determine how much to charge to insure different vehicles, and it also assists consumers in making choices of which kinds, makes, and models of vehicles to buy, for the sake of their own safety, as well as for the sake of paying lower car insurance premiums. Consumer choices in turn influence automobile manufacturers as to what kinds of safety provisions to add to their cars, in order to compete successfully for sales, leading cars in general to become safer over time. These market-imposed standards are often higher than government-imposed standards.

Between 2006 and 2007, for example, the number of motor vehicles that went through crash tests conducted by the Insurance Institute for Highway Safety and emerged with the top rating increased from 13 to 34. Over the years, motor vehicles have added many safety devices, including air bags and electronic collision avoidance systems, all of which enable more of them to meet safety standards, including some standards that did not even exist before.

Similarly, insurance companies not only offer lower premiums to insure houses built especially to resist high winds in areas subject to hurricanes, such as Florida, or houses built to resist fire, earthquakes, or other hazards in other areas, these companies also certify certain homes as having met their standards— which are often more stringent than local government building codes— thereby informing prospective buyers, who may therefore be more willing to pay extra for such housing.

To some extent, however, reducing risk through insurance may cause people to take more risks. Just as lower prices for other things usually cause more to be demanded, so lowering the costs of given risks enables people to take on additional risks. Distinguished economist Joseph Schumpeter pointed out that cars travel faster because they have brakes.

If you were driving a car without brakes, or with brakes that you knew to be less effective, it might be foolhardy to drive faster than 10 or 15 miles per hour. At a sufficiently slow speed on a sufficiently uncrowded road, you might be able to depend on simply taking your foot off the gas and letting the car coast to a stop. But, when you have well-functioning brakes as a risk-reducing device, you may well drive 60 miles an hour on a crowded highway. Thus brakes reduce the dangers in a given situation but also encourage people to drive in more dangerous situations than they would otherwise. This does not mean that safety devices are futile. It means that the benefits of such devices include benefits over and beyond any benefits from net reductions of risk. For example, because cars are able to travel at higher speeds, more extensive travel for business or pleasure becomes feasible.

Similarly, when you have automobile insurance, you may drive over to visit an old friend or family member who lives in a high crime neighborhood, where you might not risk parking your car if it were not insured, for fear of theft or vandalism. While you would still not want to have your car stolen or damaged, the chance of that happening may become an affordable risk when car insurance covers that possibility. Whether on net balance one lives a less risky life as a result of insurance is not always certain. But, even if there is no net reduction in risk, there may be other benefits resulting from the insurance. In addition to visiting places where the risk would be too great otherwise, one may live up in the hills in a home with a spectacular view, even if that home is somewhat more at risk of fire because it is surrounded by trees and is on a narrow winding road that would impede a fire truck from reaching the home in an emergency as quickly as it could down in the flatlands.

In addition to insurance companies which charge for the service of carrying other people's risks, there are businesses which incorporate charges for risk in the prices they charge for other goods and services. Indeed, all businesses must include some charge for risk in their prices, though this is usually noticeable only in businesses which charge more than usual for the same goods that are available more cheaply elsewhere because local risks are different in different neighborhoods. Moreover, some risks are in effect paid for not in money, but by a reduction in the number of businesses willing to locate in less desirable neighborhoods, or in countries where debts are hard to collect or where crime, vandalism, and terrorist activity reduce personal safety.

In some low-income neighborhoods with a history of riots, vandalism, and shoplifting, the local inhabitants— most of whom may well be honest and decent people— pay the costs created by those among them who are not by having lower quantities and qualities of goods and services available to them locally, and at higher prices. Many of these local inhabitants may be forced to go elsewhere for shopping or to get their paychecks cashed. For example, a study in Oakland, California, found:

> Less than half (46 percent) of Oakland's low-income consumers surveyed said that they did their banking in their neighborhoods. However, 71 percent of middle-income area respondents said that they did their banking in their own neighborhoods.

The same study found that it was six times as common among Oakland's low-income residents as among its middle-income residents to use check-cashing centers instead of banks. With shopping as well, low-income consumers have often found themselves forced to go elsewhere to get things that were either unavailable nearby or not available in as good a quality or as low a price as in higher-income neighborhoods. For example, this survey found low-income consumers spending only about a third of their money shopping in their local community and two-thirds shopping elsewhere.

While all this is easy to understand from an economic perspective, it is also easy to distort from a political perspective. Blaming the owners of local stores and check-cashing agencies for the higher charges in such places, compared to charges in safer middle-class neighborhoods, is usually more politically effective than blaming those local inhabitants who create the costs which these institutions pass along to customers— especially if the business owners are mostly of a different ethnic background than the local people. Even without the incentives of politics, many observers who do not think beyond stage one blame high prices on those who charge these prices, rather than on those who create the additional risks and costs which these prices reflect. From this it is a short step to advocating laws and policies to restrict how high local prices or local check-cashing charges or interest rates will be allowed to go.

However plausible such laws and policies might seem to those who do not think beyond stage one, the net result of preventing local businesses from recovering the higher local costs in the prices they charge is likely to be a reduction in the number of businesses that can earn as much locally as elsewhere— or that can even earn enough to survive locally. Given the existing meager availability of businesses in many low-income neighborhoods, anything that forces more local businesses to close aggravates the problems of the people living there.

Banco Popular, which operates a check-cashing service in low-income Hispanic neighborhoods, has charged 1.1 percent of the value of the checks it cashes, plus 20 cents a check. This means that someone earning $300 a week pays $3.50 per week to get a paycheck cashed. Meanwhile, someone earning ten times as much money probably pays nothing, since banks are happy to have high-income people among their customers and make money off the large savings accounts and checking accounts which such people typically have, while the dangers of default are less. For the low-income worker, the question is whether taking a bus or taxi to try to get a paycheck cashed will cost more than the $3.50 paid to Banco Popular, which has armored cars that drive up to the employer's place of business on pay day.

While Banco Popular's check-cashing service charges for what many banks provide free, it also takes bigger risks of losses. The workers who cash their paychecks may be honest and the checks genuine, but some of the employers they work for are small fly-by-night operators, who may suddenly leave town, closing their bank accounts and taking their money with them, making their workers' paychecks worthless. Just one such dishonest employer cost Banco Popular $66,000 in cashed paychecks that could not be redeemed at the bank where the employer's account had been closed before he skipped town. That is far less likely to happen with a paycheck from someone who earns $3,000 a week than with someone who earns $300 a week. Little fly-by-night operators are unlikely to be paying their employees $156,000 a year. People with such high incomes are more likely to be working for more substantial and reliable businesses and organizations.

The risks and costs of cashing checks for low-income people, or lending money to them, are inherent in the circumstances, rather than in the particular institutions which handle these risks. When a reputable bank that normally serves middle class or affluent people opens an affiliate in low-income neighborhoods, it faces those same risks— but without as much experience in dealing with them. Operating in what is called the "subprime market"— where borrowers do not have as good credit ratings as in the prime markets— these banks, as the ***Wall Street Journal*** put it, began "to realize the market was far tougher than they had expected." Even charging interest rates ranging from 12 percent to 24 percent in making riskier loans to low-income borrowers— compared to 7 or 8 percent on other loans— the higher rates of default often made these loans unprofitable.

Bank of America, for example, lost hundreds of millions of dollars on such loans. In 2001, according to the ***Wall Street Journal***, Bank of America "said its 96 EquiCredit Corp. offices across the U.S. will stop making subprime loans immediately." Other banks were apparently not quick enough in closing down such losing operations. A large Chicago bank went out of business, with losses on subprime loans being singled out as the main reason. Losses on such loans were also cited by the Federal Deposit Insurance Corporation as a factor in the closing of 7 out of 19 banks that failed. The Federal Housing Authority, which usually lends to lower-income home buyers, has had a repayment delinquency rate more than triple that of those who lend to other home buyers.

RISK-REDUCING INSTITUTIONS

Families, gangs, feudal warlords, insurance companies, partnerships, commodity speculators, and issuers of stocks and bonds are all in the business of reducing and transferring risk. All face the problem that reducing existing riskiness increases the willingness of the protected individual to take more risks. An individual who belongs to a tough gang may become more belligerent towards other individuals he encounters than he would be without the protection afforded by the gang's reputation. In medieval times, a peasant might be reluctant to farm in some areas where there were robbers and marauders around, without the protection of the armed nobility who take part of the peasant's produce as payment for their services. Though called tribute, these payments— usually in kind— amounted to insurance premiums.

Those who are in the business of selling insurance try to take into account not only the existing risks, but also the increased amount of risky behavior that the policy holder may engage in as a result of becoming insured. For similar reasons, the family— the oldest insurer of all— cautions its members, both when they are growing up and on specific occasions afterwards, against various kinds of risky behavior. When families had the burden of taking care of an unwed daughter's baby, there was more chaperoning, screening of her associates, and moral stigma attached to unwed motherhood. All these things declined or disappeared after many of these costs were shifted to government agencies.

Government Agencies

The incentives of a government agency are very different from those of a family or an insurance company. As a matter of financial self-protection, both families and insurance companies must seek to discourage risky behavior in one way or another. For a government agency, however, financed by taxpayers' money, there is no such urgency about discouraging the increased risks that people may take when those risks are covered by others. Moreover, the agency gets its biggest political support from helping those suffering the consequences of the risks they have taken, however unwisely, not by criticizing them. Thus government emergency programs to help people struck by floods, hurricanes, and other natural disasters make it easier for people whose homes have been destroyed to rebuild at the same locations, in areas where such disasters recur regularly over the years.

Similarly, government programs to develop medicines and medical procedures to deal with AIDS, at costs subsidized by the taxpayers, have led to a resurgence of the kinds of risky behaviors that can lead to AIDS. A researcher studying transportation found that government licensing of motorists likewise put little emphasis on reducing risks:

> Employees at the state (any state) motor vehicle division, good people all, will give virtually anyone with two forms of identification a driver's license so long as they are not seriously vision impaired and are able to pass a multiple-choice exam and minimum proficiency driving test. Their responsibility ends there; they have no stake in what happens after those drivers hit the road. . . . Under the current system, private insurance companies have little incentive to stop people from buying inadequate levels of insurance, since damages caused by underinsured drivers are capped and damages caused by uninsured drivers are borne by either the uninsured driver or the victim.

In other words, not only do government officials dealing with risky situations have inadequate incentives to force a reduction of risk, they are able to pass laws which also reduce private insurance companies' incentives to reduce risks, since the government puts caps on the damage awards to be paid by insurance companies to people injured by drivers with inadequate insurance coverage. In Arizona, for example, insurance companies are liable for an upper limit of $15,000 for a single death from an automobile accident and $30,000 for multiple deaths. Since a single fatality causes an estimated million dollars or more in damages, such insurance coverage is grossly inadequate, with the insured motorist being liable for the rest if the motorist has the money, and the loss goes uncompensated if the motorist does not.

Where the government does *not* shield private decision-makers from financial liability, those private decision-makers may impose more stringent safety requirements than those mandated by law. Disneyland, for example, does not allow children below a certain size, or pregnant women, on some of its rides, even though the law permits such people to ride.

If the government were to impose more stringent requirements for getting a driver's license, that would undoubtedly cause political resistance, especially by the elderly population, which is a segment of the population that usually votes. In some states, elderly drivers (including the author of this book) have been able to get their licenses renewed without getting behind the wheel of a car for a test, despite the well-known deterioration of sight, hearing, and reflexes with age and the greater likelihood of fainting, heart attacks, or other disabilities impairing motorists' ability to avoid dangers to themselves or others.

While fatal automobile accident rates are typically high among teenagers and young adults— especially males— and later decline with age, at some point the fatal accident rates begin to rise again, with very elderly drivers having fatal accident rates as high as those of teenagers. In the United States, fatality rates per vehicle miles driven start out high for 16-year-olds, decline sharply in one year, and then continue generally downward at a more moderate rate, reaching a low plateau for people in their forties. But the fatality rate begins to rise again for people in their sixties, first moderately and then steeply for people in their seventies, with people aged 75 having automobile fatality rates as high as those for 18-year-olds, and people aged 85 having the highest automobile fatality rate of people at any age.

While recklessness may be a more important factor among teenagers than among the elderly, physical deterioration can create dangers even among cautious but aged drivers. Despite spectacular examples of elderly motorists losing control of their cars and plowing into pedestrians or crashing through to the interior of buildings,[1] there is little stomach among politicians for stirring

---

[1] "An 86-year-old man drove his car the length of the Santa Monica Farmers' Market early Wednesday afternoon, apparently reaching freeway speeds as he plowed through a crowd of terrified summer shoppers, killing at least nine people, including a 3-year-old girl. More than 50 people were hospitalized, 15 of them with critical injuries. . ." Joel Rubin, et al., "Car Plows Through Crowd in Santa Monica, Killing 9," ***Los Angeles Times***, July 17, 2003, p. A1. In Shiloh, Illinois, an 84-year-old woman "smashed her car into Shiloh Elementary School, killing a second grader" and injuring two other children. Nicholas J.C. Pistor, "Report Details Fatal School Crash," ***St. Louis Post-Dispatch***, May 5, 2007, p. A17. A 93-year-old man in St. Petersburg, Florida, "hit a man crossing 34th Street S, severing the man's right leg, then drove 3 miles with the body stuck in the windshield. . . He renewed his license in 2003, at age 91. It was set to expire in 2010." Craig Basse, "Man Who Hit, Killed Another Dies at 93," ***St. Petersburg Times***, November 15, 2005, p. 7B.

up anger among elderly voters by requiring tests of physical vitality for people over a given age. The fact that someone passed a driving test at age 25 is hardly a sufficient reason for getting their license renewed at age 75, if automobile risk is the criterion. However, it may be if political risk is the criterion.

Political considerations affect how governments deal with financial risks, as well as with physical risks. Where both national and international institutions stand ready to bail out governments facing bankruptcy and likely to have defaults on their debts that would hurt banks and other investors in other countries, the prospect of such bailouts allows private financial institutions to invest in countries where it would be too risky to invest otherwise. Sporadic calls for a "restructuring" of debt[2] or a "forgiveness" of Third World debt encourage the debtor governments to borrow more money than they would if they knew that the loans would have to be repaid or an open declaration of bankruptcy announced, which would make it harder to borrow again, perhaps for many years. International financial crises, especially those involving poorer countries, often bring out one-stage thinking among those who wish to help less fortunate people, with the longer run consequences being overlooked.

Since risk is inescapable, the question of how much risk to tolerate is a question of weighing one cost against another. Often this is not done, especially when those who make such decisions do not pay the costs of these decisions and do not think beyond stage one. For example, when a certain number of children receive injuries from playing in a particular playground, then the swings, seesaws, or other equipment in that playground may be blamed and perhaps removed, or those responsible for the playground may be sued. But, if the offending equipment is removed or the playground shut down because of lawsuits or the fear of lawsuits, will the children be safer? Suppose that X percent of the children will receive serious injuries if they play in this particular playground and 2X percent will receive equally serious injuries if they stay home. Since no place is 100 percent safe, and none can be made 100 percent safe, the only meaningful question is the relative safety

[2] Essentially paying off old debts with new loans.

of one place compared to another and the cost of making either place safer by a given amount.

Our natural inclination may be to want to make every place as safe as possible but, in reality, no one does that when they must pay the costs themselves. We are willing to pay for brakes in our cars, but having a second set of brakes in case the first set fails would make us safer still, and a third set would result in still more reduction of risk, though probably not by a substantial amount. However, faced with rising costs and declining reductions of risk as more backup brakes are added to automobiles, most people will at some point refuse to pay any more for additional but insignificant reductions in risk. However, if someone else is paying for reductions in risk, the point at which risk reduction stops may be very different. Lawsuits can impose costs that shut down a playground that is safer than any alternative place the children are likely to be, including their homes.

The implicit assumption that zero risk can be taken as a benchmark for assessing blame for particular risks can easily lead to higher risks than if it was understood from the outset that one risk must be weighed against another, not compared to zero risk or even to some arbitrary standard of "acceptable" versus "unacceptable" risk. In India, for example, the millions of people with modest but rising incomes, in the wake of that country's faster growth rate after markets began to be freed from stifling government controls, created a market for very small and inexpensive automobiles. But some have worried about the safety of flimsy little cars, which have higher rates of injury and death in accidents. However, the key question here, as in many other situations involving risk, is: ***Compared to what?*** Current transportation for millions of Indians is hardly a model of safety:

> Currently, entire families commute on scooters, with the man of the house driving, his wife sitting side-saddle on the rear, and as many as three children wedged in between.

Ownership Sharing

As already noted, back in the days when the danger of a ship's sinking was higher than today, investors protected themselves by owning shares of a number of ships, instead of owning a given ship outright. Modern corporations similarly make it possible for individuals to spread their risks by owning stock in a number of different businesses, without owning any particular business outright. However, employees who own stock in the businesses they work for do not get the full benefits of risk spreading, since both their jobs and the money they will depend on when they no longer have jobs— whether due to unemployment or retirement— depend on the fate of the same company. The consequences of concentrating risks, instead of spreading them, proved to be catastrophic for many employees of corporations that went bankrupt amid various well-publicized scandals among American corporations in 2002.

Not only businesses, but workmen as well, have long pooled their risks as a way of making them less onerous to individuals. Mutual aid societies arose among workers in a given occupation or industry, or members of a particular ethnic group, or residents in a given neighborhood. By paying small amounts into a common fund, members of mutual aid societies enabled those among them who were stricken by illness or disabled by injuries to have the financial consequences cushioned by payments from the fund. Here the dangers of deliberately engaging in more risky behavior were minimized, first of all by the prospect of pain and death, but also by the fact of being known by other members of the mutual aid society, who could monitor malingering or fraudulent claims better than larger and more impersonal institutions could.

Safety Movements

A very different kind of institution for dealing with risk has arisen in more recent times. This is the private organization or movement devoted to imposing safety requirements through publicity, litigation or the promotion of government regulation. These include "public interest" law firms, ideological organizations and movements, such as the so-called Center for Science in the Public Interest, and government agencies such as the National Highway Traffic Safety Administration. Since these organizations do not charge directly for their services like mutual aid societies or insurance companies, they must collect the money needed to support themselves from lawsuits, donations, or taxes. Put differently, their only money-making product or service is fear— and their incentives are to induce as much fear as possible in jurors, legislators, and the general public.

Whereas individuals weighing risks for themselves are restrained in how much risk reduction they will seek by the costs of reducing those risks, there are no such restraints on the amount of risk reduction sought by those whose risk reduction is paid for with other people's money. Nor is there any such inherent restraint on how much fear they will generate from a given risk or how much credit they will claim for whatever risk reduction may take place, regardless of what the facts may be.

Automobile safety is a classic example of third party safety decisions by organizations and movements whose money and power come from producing fear. Third-party safety crusades operate in some ways the opposite from risk-reduction processes in which those who are at risk choose alternatives for themselves and pay the costs themselves. The central question of how much risk is to be reduced at what costs is usually not raised at all by third-party safety organizations or movements. Nor are alternative risks weighed against one another. Instead, the theme is that something is "unsafe" and therefore needs to be made safe. The argument is essentially that existing risks show that current safeguards are inadequate and/or the people in control of them are insufficiently conscientious, or both. Therefore power and money need to be vested in new people and new institutions, in order to protect the public— according to this argument.

This kind of argument can be applied to almost anything, since nothing is literally 100 percent safe. It has been used against medications, pesticides, nuclear power, automobiles, and many other targets. Where the issue is the safety of nuclear power plants, for example, the answer to the question whether nuclear power is safe is obviously *No*! If nuclear power were safe, it would be the only safe thing on the face of the earth. This page that you are reading isn't safe. It can catch fire, which can spread and burn down your home, with you in it. The only meaningful question, to those who are spending their own money to deal with their own risks, is whether it is worth what it would cost to fireproof every page in every book, magazine, or newspaper, not to mention paper towels, stationery, notebooks and Kleenex.

In the case of nuclear power, the question of safety, in addition to cost, is: ***Compared to what?*** Compared to generating electricity with hydroelectric dams or the burning of fossil fuels or compared to reducing our use of electricity with dimmer lights or foregoing the use of many things that are run by electricity and taking our chances on alternative power sources? Once the discussion changes to a discussion of incremental trade-offs, then nuclear power becomes one of the safest options. But neither it nor anything else is categorically safe.

These kinds of questions, which are central to safety decisions made by those who pay the costs, are conspicuous by their absence in third-party safety crusades. The rise of third-party safety advocates in the latter part of the twentieth century has brought with it categorical rhetoric in place of incremental analysis, and incentives to maximize fears rather than to minimize net injuries and deaths.

A landmark in these trends was the 1965 book ***Unsafe at Any Speed*** by Ralph Nader, attacking the safety of American automobiles in general and a car called the Corvair in particular. This book was not only historically important, as the beginning of a major political trend, but was also important in setting a pattern in methods of persuasion that have been followed by many other publications, politicians, and organizations in dealing with issues of risk and safety. That pattern is therefore worth scrutinizing, even many decades later. The thesis of ***Unsafe at Any Speed*** was that American cars were unsafe because safety was neglected by automobile manufacturers, in order to save on manufacturing costs and not interfere with styling, as some safety devices might. Consumers were depicted as helpless to do anything about safety and therefore as needing government intervention for their protection.

According to Nader, "users of vehicles" are "in no position to dictate safer automobile designs." Put differently: "The American automobile is produced exclusively to the standards which the manufacturer decides to establish." More generally, a "great problem of contemporary life is how to control the power of economic interests which ignore the harmful effects of their applied science and technology."

Unsafe at Any Speed was a masterpiece in the art of insinuation, successfully establishing several crucial beliefs about the automobile industry in general, and about the Corvair in particular, in the media and among the public, without hard evidence being either offered or asked for. The first of these beliefs was that American automobiles were dangerous and becoming more so. As Nader put it, in the first sentence of his preface:

> For over half a century the automobile has brought death, injury, and the most inestimable sorrow and deprivation to millions of people. With Medea-like intensity, this mass trauma began rising sharply four years ago reflecting new and unexpected ravages by the motor vehicle.

Anecdotes and selective quotations abounded to ***insinuate*** the conclusions reached, but nowhere did this book present automobile accident fatality rates in America over time, for the United States compared to other countries, for the Corvair compared to other automobiles, or for countries where automobiles are produced under capitalist incentives compared to countries where the industry is under socialist management and therefore not influenced by the profit motive. Such data would have supported none of the conclusions reached. The masterpiece was in making such empirical support unnecessary through various rhetorical devices. For example, he quoted a critic who characterized the Corvair as "probably the worst riding, worst all-around handling car available to the American public," and Nader attributed this to "engineering and management operations within General Motors which led to such an unsafe vehicle." Experts who assessed the Corvair and its handling more favorably— some enthusiastically— were simply not quoted.

Despite Nader's sweeping assertions about what had been happening over a period of "half a century," he offered no statistical data covering that span and the data that were available showed long-term trends that were the direct opposite of what *Unsafe at Any Speed* implied. While it was true, as Nader claimed, that automobile accidents were rising, it was also true that the population of the country was rising, the numbers of cars on the road were rising and the miles they were traveling were rising. In proportion to the number of vehicles, automobile fatality rates when ***Unsafe at Any Speed*** was published in 1965 were less than half of what they had been back in the 1920s. In proportion to millions of vehicle-miles driven, the fatality rate was less than one-third of what it had been in the 1920s. Apparently something was causing automobile manufacturers to produce safer cars, contrary to Nader's thesis.

There are fluctuations in accident fatality rates, as with most statistics over long periods of time, and in the years immediately before publication of ***Unsafe at Any Speed*** there had been a slight upward trend. But during all the previous decades of presumably helpless consumers, corporate greed, and inadequate government regulation, the safety of American automobiles had been improving dramatically, as shown by fatality rates a fraction of what they had once been, despite more crowded roadways and higher speeds. Yet the continuation of this decades-long trend toward reduced automobile fatality rates was later credited by safety advocates and much of the media to the creation of a federal agency to regulate automobile safety, in response to Ralph Nader's book. This conclusion was reached by the simple expedient of ignoring the previous history and counting the "lives saved" as the long trend of declining fatality rates continued.

What of the Corvair? Here Nader scored his greatest success. The bad publicity he unleashed was reflected in falling sales that forced General Motors to discontinue production of the car. Years later, extensive tests by the U. S. Department of Transportation showed that the Corvair's safety was comparable to that of similar cars of its era, and concluded that the performance of the Corvair "is at least as good as the performance of some contemporary vehicles both foreign and domestic." By then, of course, this information was much too late to matter. The car was extinct— killed off by a safety crusade that set the pattern for later such crusades inspired by Nader's example.

Because of its rear-engine design, the Corvair was indeed more prone to some particular kinds of accidents— and less prone to other kinds of accidents. No matter where an engine is placed, its location affects the physics of the automobile, and therefore the kinds of accidents to which the car is more susceptible and those to which it is less susceptible. Simply by emphasizing the first kinds of accidents— complete with gory examples— and ignoring the second kind, the Corvair was portrayed as an unsafe car. By similar tactics, almost anything can be made to seem unsafe because ultimately everything is unsafe, if you ignore questions of degree and alternatives.

There are trade-offs not only as regards the placement of an engine, but also as regards the willingness of consumers to pay for all the safety devices that third parties can think of putting on an automobile at someone else's expense. However, a trade-off perspective would undermine many, if not most, safety crusades— and not just those about automobiles. Nader dismissed talk of trade-offs as "auto industry cant"— a rhetorical response making a factual or logical response unnecessary, and another example of why his book was a masterpiece in the art of insinuation and a model for later safety crusades.

Much the same approach has been taken by safety crusaders when it comes to the safety of vaccines and medications, which both save lives and cost lives. No matter how many lives they save, there will still be the inevitable tragedies because some few individuals die as a reaction to being either vaccinated or medicated. (Even a substance as common and generally harmless as peanut butter is literally fatal to some people.) If a particular vaccine is administered to millions of children, for most of these children it may have no effect at all— that is, they were not going to catch the disease anyway and they suffer no side effects from the vaccination. But of course no one has any way of knowing in advance which children will be the ones for whom the vaccine will make a difference, one way or another. If 10,000 of those children would have been fatally stricken by the disease from which the vaccine protects them, perhaps 20 will die from their reaction to the vaccine, including some who may catch the disease from the vaccine itself.

Nothing is easier than having a television camera capture the anguish of a mother of one of the 20 dead children, crying and inconsolable in her grief, perhaps blaming herself and wondering aloud whether her child would still be alive if she had not had that child vaccinated. There is no way to know who are the 10,000 other mothers who were spared this anguish because they ***did*** have their children vaccinated. Nothing is easier for a safety crusader than denouncing the company that produced an "unsafe" vaccine or medicine, without telling the television viewers that there are no other kinds of vaccines or medications— or anything else.

Insurance and Re-insurance

The role of insurance companies is not simply to pay their policy-holders who have suffered various misfortunes. Like families, they seek to reduce the risks that lead to these misfortunes in the first place. While families have more ability to caution and monitor their members than insurance companies have to restrain the risks taken by their policy-holders, insurance companies try to protect themselves financially in other ways. One way is by making the reduction of risk a precondition for issuing an insurance policy or varying the amount charged according to the level of risk. Smokers may be charged higher life insurance premiums than non-smokers. Homeowners may also be required to take precautions, as the ***Wall Street Journal*** reported:

> In many Western states, where wildfires are a growing menace, some homeowners are being required to clear brush over large areas around their houses, or even to install a new fire-resistant roof. In hurricane prone areas of Eastern and Gulf states, some insurers are requiring that certain properties have storm-resistant window shutters in order to be insured.

As private insurance companies have been withdrawing from insuring properties along Gulf coast and east coast shorelines, where government regulation often prevents them from charging premiums high enough to cover the risks in such places, both state and federal insurance programs have been acting increasingly as insurers of last resort, transferring the risks to taxpayers.

Here, as elsewhere, the incentives facing political decision-makers are very different from the incentives facing economic decision-makers. Private insurance companies must either charge enough to cover the cost of dangerous situations or impose requirements to reduce those dangers, while political decision-makers can base their decisions on what will make them look compassionate— and hence more re-electable— while leaving the costs of future disasters to be paid, perhaps long after stage one, by taxpayers. If insurance companies followed the same policy, reactions from investors and financial institutions— which monitor businesses much more closely than voters can monitor government— would ***immediately*** cause the value of the company's stock and the ratings of their bonds to drop dramatically, putting the jobs of the company executives in immediate danger. In short, both the political decision-makers and the business decision-makers are protecting their own jobs, though that requires very different decisions in these different institutions.

In addition to specific safety precautions, insurance companies' policies often require the policy-holder to share the costs of risky behavior by paying a fixed amount of the damages incurred— the "deductible"— before the insurance company pays the remainder.

Like a family, an insurance company also reduces its risks by providing individuals with information about those risks. Thus insurance companies often publish booklets on healthy living, safe driving, and ways of avoiding fires and other hazards. Trade associations in the insurance industry test various makes and models of automobiles in crashes and publicize the results, thus informing the public and thereby putting pressure on automobile manufacturers to produce safer cars, in addition to supplying the insurance companies with information on which to base the premiums charged for insuring the different kinds of automobiles. Data on declining automobile fatality rates over time suggest that automobile manufacturers have in fact responded to consumer desires for safety, despite Ralph Nader's rhetoric to the contrary.

Insurance not only reduces risks but transfers those risks to where they can be borne at a lower cost. No one knows when his home might catch fire or his automobile might have an accident but, when an insurance company insures millions of homes and automobiles, its ability to predict in the aggregate is much greater than an individual's ability to predict what will happen individually. Another way of saying the same thing is that the cost of setting aside resources to cover the losses is less for an insurance company than the total of all the resources required to be set aside by each of the insured individuals to produce the same probability of being able to cover the same costs. These are not just financial arrangements that benefit particular insurance companies or their policy-holders. From the standpoint of society as a whole, fewer resources are held idle in the economy as a whole when insurance reduces risks and the costs of those risks.

Just as owners of homes and businesses transfer their risks of fire, flood, and other damage to insurance companies by paying premiums, so the insurance companies themselves can transfer part of their risks to ***re-insurance*** companies, at a price. In both cases, risks are not simply transferred but reduced. If a given insurance company located in the American Midwest has a concentration of homeowners' policies in the Ohio valley, a flood in that valley could be financially devastating to that insurance company. However, if it transfers a major part of its liabilities to a re-insurer like the Swiss Reinsurance Company (better known as "Swiss Re"), then this international re-insurer's risk of simultaneous floods in the Ohio valley, the Rhine valley, the Nile valley, the Danube valley, etc., is far less than the local insurance company's risk of a flood in its region.

Since there are well over a hundred re-insurance companies around the world, no single re-insurer may have taken on all the liability for the Ohio valley, and each re-insurer will have a geographically more widespread set of risks than a local primary insurance company has. In short, the whole insurance and re-insurance industry will have lower risks than any given primary insurance company would have, especially if the primary insurance company has customers concentrated in a particular geographic area. Therefore it is relatively cheaper to insure homes and industries along the banks of various rivers around the world than to insure those along the banks of any one of those rivers.

Put differently, in the absence of re-insurance, enterprises and households in China have to put aside more money, or the physical resources that money represents, to guard against risks than if part of those risks were carried by a company located in Switzerland or the United States, which simultaneously re-insures enterprises and homes in Argentina, Egypt, Australia, Denmark, and Fiji, as well as in China. The amount of equipment and supplies needed to be stockpiled to cope with the risk of floods along the Yangtze River—tents to house people forced from their homes, canned or other preserved food to feed them, equipment to repair the damage and rebuild— would be much less if instantaneous electronic transfers of money from Swiss Re could purchase equipment and supplies to be flown in from Japan to China in a matter of hours, if and when they are needed.

As the London magazine ***The Economist*** put it, "China is therefore wasting capital that could be used for other things" when it puts aside larger amounts of capital to guard against floods, fires and other catastrophes than it would if it were re-insured by international re-insurers. Insurance, re-insurance and other risk-sharing activities mean that fewer idle resources are necessary around the world to provide a given level of protection against risks. That in turn means that the resources no longer kept idle can be used for other things, such as raising living standards, supporting medical research, or promoting greater economic development.

Lower risks mean lower costs, and market competition among insurance and re-insurance companies means that those lower costs must be passed on to customers in lower premiums, in order to get their business.[3] While geographic distributions of risks provide one reason for re-insurance, that is not the only reason. For example, more than four-fifths of American life insurance companies also have re-insurance. Thus the financial risk of a local epidemic with many fatalities is spread among re-insurance companies around the world, just as the risk of local flooding is.

Political incentives in response to natural disasters can be very different from market incentives. The government of India's response to the cyclone that struck India in 1999 was to save face for the authorities, according to India's own media, rather than to rescue the victims as quickly as possible by seeking help from other nations or from international agencies— which would be politically embarrassing because it would call into question the capability of India's own government. Similarly, the Russian government declined offers of help from the American and British navies when one of

[3] For example, ***BusinessWeek*** magazine reported in its March 4, 2002 issue: "Premiums for reinsurance industrywide had already gone into a tailspin as strong profits attracted more competitors who slashed prices to gain market share." (page 77).

its submarines was trapped under the ocean, leading to the loss of the lives of all those on board. Only massive public outcries led the Russian government to accept the British navy's rescue offer the next time they were presented with a similar disaster.

In a competitive marketplace, however, a private insurance company's reputation for quick response is an enormously valuable asset to the company. It was the Swiss Reinsurance Company's swift response in getting money to the victims of the devastating San Francisco earthquake and fire of 1906 which gained them international renown and promoted the spread of their business around the world. Although paying off the huge claims resulting from the massive 1906 San Francisco disaster took half of Swiss Re's annual income from fire insurance premiums, the subsequent growth in their business as a result led eventually to its becoming the world's largest re-insurance company between the two World Wars.

Government Regulation of Insurance

Insurance companies, like other businesses, tend to respond to the economic incentives of the market, while government agencies that regulate the terms and conditions of insurance policies tend to respond to political incentives. Ideally, the costs created by given risks would be reflected in the prices charged to insure against those risks, but neither the market nor the government always provides incentives for that to happen. Indeed, there are both economic and political incentives to behave in ways that make it more difficult, or in some cases impossible, for the relative costs of various risks to be reflected in the relative prices charged for insuring against those particular risks.

Two main problems affect insurance companies in a free market: One already discussed earlier is that people who are insured may choose to engage in more risky behavior as a result. This is called "moral hazard." Another is that, when some people choose to be insured for some things and others choose not to be insured, those at the greatest risk are more likely to choose to be insured, so that general statistics on the risks to the population at large are misleading as to the risks of those who choose to buy insurance.

That is called "adverse selection." Both these factors mean that statistical data based on what currently happens in the general population are not always reliable predictors of what is likely to happen to those people who are insured.

Government regulation of risky behavior— laws against storing flammable materials in homes or driving under the influence of alcohol, for example— can reduce the risks arising from moral hazard, while laws requiring everyone who drives to have automobile insurance can reduce the problem of adverse selection. As in other situations, however, the fact that the government ***can*** sometimes improve on the situation that would exist in a free market does not mean that it ***will*** in fact restrict its activities to such useful things. When the counterproductive interventions of government in the market are added to its beneficial interventions, it is by no means always clear what the net balance will be.

Many of the counterproductive effects of government regulation come from allowing other factors to override the risk factor which is at the heart of insurance. For example, some people consider it "unfair" that individuals are charged higher premiums, or are denied insurance coverage, because of things that are not their fault and may be beyond their control. But risk and fault are not the same thing, and the costs created by particular risks do not depend solely on the policy-holder's behavior.

A safe driver with an unblemished record may nevertheless be charged a higher premium for automobile insurance because that driver happens to live in a particular neighborhood where others have more accidents than usual. But the risks to an automobile do not depend solely on its owner or driver, but also on others who create dangers of accidents, theft, or vandalism. If drag racing or drunk driving are more common in that neighborhood, then the risks to an automobile driven by a safe driver living there are higher than they would be in some other neighborhood. Similarly, if thefts or vandalism are more common in the neighborhood where the insured driver lives, then the costs of insuring drivers in that neighborhood will be higher, even if those drivers take the normal precautions that would be more effective in a different community. Obvious as such considerations may seem, or even be demonstrable in hard data collected by statisticians, most people are not statisticians and their sense of what is fair or unfair, whether logical or not, carries political weight in government agencies regulating insurance companies.

The laws and regulations imposed by state or federal agencies in the United States, or by governments in other countries, often forbid insurance company practices considered unfair to individuals, even when those policies accurately reflect differences in risks among different ***categories*** of people—and it is only among categories of people, not individuals, that risks can be calculated, which is why there is insurance in the first place. But people resent being charged for things which they believe, or claim, do not apply to their particular situations. This issue has arisen, for example, among people who own pit bulls or other aggressive breeds of dogs, as reported in the ***Wall Street Journal***:

> There is a push by lawmakers and animal-welfare groups to ban the growing insurance-industry practice of refusing to write homeowners' policies for people who own dogs of certain breeds. Some big insurers, including Allstate Corp. and Farmers Insurance Group, won't cover homes in some states if certain breeds are present. Others exclude the breeds form liability coverage or charge extra for it.

Although the Centers for Disease Control and Prevention report that more than half the deaths from dog attacks, over a twenty year period, have come from pit bulls and related breeds or from Rottweilers, owners of these and other breeds excluded from insurance coverage protest that their particular dogs don't bother anybody. But of course insurance exists precisely because risks for groups are more predictable than risks for individuals. Nevertheless, political responses to dog owners have led to bills in a number of states to forbid insurance companies from restricting their coverage of owners of these particular breeds of dogs. Among the consequences of this are that more people are able to afford to keep more dangerous dogs, the price of which is paid both in money by other policy-holders (since the over-all costs of the insurance company are higher) and in injuries or death by those attacked by these dogs.

In general, political incentives are to force insurance companies to cover more things than they would cover otherwise, whether dog attacks, wind damage to homes, or more medical procedures or conditions than they would otherwise cover. Human interest stories about particular individual misfortunes are seldom lacking in the media to justify such additional compulsory coverages. What is usually lacking, in both media and political discussions, is any consideration of how much this additional coverage will cost and who will pay those costs. If critics raise the question of costs, this can usually be dismissed rhetorically by saying that multi-billion dollar insurance companies can surely afford these costs and have a "social responsibility" to do so— "social responsibility" being one of those opaque imperatives for which neither logic nor evidence is considered necessary.

What is in fact likely to happen is that benefits mandated in stage one lead to higher premiums to be paid by policy-holders in stage two. This in turn means that many people who might be able to afford insurance for basic risks cannot afford the higher costs of insurance whose coverage has been politically expanded to include things of marginal concern to most policy-holders. Moreover, the same politicians whose laws have contributed to an increase in the number of people who are uninsured can depict "the uninsured" as yet another problem which they will "solve."

The ignoring of risks in favor of some notion of "fairness" takes many forms. When women in general live longer than men, that makes it more costly for an insurance company to provide life insurance to a man than to a woman, and more costly for the insurance company to provide an annuity to a woman than to a man. If such things are left to be determined by economic criteria in the competition of the market, that would result in higher premiums being charged to a man for a given amount of life insurance coverage and higher prices being charged to a woman for a given amount of annual income from an annuity. But, where popular notions of "fairness" lead to political demands for women and men to be treated the same, laws may forbid different prices from being charged to different sexes, as has happened in France. Here again, the net result is an increase in costs for both insurance policies and annuities, and those costs end up being paid by the policy-holders in general.

Because it is not possible to predict the ratio of women to men who will choose to buy any particular insurance company's life insurance or annuities, there is a larger penumbra of uncertainty surrounding calculations of costs, meaning that there are more risks than if each sex paid only the costs calculated on their own life expectancies. But each insurance company must charge enough extra to cover the possibility that more men than women will buy their life insurance and more women than men will buy their annuities. In short, an additional risk has been created for insurance companies without any additional benefit to policy-holders as a whole, who end up paying more for both insurance and annuities as a result of politically imposed notions of fairness.

While opinions are free, including opinions as to what constitutes "fairness," the consequences of opinions translated into laws have costs, and someone has to pay those additional costs. The same is true when different racial or ethnic groups have different life expectancies or different rates of contracting various diseases, while laws forbid "discrimination" in the prices charged or the coverage offered. Higher automobile accident rates in particular age brackets may also lead to higher premiums for those in these brackets, even when the individual has an unblemished safety record. But state laws and regulations may forbid insurance companies from making some or all of these distinctions among people when charging premiums to different policy holders.

However irrational such results might seem in economic terms, they are perfectly rational in political terms, for the government officials who impose such requirements benefit politically in stage one, even if both the insurance companies and their policy-holders end up worse off in stage two. Political incentives also make it rational to mandate insurance coverage for things that would not be covered by insurance on economic grounds, since those things are not matters of risk. For example, the cost of annual medical checkups is not a risk, since it is known in advance that these checkups occur once a year. To have health insurance cover such things would be like having automobile insurance cover annual smog checks or routine oil changes. But, because of the stronger emotions involved in medical issues, annual checkups are more readily depicted as a "good thing"— and therefore as a justification of a government mandate.

Although "fairness" is a sufficiently vague word to serve as a rationale for government intervention to change economic outcomes in a wide range of contexts in the insurance industry, as in other industries, there is much other intervention, even in situations where the regulatory agency simply chooses to impose whatever it may consider to be a more "reasonable" set of practices than those that would emerge in a free market.

When the price of auto insurance is set by state officials, often they will not let the price rise to as high a level as it would reach in a free market when insuring drivers with a record of repeated accidents or serious traffic violations. Since insurance companies will not want to insure such drivers when the premiums they pay are unlikely to cover all the costs caused by these kinds of drivers, a common political "solution" is to create a special pool of drivers unable to get insurance through regular channels or unable to afford it. Insurance companies are then forced to share high-risk drivers among themselves, and rates in general are then set at levels which will enable the insurers to cover the losses created by all their drivers, including those in the high-risk pools.

What this means is that other drivers are subsidizing high-risk drivers. Looking beyond stage one, what this also means is that more pedestrians and motorists are likely to suffer injuries or death because more high-risk drivers can afford to be on the roads and highways than could do so if auto insurance rates were allowed to rise to the very high levels required to compensate for all the damage caused by reckless drivers. Among the other consequences is that, as premium costs continue to rise to safe drivers, in order to compensate for losses due to unsafe drivers, a larger and larger percentage of safe drivers will be unable to afford the ever more costly insurance through the regular channels— and therefore end up being covered in the subsidized pool initially established for high-risk drivers.

In New Jersey, for example, only 12 percent of high-risk drivers were in the subsidized pool in the early 1970s but, a decade later, nearly half of all cars were insured in the subsidized pool. New Jersey's experience with automobile insurance regulation has not been unique. Nor has automobile insurance been unique in having political criteria over-rule economic criteria in setting insurance rates. The net effect, with other kinds of insurance as well, is to have those with lower risks subsidize those with higher risks, leading to higher insurance costs over all and more risky behavior, whose consequences can cause both financial losses and losses of life and limb to third parties. While government has the power to reduce the risks of "adverse selection" by mandating that everyone have automobile insurance, that benefit may be nullified by imposing insurance rates that make insurance more "affordable" to unsafe drivers or by failing to impose sufficient sanctions on drivers who violate the law and drive without insurance.

None of this is unique to the United States. Similar political incentives produce similar government actions and inactions elsewhere. The London magazine ***The Economist*** reports that "driving without insurance is not treated very seriously" by the law in Britain, with the predictable result of rising amounts of compensation having to be paid to people injured by uninsured drivers:

> The Motor Insurers Bureau, an outfit financed by a levy on the whole industry that pays out when such drivers hurt someone, paid out just £11m in 1988. By 2000 that had risen to £225m.

Here, as in other situations, the fact that the government ***can*** have a beneficial effect by intervening in the market— in this case, to reduce "adverse selection"— does not mean that it ***will*** in fact have that beneficial effect on net balance, or even that it will avoid having a detrimental effect. That depends on the political incentives and constraints, and especially on such incentives and constraints as they exist in stage one, often ignoring the repercussions in later stages.

With scientific advances in the study of DNA, the possibilities of predicting the likelihood of people with particular DNA becoming afflicted with particular diseases raises again the question whether the terms and conditions of insurance policies should be allowed to reflect those different risks. Arguments familiar in other contexts are already being made on both sides of this issue in various countries. According to ***The Economist***:

> Rosanna Capolingua, the head of the Australian Medical Association, warned in June that the rising tide of genetic data could be used by insurance firms to discriminate against those with higher risks of certain illnesses. . . Soren Holm, a lawyer at Cardiff University, argues that genetic data are not, in principle, different from other sorts of medical data, such as family history or cholesterol level. Insurers should therefore be allowed access to them.

The issue of "genetic discrimination" has also been raised in the United States. A front-page story in the *New York Times* began:

> A bill that would prohibit discrimination by health insurers and employers based on the information that people carry in their genes won final approval in Congress on Thursday by an overwhelming vote.
>
> The legislation, which President Bush has indicated he will sign, speaks both to the mounting hope placed in genetic research to greatly improve health care and the fear of a dystopia in which people's genetic information could be used against them. On the House floor on Thursday, Democrats and Republicans alike cited anecdotes and polls illustrating that people feel they should not be penalized for what is in their genes.

THE ECONOMICS OF RISK

Safety might seem to be something that you cannot get too much of. Yet everything we do in our everyday lives belies that conclusion. Often what we do makes more sense than what we say.

Reducing risks has costs— some of which we are willing to pay and some of which we are not willing to pay. Moreover, not all costs are money costs. For many people, the cost of reducing risks would be giving up the enjoyment they get from skiing, boating, rock climbing, skateboarding, and other risky activities. In fact, ultimately there are only risky activities, since nothing is 100 percent safe. Yet no one suggests that we retire into passive inactivity— which has its own risks, and which would also have to be away from sunlight if we were consistent, since sunlight increases the risk of skin cancer. On the other hand, most of us are not prepared to take a short cut by walking across a freeway during the rush hour. In other words, there are risks we are willing to take and risks we are not willing to take, varying somewhat from person to person, but involving a weighing of benefits and costs in any event. We do not drive to work in tanks, even though tanks would be safer than automobiles, because we are not prepared to pay the costs in money, commuting time or parking space problems.

Trade-Offs

However much we may agree with sweeping rhetoric about safety, or even vote for those who use such rhetoric, nevertheless when faced with choices in our own lives we weigh incremental safety against incremental costs. We may consider it worthwhile to avoid one chance in six of getting killed from playing Russian roulette, but not worth it to pay a thousand dollars to avoid one chance in six million of getting killed by some fluke occurrence. Indeed, if the cost of avoiding one chance in six million is merely an inconvenience, some may still refuse to pay it. In short, even those who talk about safety in categorical terms— "if it saves just one life, it is worth whatever it costs"— actually behave in their own lives as if safety is an incremental decision, based on weighing costs against benefits, not a categorical decision.

One of the costs of any given kind of safety may be an increase in other kinds of dangers. It is always possible to make subways safer by having the trains go more slowly, increasing the distances between trains, and having fewer cars per train, in order to reduce the train's weight and hence reduce the distance required to bring the train to a stop. However, all these things reduce the number of passengers who can be carried during rush hours and— since people have to get to work somehow— force some of those passengers to try other means of transportation, most of which involve greater risks of death than subway trains do. In short, you can always reduce the risks in subways by policies which increase the risks elsewhere.

One of the problems of risk management through political institutions is that reducing a given risk is newsworthy, while the increases in other risks that this may entail are not. In 2008, for example, under pressure from Congress, the Federal Aviation Agency forced airlines to cancel thousands of flights in order to take care of overdue inspections and corrections before their planes could fly again. At this point, there had not been a commercial airline crash in the United States in seven years, so the items awaiting inspection could hardly have been major hazards. However, by suddenly stranding hundreds of thousands of passengers without warning, the grounding of so many airliners undoubtedly led many people to get to their destinations by automobile— and the fatality rate per mile is several times as high for cars as for planes. In short, reducing whatever residual dangers there may have been from uninspected items on airliners meant increasing the risk of fatalities on the highways.

There are many contexts in which reducing one kind of danger entails increasing another kind of danger. During the Second World War, Japanese fighter pilots usually chose not to wear parachutes when going into aerial combat, even though parachutes are obviously a safety device. As one of these pilots explained after the war, although every pilot was provided with a parachute, "the decision to fly without them was our own" and was made because parachutes "hamstring our cockpit movements in a battle," when split-second responses can be matters of life and death, and it "was difficult to move our arms and legs quickly when encumbered by chute straps." In other words, wearing a parachute increased the chances that you would get shot down.[4] Increasing one kind of safety can increase other risks, just as with subway trains, commercial airliners and other things.

Politics versus Economics

A crucial distinction in decision-making processes is the distinction between individuals making decisions for themselves and third-parties making decisions for others. Subway passengers always have the option of using other means of getting to work, but they are very unlikely to hold subways to a standard of 100 percent safety and go elsewhere if this standard is not met. But what of those who are making decisions for others? If there has recently been a tragic and highly publicized subway accident with a

---

[4] Another reason was that Japanese pilots were usually fighting air battles over enemy territory and bailing out would mean being captured by the enemy, which was "unthinkable" to a Japanese pilot.

number of fatalities, political outcries for more subway safety may well cause the authorities to order the trains slowed down, fewer cars to be attached to each train, and greater distances maintained between trains.

Moreover, after the passage of time shows that these policies have reduced accidents and injuries in the subways, officials who instituted such policies are unlikely to be shy about claiming credit. Nor are most voters likely to inquire about the total number of injuries and deaths during rush hour on all modes of transportation put together. That would require thinking beyond stage one. In short, third-party decision-making, based on categorical reasoning and one-stage thinking, often succeeds in the political arena, even though individual decision-making for oneself is more likely to involve an incremental weighing of benefits against costs. Those skilled in rhetoric, such as politicians, can easily ignore hidden costs which those faced with decisions for themselves are more likely to take into account.

There are other situations in which caution— at stage one— can turn out to be dangerous in the long run. Nor are these situations confined to economics. In the American Civil War, for example, General George McClellan's cautious use of the Union army has often been blamed for more fatalities than if he had been more aggressive and not let defeated Confederate troops escape to fight another day. McClellan's insistence on waiting to get his forces organized before launching another attack allowed the Confederates time to both escape and dig in to create stronger defensive positions, from which they could later more readily kill more Union attackers.

Another and more general way in which one kind of safety increases other risks involves the role of wealth. Reconsider the common statement, "If it saves just one life, it is worth whatever it costs." This sacrifice of wealth would make sense from a safety standpoint only if wealth saved no lives. But, in reality, wealth is one of the biggest life-saving factors, so that sacrificing wealth costs lives. The role of wealth in saving lives can be dramatic, whether comparing rich and poor in a given society or comparing prosperous nations with Third World nations. An economist in India has pointed out that "95 percent of deaths from natural hazards occur in poorer countries." Since virtually all countries were poorer in the past, this also implies that deaths from natural disasters have been declining over time, for both rich and poor countries. Empirical evidence supports that conclusion.

Six to eight thousand people perished in a hurricane that struck Galveston, Texas, in 1900 but fewer than 50 died when Hurricane Andrew hit Florida in 1992— even though Andrew was a far more destructive hurricane. The difference is that the United States was a much richer country in 1992 and therefore had many more options as to warnings that could be spread beforehand and actions that could be taken afterwards. Similarly in India where, as Indian economist Barun Mitra put it, a drought in the year 2000 was dubbed the worst of the century by the media, which "struggled to identify even one victim, while quietly forgetting the past famines that cost the lives of millions." Medical, automotive, and other hazards are likewise affected by the wealth of the people and nations where they occur.

While the richest countries suffer the largest financial losses from natural disasters, it is the poorest countries which suffer the largest losses of life. In 2005, for example, Hurricane Katrina cost $135 billion in damages to the United States and the Bahamas— several times more financial damage than any other natural disaster anywhere else in the world— but an earthquake that struck India and Pakistan claimed more than 73,000 victims dead or missing, compared to fewer than 1,500 victims of Hurricane Katrina in the United States and the Bahamas, even though Katrina was an unusually destructive hurricane with unusually large numbers of victims, by American standards.

Not all risks are physical risks to life and limb. Financial risks are also different when they are dealt with through political institutions than when they are dealt with through economic institutions, responding to the economic forces of the market. Banking is a classic example of an industry where risk-assessment is crucial to survival, much less success. But, because banks have long been regulated by government, their riskiness can vary widely according to the extent to which political controls influence or override the decisions that banks themselves would be led to make by market conditions.

For most of the history of the United States, there have been restrictions on banks having multiple branches, at least in some states. Whatever the political reasons for these restrictions, the economic consequence has been to make banking more risky. A bank located in the middle of a wheat-growing region has its fate heavily dependent on the market for wheat, since both its depositors and borrowers are likely to consist to a disproportionate extent of people whose incomes are dependent on the wheat market. If this bank had branches located in other regions where oil, silver, or a variety of other products were bigger parts of the economy, its risks would be more diversified and therefore less risky over-all.

Banks with only one location, called "unit banks," lose money when something goes wrong with the economy at their one location, because that makes it difficult for their borrowers to make the payments on their loans, while at the same time depositors have less income to deposit. However, the loss of profits is not the biggest danger. Since banks lend out much of the money that has been deposited in them, no bank has enough cash on hand to pay all their depositors if they all demand payment at the same time. When an economic downturn in a given area leads to fewer borrowers being able to make their loan payments and more depositors withdrawing money to cover expenses no longer covered by their declining incomes, there is also a danger of additional drains on the bank's money supply by a run on the bank by people fearful of a bank collapse— and such a run on a bank will in fact make such a collapse more likely.

The special risks of these "unit banks" became painfully apparent during the Great Depression of the 1930s, when thousands of banks failed. These were risks not only to the banks themselves but to the economy as a whole, since their failures entailed a reduction of the aggregate demand in the economy, making it harder for the country to get out of the depression. These bank failures were not random but were concentrated in unit banks:

> Small unit (one office) banks, which accounted for about 90 percent of bank failures, began lobbying for federal deposit insurance to assure customers that they needn't worry about their deposits. Big banks with many branches didn't seek such insurance since they had a diversified business and were financially sound.

Previously, 14 state governments had had their own deposit insurance. All of these were states with laws requiring unit banking and most of these states had large numbers of bank failures. In other words, these states' deposit insurance was a way of dealing with special risks created by the state governments themselves. Moreover, this solution was by no means costless, since banks had to pay deposit insurance premiums to protect themselves from risks created by politicians. At the federal level, big banks with multiple branches saw no need to pay premiums for deposit insurance, but creation of the Federal Deposit Insurance Corporation made it legally obligatory for them to do so anyway.

Federal deposit insurance greatly reduced the danger of a run on banks, since people knew that their deposits were safe, even if the bank failed. This reduced likelihood of a run on the bank reduced the dangers of a great contraction of the money supply and of aggregate demand, such as occurred in the 1930s. Many have regarded this as a major contribution of the government to the long-run stability of the economy. However, the federal government was solving a problem created by previous governmental restrictions, and at a cost that big, multi-branch banks did not need to pay, for a problem that they had not had, even in the depths of the Great Depression. The extension of the same deposit insurance protection to savings and loan associations eventually cost the taxpayers more than half a trillion dollars in the 1980s, when many of these institutions failed. Apparently the premiums they had paid were not sufficient to cover the losses but the protection of the insurance made both depositors and the bank directors less cautious. People who run financial institutions, like other people, tend to take more risks when they are insured.

"SOCIAL INSURANCE"

Everything that is called insurance is not in fact insurance. In the countries of the European Union, government retirement programs account for 90 percent of all retirement income, often under the name "social insurance." But real insurance is very different from these government pension programs. Real insurance is based on careful mathematical and statistical calculations of risks and of the premiums required to cover those risks. These are known as actuarial calculations and only when the assets of insurance companies are large enough to cover their liabilities are they said to be actuarially sound. Their assets include the premiums they have received, the physical assets and financial assets they have purchased with this money, and the additional earnings from these investments. Whatever they are obligated by law to pay to their policy-holders are the insurance company's liabilities.

Government-run social insurance programs seldom have enough assets to cover their liabilities, but rely instead on making current payments out of current receipts. These are called pay-as-you-go programs— and sometimes they are also called pyramid schemes. Pyramid schemes are privately run pay-as-you-go plans— and they are illegal because of their high risk of default and the opportunities for those who run them to take part of the money for themselves. The most famous pyramid scheme was run by a man named Charles Ponzi, who went to jail back in 1920. He used the same principles behind the pension plans of many Western governments today.

Ponzi had promised, within 90 days, to double the investment of those who paid into his program. The first investors who were not deterred by warnings from skeptics were in fact rewarded by having their investments pay off double in 90 days. Ponzi simply paid the first wave of investors with money received from the growing second wave of investors, and the second wave from the even larger number of those in the third wave, as enthusiasm for his plan spread. So long as the number of people attracted to this plan formed an expanding pyramid, both the earlier investors and Ponzi profited handsomely. But, once the pyramid stopped growing, there was no way to continue to pay off those who sent Ponzi their money, since his scheme created no new wealth.

The American Social Security pension system and similar government pension systems in the countries of the European Union likewise take in payments from people who are working and use that money to pay the pensions of people who have retired— paying the first generation of workers who paid into these pension plans with money received from the second generation, and so on.

Unlike Ponzi's pyramid scheme, these government pension plans have much longer than 90 days before the promised pensions are scheduled to be paid. They have decades before they have to redeem the promises of the system to workers after they retire. Moreover, the small generation of people working in the 1930s, when Social Security began in the United States, was succeeded by a much larger "baby boom" generation after World War II, so the pyramid of contributors was predestined to grow. The economies of countries with such programs also grew, allowing working people with much higher incomes to be taxed to cover pensions based on the much lower incomes of the 1930s generation. The promises not only were kept, the benefits were often expanded beyond those initially promised. Like the Ponzi schemes, these pension plans paid off handsomely to the first wave of participants.

Those who warned that these government pension plans were essentially Ponzi schemes without enough assets to cover their liabilities— that they were "actuarially unsound" in the financial jargon— were either not believed or were brushed aside for having made objections that were theoretically correct but in practice irrelevant. One of those who brushed these objections aside was Professor Paul Samuelson of MIT, the first American winner of the Nobel Prize in economics:

> The beauty of social insurance is that it is actuarially unsound. Everyone who reaches retirement age is given benefit privileges that far exceed anything he has paid in. . . . Always there are more youths than old folks in a growing population. More important, with real incomes growing at some 3% a year, the taxable base upon which benefits rest in any period are much greater than the taxes paid historically by the generation now retired. . . A growing nation is the greatest Ponzi game ever contrived.

By the end of the twentieth century, however, the day of reckoning began to loom on the horizon for these government pension programs, as it had for the original Ponzi scheme. Contrary to Professor Samuelson's assertion, there are not ***always*** "more youths than old folks." As birth rates declined in the Western world and life expectancy increased, vastly increasing the number of years in which pensions would have to be paid to growing numbers of people, it became painfully clear that either tax rates were going to have to rise by very large amounts or the benefits would have to be reduced in one way or another— or both— or the system would simply run out of money.

In 2002, the credit-rating agency Standard & Poor's calculated the liabilities representing promised pension benefits to add up to more than the annual Gross Domestic Product of nine of the 15 European Union nations. These were the kinds of overwhelming debts usually run up in fighting a major war. Moreover, wars usually end in a few years, so that these debts can begin to be paid off, while there are endless generations of retirees ahead, living longer and longer. Demographic projections showed the size of the population of retirement age, compared to the size of the working-age population, to be rising sharply for the first half of the twenty-first century, not only in the European Union countries, but in Japan and the United States as well.

The underlying reason for the crisis atmosphere surrounding many discussions of how to "save" Social Security in the late twentieth and early twenty-first centuries came from the fact that the contributions paid by workers were not invested, like insurance premiums, but spent. Because there was no real fund of wealth to draw on in pay-as-you-go government pension plans, these plans had the same fatal weakness as the original Ponzi scheme. Yet none of that became obvious in stage one. Decades passed before a financial crisis developed, and even then the reason for the crisis was not obvious to many people. The crisis was often blamed on changing demographics, rather than on those who set up a scheme that could work only so long as demographic trends did not change— even though demographic trends had been known to change many times in the past.

Chapter 6

The Economics of Immigration

No-one can know enough to be categorical about the pros and cons of mass immigration.

Wolfgang Kasper

While there are certain patterns that can be seen in the history of immigration and certain economic principles behind some of those patterns, there cannot be any blanket conclusions about immigrations in general because there is no such thing as immigrants in general. The international migration patterns of Italians have been very different from the international migration patterns of the Irish, and these in turn have been very different from the international migration patterns of emigrants from India. These patterns have also differed over time as the changing technology of transportation— from wind-driven ships to steamships, and later to airplanes— has changed both the origins and the destinations of international migrants. In addition, refugees differ from sojourners, and people expelled en masse— as Asians were expelled from Uganda in the 1970s or Jews from parts of Europe in medieval times— have yet another pattern of resettlement. All this is in addition to the fact that different groups of immigrants bring different languages, cultures and skills.

There are an estimated 200 million immigrants today worldwide. They outnumber the total population of every nation except four— China, India, the United States and Indonesia. Yet immigrants are only three percent of the world's population. While the general pattern of international migrations today, as in the past, has largely been from poorer countries to more prosperous countries, it has by no means always been the poorest people in a country who immigrate, since migration itself costs money. From some less prosperous nations, their most skilled and highly educated people are most likely to emigrate. As the distinguished British magazine *The Economist* reported:

> In South Africa, although universities churn out graduates at a fast clip, many well-qualified people promptly depart for Britain or Australia, leaving tens of thousands of jobs unfilled at home. In Morocco those with science and engineering degrees, computer skills and languages go to France, the Netherlands and Canada, whereas the students of literature and public administration stay at home. Professor Mohamed Khachami, of AMERM, a migration think-tank in Rabat, laments that his country lacks people to build better internet connections, yet Paris now has an association for Moroccan IT engineers. Hospitals and clinics in southern Africa struggle to cope with huge public-health problems as doctors and nurses pack their bags for jobs in the Gulf, Europe and elsewhere. It is a similar story for schools. . . Small countries such as Jamaica, Trinidad and Senegal have seen half to three-quarters of all their graduates move abroad.

To make a complex subject like immigration manageable, it is necessary to break it down into segments that can be examined one at a time. We can begin with historical patterns of migrations and then consider the economic factors affecting those patterns.

HISTORY

Migrations of peoples have taken place throughout thousands of years of recorded history, and archaeological studies indicate that people migrated before history was being written. Migrations antedate national boundaries, so the distinction we make today between internal migrants and international emigrants would have had no meaning in those early times.

Why do people move?

Individuals may move for any of a wide variety of reasons but the migrations of whole peoples have usually been for very visible and very powerful reasons. In those times and places where the land would produce enough food to feed the population for only a limited number of years before the nutrients in the soil became exhausted, human survival required moving on to new land while the old land recovered its fertility over the years by absorbing nutrients from the environment. Some people migrated to escape invaders, as the Slavs were pushed westward by the invading Mongols in medieval times or as the indigenous peoples of the United States were pushed westward by the invading Europeans. The invaders themselves were also migrants, moving in search of land, people, and wealth to conquer. Some people were moved by others. At least a million Europeans were captured and brought as slaves to the Barbary Coast of North Africa from 1530 to 1780. That was twice as many people as were brought as slaves from Africa to the United States and to the 13 American colonies from which the United States was formed.

The migrations of modern times have usually had different reasons and different patterns. Most were not fleeing invaders or exhausted land, and most migrated of their own free will. While the decision to move was usually an individual or family decision, they were not random decisions and their patterns varied from group to group, from country to country, and from one time period to another.

Origins and Destinations

For most of the past three centuries, the United States has received more immigrants than any other country. As of 2007, there were 38 million people living in the United States who were not born there. That was about 20 percent of all the migrants in the world. As for countries of origin, no single country has supplied such a high percentage of all the migrants in the world for as long as the United States has remained the leading destination of immigration. However, the continent of Europe was the principal supplier of emigrants for centuries, though these emigrants came from different countries in Europe at different times, and none of these countries remained as prominent among the countries sending emigrants as the United States has been among countries receiving them. Among European immigrants to the United States, for example, the most numerous were from Ireland in 1850, Germany in 1880, and Italy in 1930.

Although we may speak of emigrants from one country going to another country, the history of their origins and destinations is usually much more specific than that. Germans did not migrate randomly from across Germany to settle randomly across the United States. Quite the contrary. Frankfort, Kentucky, was founded by people from Frankfurt, Germany. The town of Lomira in Wisconsin was settled almost exclusively by people from Brandenburg. A study found whole villages in Germany transplanted to rural communities in Missouri. Nor was this pattern peculiar to Germans or to the United States. At one time, most of the fisherman in the Australian port of Freemantle came from just two towns in Italy. Immigrants from particular towns in Lebanon often settled together in particular towns in Colombia. Other examples from around the world could be multiplied almost without limit.

The origins of immigrants are often specific in another sense. Neither the geographic nor the social origins of immigrants are random. The population of the original thirteen American colonies was not a random sample of the population of Britain. Colonial America has sometimes been referred to as a "decapitated" society, since the wealthy elites were seldom known to take on the hazards of an Atlantic crossing, followed by the uncertainties and hazards of pioneering in creating a new society in an unfamiliar land among an unfamiliar indigenous population. Geographically, the people who settled in the South came from different parts of Britain than those who settled in New England, and rates of illiteracy, violence, and unwed motherhood varied widely between these two groups, on both sides of the Atlantic. Sephardic Jews and Ashkenazic Jews settled in separate communities, whether in Argentina, Brazil, or even on the small Dutch island of Curaçao. Similarly with immigrants from various parts of China living in various countries in Southeast Asia.

Migration is more than relocation. Internationally, and sometimes even domestically, it involves having to learn innumerable new things about a new society, including a new culture and in many cases a new language, as well as such mundane but urgently important things as where and how to get a job and find a decent and affordable place to live in the new community. For the new migrant, the cost in time and money of doing all these things is lower where a family member, or at least someone from the old community, is already living in the new community and can serve as a guide— and, if need be, offer financial or other help in case of emergency. This was especially important during the long era when people arrived in a new place with very little money and so had very little time before having to find a job that would support them and an affordable place to live. The concentration of immigrants from a given locality in the country of origin in a given locality in the country of destination was one consequence of these considerations.

Another fact leading many new emigrants from Europe to follow in the footsteps of fellow countrymen who had immigrated before them was that their passage across the Atlantic was paid by family or other countrymen already living in the United States. During the era of mass emigration from Europe, about 30 percent of the emigrants from Finland traveled on prepaid tickets, as did 40 percent of Norwegian emigrants and 50 percent of Swedish emigrants. More than half of the emigrants fleeing the 1840s famine in Ireland had their passage across the Atlantic prepaid by the Irish already living in the United States. Similarly, more than half of the Eastern European Jews fleeing persecution and violence in Eastern Europe in the early twentieth century had their Transatlantic passage paid by Jews already living in the United States.

These prepaid fares were a symptom of a larger pattern of family and other ties linking particular individuals in the country of origin to particular people in the country of destination. These ties have long been a key factor in creating migration chains between highly specific locations in one country to highly specific locations in another. Nor were such "chain migration" patterns peculiar to the United States. At one time, it was common for Lebanese businessmen in West Africa or Indian businessmen in East Africa to provide jobs for younger family members who later followed them to their new country of settlement, and Chinese businessmen have done the same in Southeast Asia. Over a period of half a century, more than 90 percent of the immigrants to Australia from southern Europe came via the chain migration process. Modern communications and transportation facilitate the maintenance of such ties, as *The Economist* magazine noted: "The fall in transport costs has made it cheaper to risk a trip, and cheap international telephone calls allow Bulgarians in Spain to tip off their cousins back home that there are fruit-picking jobs available."

Other important and continuing ties of immigrants with people in their countries of origin have also been shown by the sending of money back to them. Such international remittances have been estimated at $318 billion worldwide in 2007, mostly— $240 billion— to poorer countries. These remittances from their own citizens living abroad have been more than twice as large as all the foreign aid the poor countries receive. Often these remittances have also been a significant proportion of the total income of the countries receiving them— 17 percent of Gross Domestic Product in Serbia and Jamaica, 20 percent in Jordan and 25 percent in Haiti. A study of 9,000 African doctors in America found that they sent home an average of $20,000 a year, some of them even after living overseas for 20 years.

The origins and destinations of migrants are affected by the transportation available to them, both technologically and economically. During the long eras when most people in most societies were poor, many of these people did not move much at all, but lived and died within a radius of perhaps 50 miles of where they were born, often in the same home in which their parents and grandparents had lived. Those who did migrate, then or in later times, did so within limits determined by the availability of transportation that they could afford. For example, during the early centuries of the American colonies, and then of the United States formed from these colonies, most of the immigrants came from Europe and, more specifically, from northern and western Europe. That was because ports in these parts of Europe were the most frequent destination of cargo ships that crossed the Atlantic to and from America.

Because Americans during this era were usually exporting agricultural products and importing manufactured products from Europe, the United States traded primarily with the industrial nations of Europe. Therefore this international exchange of products of similar value meant an exchange of products of very different size and weight. Ships carrying American produce to Europe usually returned with unfilled space because manufactured goods took up less space than the agricultural products that paid for them. As a result, this empty space was available at low cost to people who wanted to immigrate to America— provided that they lived where Americans were shipping cargo. As already noted, that was primarily northern and western Europe. More specifically, it was the port cities of northern and western Europe and the hinterlands from which these ports were readily accessible to people wanting to emigrate.

The economics of the situation largely determined where the immigrants settled, as well as where they originated, because they had to land wherever the cargo ship was going, and could move on to other destinations only if and when they had enough money to do so. For very poor people, that meant landing and settling largely in big east coast ports like Boston, New York, and Philadelphia, from which many cargo ships went back and forth to Europe. Boston, for example, initially had relatively little to offer the destitute immigrants fleeing from famine-stricken Ireland in the 1840s, but that is where many of the cargo ships from their part of the world landed, so that is where many of the Irish settled and tried to make the best of an unpromising situation.

Later in the nineteenth century, the development of the steam engine and the replacement of wind-driven ships by steam-powered ships revolutionized migrations to the Western Hemisphere.

The drastic reduction in the amount of time required to cross the Atlantic in steam-powered ships lowered the cost of migrating, not only as regards the fares charged, but also the costs of food and other necessities used during the voyage and the time lost in idleness aboard ship without a job to bring in income. These lower costs greatly increased the amount of Transatlantic migration— and also shifted the origins of the migrants from Northern and Western Europe to Southern and Eastern Europe. At the greatly reduced costs of crossing the Atlantic, the poorer people of these other regions of Europe could now afford to migrate and it was no longer necessary to find cargo ships with empty space. They could afford to travel on passenger ships and therefore choose their own destinations independent of cargo trade routes. The decade of the 1880s was the last decade in which most immigrants to the United States came from northern and western Europe.

Now a growing mass migration was dominated by Italians, Slavs, Jews and other peoples from those parts of Europe from which few people had been able to afford to migrate before. Moreover, the drastically reduced cost of Transatlantic migration led to a new phenomenon— people who migrated to the Western Hemisphere, not in order to settle permanently, but to work for a while where they could earn higher incomes than at home, and then return to Europe with their savings. Italians were especially prominent as sojourners in the United States, Argentina, and other countries, repeating across the Atlantic a long-established pattern of Italians sojourning in various other countries in Europe.

Sojourners sometimes stayed for a number of years before returning home, but sometimes just for one season, for those who did such seasonal work as agricultural labor or construction. The fact that South America's seasons were the opposite of those in Italy made seasonal sojourning especially attractive for workers who might otherwise have had trouble finding work at home during the winter months. Sojourning was not confined to Italians, however. On the other side of the world, there were many Chinese sojourners in various countries in Southeast Asia, and massive migrations of plantation laborers on fixed terms of indenture from India to countries around the world, including Fiji in the South Pacific and countries in Africa and the Caribbean. Sometimes people who came as sojourners decided to stay rather than return home as planned. So many people from India remained in Fiji that they became as numerous as the native Fijians, and in British Guiana they became as numerous as the initially predominantly black population of that country.

The same drastic reduction in ocean voyage costs which enabled people to cross the Atlantic who could not have afforded to do so before likewise reduced the cost of crossing the Pacific, bringing in significant numbers of immigrants from China and Japan to the west coast of the United States, as well as to the Caribbean and South America. The Japanese population of Brazil became the largest outside of Japan, and they eventually owned about three-quarters as much land in Brazil as there was cultivated land in Japan.

Still later, in the twentieth century, the invention of the airplane and the spread of commercial aviation internationally once again changed the origins and destinations of migrants, making possible migrations and sojourns that had not been available to most people before. In the last third of the twentieth century, more immigrants came to the United States from Asia than from Europe.

During the era of mass emigration from Europe between 1850 and 1914, about 55 million Europeans migrated to the Western Hemisphere and Australia. Earlier migrations to the Western Hemisphere were dominated by the involuntary emigration of slaves from Africa and later, after the middle of the twentieth century, emigrants from Asia. In short, the origins, destinations and cultures of immigrants changed greatly over time.

Cultures

Migrations, and especially international migrations, are not simply a movement of people. The cultures of those people move as well. Some of these cultures erode as the migrants and their descendants absorb the culture of the society around them but other cultures can persist for generations, or even centuries, despite being surrounded by millions of people with a very different culture. Indeed, the same culture may persist in one society and erode in another. There are reasons for both patterns.

Among Lebanese immigrants, for example, assimilation tends to be greater in the United States or Australia than in Latin America, and least in West African nations such as Sierra Leone or the Ivory Coast. America and Australia have been characterized historically as societies in which "there is a single culture, that of the dominant social group, to which all others try to assimilate." An implicit corollary to this is that those who do assimilate tend to be accepted into that culture, which is what makes assimilation worthwhile to them. Latin America has been characterized as a place "where society is not only mixed in origin but mixed in culture as well; different cultures are accepted as being on the same level and capable of contributing something to the common stock." This is essentially the "multiculturalism" philosophy which has in more recent times become a major, if not dominant, philosophy in most of the English-speaking countries as well. Finally, in West Africa, "the culture of the indigenous majority is not communicated to immigrant groups"— or perhaps the Lebanese and other immigrants do not choose to become like the indigenous peoples.

These suggestive characterizations reflect a pattern of assimilation not confined to Lebanese emigrants or to these particular regions. Once the Chinese were socially accepted in the United States in the second half of the twentieth century, they assimilated into American society both culturally and biologically far more rapidly than they did in Malaysia, where they had been living longer and in larger numbers. Most Chinese Americans speak English, while few Chinese in Malaysia speak Malay. Rates of intermarriage of Chinese Americans with white Americans have been far higher than rates of intermarriage with Malays. Assimilation requires not only that acceptance be mutual but also that there be tangible benefits to those immigrants who decide to assimilate. Where the local culture is regarded as inferior, the immigrant culture can persist indefinitely, as the culture of German enclaves in Russia and Argentina persisted for centuries, even as Germans in Australia and the United States eventually came out of their enclaves and became English speakers and were absorbed into the larger society around them.

Sojourners tend not to assimilate as quickly or as thoroughly as immigrants who plan to settle permanently. Nor do immigrant cultures give way as readily to the culture in their country of destination when the immigrant culture is constantly reinforced by new arrivals from the country of origin, or among people who move readily back and forth between their country of origin and the country to which they have immigrated. The drastic reduction of immigration to the United States, as a result of restrictive laws passed in the 1920s, has often been credited with the assimilation of various immigrant groups once regarded as inassimilable by many Americans a generation earlier. In short, there is no single pattern of cultural or biological assimilation, even for a given group settling in different countries or at different times in the same country, much less among immigrants from lands around the world.

Cultures are among the many reasons for not being able to discuss immigration in the abstract. Germans who settled in Brazil were not like the original Portuguese settlers. At one time, the rulers of Brazil were quite clear and quite candid about that, and deliberately sought to encourage immigration from parts of Europe different from those from which the first settlers came. There were vast undeveloped areas of Brazil, and the existing population showed no real interest in taking on the arduous task of becoming pioneers in opening up those regions, while Germans had done such things in Russia, the United States and elsewhere. Likewise, Italian immigrants, both in Argentina and in neighboring Brazil, were far more willing to do hard and "menial" work than were the descendants of the Spaniards and Portuguese who had settled these countries. Italians were also as well known for being thrifty as the Argentineans of Spanish origin were for being free spenders, so that even though most Italians arrived in the country very poor, they soon had more bank accounts in Buenos Aires than the native Argentines did.

Ultimately the Italian immigrants became more successful than the native-born population, whether in agriculture, commerce or industry. None of this was peculiar to Italians or to Argentina. In centuries past, it was not uncommon for the Jewish minority in a number of countries to be literate, even when surrounded by a much larger population that was almost totally illiterate. Nor was this simply a matter of having money to be able to afford education. In colonial Malaya, government schools were provided for the indigenous Malays but not for the Chinese minority; yet the initially poor and often illiterate Chinese created their own schools as they rose economically and became better educated than the Malays. In late eighteenth century Scotland, people who could not afford to buy books were nevertheless able to use lending libraries that were widespread across the country because of the widespread demand for books. Yet when Frederick Law Olmsted made his celebrated excursions through the antebellum South in the nineteenth century, he seldom saw books even in the homes of slaveowners who could easily have afforded them.

In short, culture is a major factor in the behavior of different groups of people, often overriding even economic factors. This applies both to migrants and non-migrants, as well as distinguishing one group of migrants from another. It is one of many reasons why it can be misleading to refer to immigrants in general, when they vary so much from one another according to cultural specifics.

Cultures also change over the generations, whether for better or for worse, and at different speeds for different groups. Emigrants from the Scottish lowlands were more readily assimilated into English-speaking societies in the United States, Australia, and New Zealand than were Scots from the highlands. German emigrants, on the other hand, maintained their language and culture for centuries, living in their own ethnic enclaves in Eastern Europe, Brazil, and Argentina. Yet, despite this enduring loyalty to their own culture, most had no similar political loyalty to Germany and became patriotic citizens of the countries in which they settled. Key American military leaders in both World Wars were of German ancestry, including Generals John J. Pershing (whose ancestors' name was Pfoerschin), Dwight D. Eisenhower, and Carl Spaatz, whose bombers pulverized Germany, and Admiral Chester Nimitz.

Others, including Japanese emigrants to Brazil, maintained both cultural loyalty and political loyalty to their country of origin. The Japanese in Brazil even refused to believe that Japan had been defeated in World War II— with extremists among them assassinating fellow Japanese in Brazil who publicly said that they believed the news of Japan's defeat. By contrast, those Japanese emigrants who went to the United States did so during a previous era in Japan, when American society was greatly admired by the Japanese, so that they arrived in the United States predisposed to become loyal Americans, and largely remained so despite encountering more discrimination than other Japanese encountered in Brazil. Among other things, this also indicates that a group's behavior is not simply a function of their treatment by the society around them but also reflects internal cultural patterns.

Few, if any, American or Brazilian authorities were aware of this cultural distinction among Japanese who emigrated from Japan during radically different cultural eras, so that Japanese Americans were interned, as other enemy aliens were interned in wartime in other countries, including German Jews interned in Britain at the beginning of World War II, despite the extreme unlikelihood that German Jews would aid the Nazi cause. Many decisions made during the exigencies of war reflect a need for speed rather than deliberation, and for erring on the side of the country's interests, rather than those of individuals or groups.

Some major cultural changes within an immigrant group can take place in a single generation. It has not been uncommon in the United States, for example, for the first generation of immigrants to continue speaking their own language, either predominantly or exclusively, while the second generation speaks primarily English, with some knowledge of the language of their parents, and the third generation to speak English only. Yet, in other ways, the second generation may adjust less readily to American society than did the immigrant generation. Those who had fled either poverty or oppression in their native lands tended to be keenly aware of the advantages of living in American society. But their children, who never experienced the life that their parents lived in other countries, may tend to compare their lot with that of other Americans around them, and often develop resentments and bitterness at their own lower economic or social status.

It was from the second generation of Eastern European Jews that leading criminals emerged to dominate organized crime in the United States before they were replaced by second-generation Italian criminals. In a later era, it was the offspring of refugees from China during the era of Mao Zedong who often became Maoists in the United States— admirers of the very system their parents had fled— and criminals as well. Similarly in France, where the first generation of emigrants from North Africa were described as "better Frenchmen than either their children or grandchildren: they would never have whistled and booed at the ***Marseillaise***, as their descendants did before the soccer match between France and Algeria in 2001, alerting the rest of France to the terrible canker in its midst." Subsequent Muslim riots that rocked France in 2005 only validated this assessment. Two years later, there were fewer riots but they were more deadly. The *New York Times* reported:

> The onetime rock throwers and car burners have taken up hunting shotguns and turned them on the police.
>
> More than 100 officers have been wounded, several of them seriously, according to the police. Thirty were hit with buckshot and pellets from shotguns, and one of the wounded was hit with a type of bullet used to kill large game, Patrice Ribeiro, a police spokesman, said in a telephone interview. One of the officers lost an eye; another's shoulder was shattered by gunfire.

Crime rates among Mexican immigrants in the United States showed a familiar pattern: "Between the foreign-born generation and their American children, the incarceration rate of Mexican Americans jumps more than eightfold." The *Washington Post* reported another similarity with France:

> Many new immigrants are not assimilating. When the U.S. soccer team played Mexico in the Los Angeles Memorial Coliseum a few years ago, our national anthem was booed and our team was showered with garbage.

Among Muslims in the United States, a poll by the Pew Research Center found that one out of four respondents under the age of 30 accepted suicide bombing.

Return Migration

Twenty thousand people of Indian descent were reported to have returned to India in 2005-2006, and China had 40,000 returnees in 2006 alone. Looking at longer spans of time, more than 8.5 million emigrants returned to Italy during the period from 1905 to 1976. During the era of British rule in India, vast numbers of Indians left their native land— often as indentured laborers, to work in other parts of the worldwide British

Empire— and then returned home after their years of indenture were over. During the century between the mid 1830s and the late 1930s, an estimated 30 million people left India and nearly 24 million returned.

Here, as elsewhere, it is not possible to speak of immigrants in general, for the extent of return migration varied greatly from one immigrant group to another. Refugees fleeing either natural disasters, such as the 1840s famine in Ireland, or the persecutions and violence of the people around them, such as the Jews of Eastern Europe in the last decades of the nineteenth century, returned to the land from which they had emigrated far less often than people who migrated for economic reasons and later returned after achieving a level of prosperity abroad that they could not have achieved at home. Whatever their reasons, the rate of return migration has varied greatly among emigrants from different countries, ranging during the era of mass emigration from Europe from about 5 percent among emigrants from Russia, Ireland, and Scandinavia to nearly half among Italians.

Just as immigrants bring a particular culture with them when they enter a new country, so returnees have often brought back with them part of the culture of the country in which they had sojourned, especially when they have had a lengthy stay abroad. Many Italians who had stayed some time in the United States returned to Italy not only with more money earned in the United States, but also with American ideas of equality that made them no longer willing to be deferential or subservient to local elites, and with an American emphasis on education that now led them to want their children educated. In various places, these returnees had become so different from those they had left behind in Italy, that they tended to settle together in enclaves of returnees.

Diseases

Just as cultures migrate with people, so do diseases. Indeed, diseases had much to do with the relative ease with which European invaders conquered vastly larger populations of indigenous peoples in the Western Hemisphere. Diseases which had spread across the Eurasian landmass in previous centuries proved to be far more devastating to the native populations of the

Western Hemisphere than the diseases peculiar to the Western Hemisphere were to the European invaders. Death rates of 50 percent of the native populations, as a result of contracting European diseases, were not uncommon, and death rates as high as 90 percent in some places were not unheard of. The fact that more soldiers have died from diseases than from enemy action in many wars was especially so for the indigenous peoples of the Western Hemisphere. European invaders not only had the advantage of gunpowder weapons and horses, they had millions of microscopic allies whom neither they nor the indigenous peoples were aware of at the time.

Diseases were also a factor in the otherwise puzzling fact that Europeans began conquering the Western Hemisphere centuries before they conquered sub-Saharan Africa, even though they knew of Africa's existence more than a thousand years before they discovered the Western Hemisphere. In Africa, the indigenous diseases were far more devastating to Europeans than the European diseases were to the Africans. At one time, the average life expectancy of a white man in sub-Saharan Africa was less than one year. Only after European medical knowledge had advanced to the point of being able to cope with the many tropical diseases of Africa were widespread European conquests on that continent possible.

It is not only with migrations based on conquests that diseases have been a factor. Refugees have fled from epidemics as they have fled from famines and other natural disasters. In the case of diseases, however, those who migrated to escape have often transmitted those diseases to the people living in the places to which they fled. Even migrations for economic or other reasons have often brought people with unfamiliar diseases into the society in which they have settled. As noted in Chapter 4, cholera was unknown in American cities before the Irish settled there in the nineteenth century. Here it was not only the disease itself that was brought by Irish immigrants but a whole way of life that allowed the disease to persist and spread amid strewn garbage that supported large rat populations, which in turn spread the cholera.

A similar problem continues today in many countries. In Britain, for example, over a four-year period, "95 per cent of all new cases of Hepatitis B have arrived from abroad" and "Africans in 2001 accounted for 34.7 per cent of all HIV infections— although they make up less than 1 per cent of the population." The treatment of Hepatitis B in Britain has been estimated to cost the taxpayers about £10,000 per infected immigrant per year. Medical treatment for one family of Sudanese immigrants with HIV cost £80,000 a year. But the financial costs are not the only cost. Britain's free, government-run medical care system attracts people with diseases from other countries, and these include communicable diseases that spread to the British population, which may have little biological resistance to diseases from very different parts of the world.

In the United States as well, immigrants have brought in diseases seldom found among twenty-first century Americans. In Loudoun County, Virginia, for example, 86 percent of the tuberculosis cases in 2005 originated in foreign countries and in Fairfax County immigrants accounted for 93 percent of the tuberculosis cases in 2004. In Texas, the proportion of the Hispanic population with hepatitis A is several times the proportion of either black or white Americans with that disease. A sample of African immigrants in Minneapolis showed them to have rates of infection of hepatitis A, B and C similar to those in East Africa, despite being "neither malnourished nor chronically ill in appearance."

This problem is not unique to either Britain or the United States but has become common in Western nations receiving large numbers of immigrants from poorer countries. A study in the ***American Journal of Tropical Medicine and Hygiene*** reported:

> In Western countries, an increase in typically tropical diseases, such as malaria or filariasis, and a return of other formerly common ones, such as tuberculosis or viral hepatitis, are being observed as a consequence of growing migration from less developed countries.

ECONOMICS

Economics affects both the decision to emigrate and the decision of the receiving country to accept immigrants, just as it affected the origins and destinations of European immigrants before and after the change from sailing ships to steamships. More fundamentally, immigrants bring both benefits and costs to the countries they enter, creating the classic economic problem of trade-offs. In addition, these benefits and costs vary greatly from one group of immigrants to another. For example, in the early twenty-first century, 45 percent of the immigrants from Asia had a college degree compared to just 4 percent among immigrants from Mexico.

Differences among Immigrants

Sometimes different groups of immigrants from the same country have very different characteristics, which affect their role in the economy and the net balance of costs and benefits to the country receiving them. People who emigrated from the Scottish highlands in the nineteenth century took with them a different culture from that of people who emigrated from Scotland's lowlands, and that difference affected both them and the countries that received them, whether the United States or Australia. One of the most immediately observable differences was that the Scottish lowlanders spoke English while the highlanders still spoke the indigenous Gaelic of Scotland. But the differences went deeper than that. Like many upland areas around the world— Appalachia in the United States, the Rif mountains in North Africa, and the mountainous regions of the Balkans, for example— the Scottish highlands exemplified historian Fernand Braudel's principle that the mountains always lag behind the plains, culturally and economically.

The industry and commerce that spread from England to the Scottish lowlands were much slower to spread up into the highlands, where transportation costs alone could be prohibitive and where the population was largely illiterate and unskilled, in addition to not speaking English. When emigrants from these two regions of Scotland settled in the United States, they settled in communities that were separate from one another, and the highlanders remained distinct longer, since they could not communicate with either Scottish immigrants from the lowlands or with the larger American society around them. In Australia the lowlanders, who came from urban, industrial and commercial areas of Scotland, went to similar areas in Australia, where they were usually successful and welcomed. Those lowlanders who went into agriculture in Australia came from an agricultural background in Scotland, whose agriculture was advanced by the standards of its time. But most of the Scottish shepherds in Australia were highlanders, repeating in their new homeland their occupational patterns in Scotland.

Although there were complaints back in the Scottish highlands that emigration had taken away the cream of the local working population, in Australia the complaint was that the highlanders were the dregs of the Scottish immigrant population. Given the circumstances of the times, there is no reason why both complaints could not be true. With the passing years, the proportion of highlanders among the Scottish immigrants to Australia declined, so that eventually more than 90 percent of the Scots arriving in Australia were lowlanders.

With immigration, as with so many other things, a crucial distinction must be made between causation and blame. No one can choose whether to be born in the uplands or the plains, either in Scotland or anywhere else. No one can choose what language or culture to be born into, though both can have profound effects on people's prospects in life, whether at home or abroad. The inescapable facts of geography can likewise limit or promote opportunities. There was no way that an industrial revolution could have originated in either the Scottish highlands or in the mountains of the Balkans, since the raw materials needed were not present and high transportation costs made it prohibitively expensive to carry those raw materials there.

What this means more broadly is that there is little point in trying to analyze, or set legal policies for, "immigrants" in general— because there are no immigrants in general. Even groups that outside observers may lump together, whether Scots in the past or Hispanics today, can differ greatly from one segment to another. The economic history of Cubans in the United States has been very different from that of Puerto Ricans, just as the economic history of highland Scots and lowland Scots differed in the past. Moreover, the whole immigration process itself can change very substantially over time, so that the circumstances of twenty-first century immigration cannot be dealt with as if the issues that immigration raises today can be settled by referring to what happened with the immigration of a hundred or more years earlier.

Most immigrants to the United States prior to the middle of the twentieth century crossed an ocean from Europe and most had neither the means nor the desire to go back, so that the die was cast for them to become Americans. In the twenty-first century, however, the overwhelming majority of immigrants come from either Asia or Latin America and the latter, especially those from Mexico, can go back and forth innumerable times, never having to make a commitment to a new language or culture. The American society that receives immigrants today is itself very different from that of a hundred years earlier, not only in its technology, but also in its welfare state policies and in its social attitudes. The welfare state is even larger and more generous in Europe. According to ***The Economist:***

> Advertise for a cleaner in London at twice the minimum hourly wage, and you will get no response from local school drop-outs or Liverpool's unemployed. More probably, the applicants will be from Ukraine, Colombia or Poland.

At one time, it was common for nations to make distinctions among the immigrants it would admit and those it would not, even subsidizing the immigration of people they deemed especially useful to their society and economy. Thus Brazil, though first settled by Portuguese immigrants, deliberately sought immigrants from outside the Iberian peninsula, notably Germans who pioneered in developing part of that country's vast wilderness in the nineteenth century, as immigrants from Japan to Brazil were also to do. Canada, Argentina, and Australia have also been among the many nations which have subsidized the immigration of selected immigrants. In medieval Eastern Europe, whole enclaves of immigrants were recruited from Western Europe, mostly Germans, in order to bring to the less developed eastern regions of the continent some of the agricultural and other advances from the west.

After the Second World War, the policy of differentiating among immigrants from different countries tended to fall into disfavor, perhaps in reaction to the tragic consequences of the Nazi's emphasis on race. The "white Australia" policy was repealed, for example, and in the United States the new 1965 immigration laws moved away from the restrictive national quota laws of the 1920s. Various nations in Western Europe likewise began opening up immigration from regions of the world with large non-European populations, including many people from the former colonies of Britain and France. These new immigration policies brought both new benefits and new costs to the countries receiving this less restricted stream of immigrants.

Income Differences

Studies of both the mass migrations of European emigrants in the nineteenth century and of mass migrations of emigrants from Asia and Latin America in the twentieth and twenty-first centuries found that income differences between the country of origin and the country of destination were key factors in determining the direction and magnitude of migration. For example, during the era of mass migration from Europe, emigrants from the British Isles tended to settle in countries where real wages were, on average, 69 percent higher than in the United Kingdom. Over time, however, the transfers of millions of workers from Europe to the Western Hemisphere affected wage rates in both places, as the supply of labor fell in Europe and rose in the Western Hemisphere, leading to rising wage rates in Europe, while inhibiting the growth of wage rates on the other side of the Atlantic. A study of this era found "substantial per capital real income and real wage convergence in the late nineteenth century."

The convergence of wages, brought on by mass emigration, became in turn a reason for reduced emigration as the pay differential declined. Emigration from Ireland, across the Irish Sea to England, across the Atlantic to Canada and the United States, and as far away as Australia, led to pay differentials between all these places and Ireland declining substantially in the nineteenth century, as pay in Ireland rose dramatically in the wake of large-scale emigration. As economic principles would suggest, the loss of labor relative to land and capital, led not only to an absolute increase of labor's rate of pay but also to a rising share of Ireland's national income going to labor and less going to the rent of land and to the return on capital. The net result was that Irish emigration declined.

A somewhat more complicated pattern in Italy highlights other economic factors involved in decisions to emigrate. Although there was also a declining pay differential between Italy and the various destinations of Italian emigrants abroad during the nineteenth century, emigration continued to rise. While the pay differential provides an incentive to emigrate, the cost of emigration is a deterrent, especially for the poorest of those who would like to emigrate. As pay rose in Italy in the wake of an exodus of workers, that put emigration within the financial reach of more poor people, who now added to the tide of emigration. The fact that the share of Italian emigration represented by people from the poorer south of Italy increased over the years reinforces this point.

These patterns of rising wages in countries experiencing massive emigration— which was typically an emigration of young adults with high labor force participation rates, whose departures had an especially strong effect on the labor supply— were not confined to Ireland or Italy. Wages rose dramatically in Sweden, as labor flowed out and capital flowed in. For Western European nations as a whole, a statistical analysis showed "the real wage gap between Old World and New fell 36 percentage points over the 25 years up to 1895, and by 49 percentage points over the 43 years up to 1913." However, in the poorest Third World countries today, a rise in income may have an effect similar to that in nineteenth-century Italy— that is, it may enable more of the poorest people to be able to afford to emigrate.

Economic Benefits to Recipient Countries

On the whole, there have been both benefits and costs to the immigrants and to the countries that received them. These have varied greatly, depending on which immigrants, which countries, and which periods of history.

Whole new industries have been created by some immigrants. There was, for example, no watch-making industry in England before the Huguenots fled religious persecution in seventeenth-century France and brought with them to London their skills as watch-makers. This turned England into one of the world's leading watch-making centers, much like Switzerland, to which many other Huguenots fled. Virtually the entire modern industrial, commercial, and financial sectors of colonial Malaya's economy were created by foreigners— immigrants from China and India supplying most of the labor on the rubber plantations and tin mines, as well as setting up small-scale retailing and money lending businesses, while enterprises requiring large-scale investment, such as shipping, were financed and run by Europeans. German immigrants built the first pianos in Russia, as well as in England, France, and colonial America.

Lebanese immigrants created retail networks in the West African hinterlands of Sierra Leone and the Ivory Coast, as immigrants from India and Pakistan dominated retail trade in both the hinterlands of East African nations such as Kenya and Uganda and in urban centers such as Nairobi. Jews have for centuries dominated the apparel industry in countries as different as Argentina, the Ottoman Empire and the United States, as Germans have dominated beer production from the United States— where all the leading brands were created by people of German ancestry— to China, where that country's famed Tsingtao beer was also created by Germans. Similar examples of immigrant contributions could be cited for many other immigrant groups and many other countries in which they settled.

At one time, it was common to openly recognize the particular skills, talents, or work habits of particular groups, and even to selectively subsidize the immigration of such groups, for the benefit of the receiving country. Japan deliberately imported Scottish engineers in the nineteenth century to aid their industrialization, so much so that there was a Scottish church in Japan at one time. Other specialists from Europe and the United States were also brought in to help establish various industries in Japan, as sojourners there during Japan's rise from an agricultural to an industrial and commercial society.

The Japanese, however, have never encouraged or permitted large numbers of immigrants to stay in their country on a long-term basis. Japan has thus remained one of the most racially homogeneous of modern industrial nations. One of the few comparable examples would be Australia during the era of the "white Australia" immigration policy that ended in the latter part of the twentieth century. However, even during the era of the "white Australia" policy, that country permitted immigration from many countries across the European continent. But Japan's more narrowly exclusive and still continuing policy has never provoked the kind of international condemnation that Australia's immigration policy once provoked.

Isolated episodes in history do not provide as general or as reliable an account as hard statistical data on immigrants. In the United States, for example, the approximately 10 million immigrants who entered the country between 1820 and 1880 were largely from Western Europe or Northern Europe, while most of the 26 million immigrants who entered between 1880 and the legal restrictions on immigration in 1924 were from Eastern Europe or Southern Europe. Another major change in American immigration law in 1965 was followed by an even more dramatic change in the geographic origins of immigrants, as most thereafter came from either Latin America (51 percent by the year 2000) or Asia (26 percent). Immigration from Europe fell to about 15 percent of all immigration to the United States, that whole continent now sending fewer immigrants than Mexico alone (28 percent). The change, however, was more than geographic.

In the years preceding the changed immigration laws of the 1960s, the average immigrant earned higher pay in the United States than the average native-born American. But, thereafter, successive cohorts of immigrants fell successively below the income of the average American. One factor was that the education gap between post-1960s immigrants and the average American widened. By and large, both had growing amounts of education but native-born Americans much more so than immigrants. Not only geographical origins but social origins had changed and that was reflected in widening pay differences. By 1990, the average pay of immigrants from Mexico was 40 percent below that of the average American.

In short, the changing American immigration laws led to a changing mix of immigrants, letting in more people with lower levels of skills and education at precisely the time when the American economy's growing demand was for more people with more skills and more education, and when the differential pay of people with more education and less education was widening, for both domestic and immigrant workers. That this was a result of immigration laws is underscored by the very different experience of Canada during the same era. Canadian immigration laws gave preference to those who had more education, had fluency in English or French, and who were in occupations deemed more important to Canada. The net result was that immigrants to Canada had higher skills and higher wages than immigrants to the United States. The mix of these immigrants' countries of origin were also different, as a consequence of different economic and cultural criteria, rather than national quotas as such.

During the second half of the twentieth century, Western European nations pioneered in creating "guest worker" programs for immigrants who would come in and take jobs that were not attracting sufficient applicants from the native-born population— at the existing pay scales. Employer benefits were often represented politically as net benefits to the nation, implicitly assuming that the unskilled vacancies would go unfilled otherwise, rather than simply leading to higher pay scales, as in other cases of temporary imbalances between supply and demand. The combination of employer self-interest and the philosophic commitments of multiculturalists proved to be powerful, and those opposed to more open immigration policies were marginalized, often as "xenophobic" or "racist." While a poll conducted by the Chicago Council on Foreign Relations showed that 60 percent of the American general public ranked the large numbers of immigrants and refugees coming to the United States as a "critical threat," only 14 percent of elite opinion-makers saw it that way.

Typical of the new attitude toward assimilating immigrants was a comment by the head of the U.S. Bureau of the Census during the Clinton administration: "Without fully realizing it, we have left the time when the nonwhite, non-Western part of our population could be expected to assimilate to the dominant majority. In the future, the white Western majority will have to do some assimilation of its own." Such views— and the condescending and peremptory tone in which they were expressed—

have become fairly typical of elite opinion across the political spectrum, from liberal or radical publications like *The Nation* magazine to conservative publications like the *Wall Street Journal.*

Similar views prevail among elites in Britain, Australia and other Western nations, and the public backlash in a number of countries in Europe, as well as in America and Australia, is often discussed dismissively by the elites. In Britain, a 2007 article in *The Economist* magazine discussed immigration without a single mention of riots or terrorism committed by immigrants and treating resistance to more immigration as sheer inexplicable narrow-mindedness:

> Cast your eye around Europe, and you find a funk about foreigners. Denmark's voters have given the anti-immigration Danish People's Party its fourth successive rise in voting share. The Swiss gave 29% of their votes to the xenophobic Swiss People's Party. An anti-foreigner party is the second-biggest in Norway. A fifth of Flemish voters in Belgium back the far-right Vlaams Belang.

Over the years, public opinion has proven to be more subject to change in the light of changing facts than has elite opinion. In Australia, for example, in 1961 only 16 percent of the public thought the country was accepting "too many" immigrants. But, thirty years later, after Australia had accepted so many immigrants that one-fourth of the entire population of the country was born in some other country, 73 percent of the public said that "too many" immigrants had been admitted. Moreover, in Australia as in other Western nations, these new immigrants often do not seek to become part of the larger Australian society. As an Australian scholar, himself an immigrant, put it:

> To a much greater extent than previously, migrants now come from a growing diversity of cultures and failing economies. Some display hostility to Western values and mores and adhere to modes of behaviour that are counterproductive in a Western context.

In Australia, as elsewhere, the same scholar noted that debates about immigration policy are often marked by "a tendency to cast open immigration and official multiculturalism as a position that distinguishes the 'right-minded' from the ignorant, ignoble rest."

In a number of prosperous Western nations, demographic trends reinforced the arguments for "guest workers" from poorer countries. As the median age of the population rose in Europe, exceeding 40 years in Germany and Italy, while many Third World countries had median ages of around 20, or sometimes even lower, as in Yemen or Afghanistan, the argument was made that someone had to provide the services usually provided by young people. Another economic argument was that someone had to pay into the government pension systems, which were financed by taxes on the working population to pay older people who were retired. Thus the welfare state, multiculturalism, employer interests, and underfunded pension systems combined to make more open immigration policies seem not only desirable but imperative.

The real question is not have particular interests or institutions benefitted from immigration but have the countries as a whole benefitted economically from immigration. ***The Economist*** advanced a familiar argument: "Clearly immigration makes the economy bigger by adding to the workforce," leading to more total output. However, that does not say that this increased output adds to the real per capita income of the existing citizens. Recognizing that this is "what matters," ***The Economist*** estimated that an increase in the Gross Domestic Product per capita as a result of immigration "will probably be around an eighth of a percentage point" for Britain. The question is whether the costs imposed by immigration are enough to offset that, whether for Britain or in other countries.

Costs to Recipient Countries

Various attempts have been made to calculate the net costs or net benefits of immigrants to the United States by counting the taxes they pay, the contributions they make to Social Security, and other benefits they provide, versus the costs they entail through increased welfare spending, the costs of schooling their children, and the disproportionate numbers of immigrants among prison populations. Different studies have arrived at very different conclusions, some concluding that immigrants have a net positive effect economically of some billions of dollars, while other studies conclude the opposite, that immigrants impose billions of dollars of additional burden on American taxpayers. Much depends on the implicit assumptions behind the analysis of the relevant statistics. Similarly conflicting conclusions have come from attempts to determine whether immigrants tend to cause American workers in general, or low-income workers in particular, to have lower pay levels than they would have had otherwise.

Considering the strong evidence on the effect of massive nineteenth century European emigration in narrowing the gap between wages in Europe and wages in the countries to which Europeans were immigrating, it might be expected that there would be similarly clear evidence on the effect of contemporary immigration to the United States on either the incomes or unemployment rates of American workers in general, or low-income workers in particular. But here, again, studies have reached conflicting results. Part of the problem in this case is that many of the studies have been local area studies in places with large concentrations of immigrants. While workers in those particular areas may not be much affected, if ample supplies of immigrant workers have kept wages low in a particular area, that provides an incentive for American workers in similar occupations to avoid moving to such areas or to leave such areas if they lived there before. Thus a lack of a substantial pay differential between immigrants and those native-born workers remaining within the locality does not necessarily mean that immigrants have had no effect on American workers as a whole.

Part of the problem of determining the net economic effect of immigrants in general is that there are no immigrants in general and that the economic and cultural characteristics of immigrants from different countries and different regions of the world differ greatly in such things as education and job skills. Moreover these differences have varied greatly over time. Before the 1960s, immigrant men had higher pay levels in the United States than the pay levels of native-born American men. But, since the changed immigration laws of that decade led to changed origins of immigrants, the pay levels of native-born American men have exceeded the pay levels of immigrant men by larger and larger amounts.

Among the costs imposed by immigrants that do not get counted in the marketplace are the unpaid services of hospital emergency rooms, schools, and law enforcement. However, it would be difficult, if not impossible, to get comprehensive and accurate data on all these things. In the absence of such data, conflicting estimates tend to be inconclusive. Moreover, many of the costs created by immigrants are not money costs, but are no less important.

Whatever the arguments for or against the importation of more workers, the importation of people has remained, as it had always been, an importation of their cultures as well. Many of the immigrants who flowed into Europe after the lowering of immigration barriers came from Muslim countries with lower standards of living— Turks to Germany and Algerians to France, for example— and brought with them a culture with values that raised barriers to assimilation into the new society, even as the barriers to immigration were lowered. The net result has been a growth of separate ethnic enclaves in Western European countries, not only different from but in many cases hostile to the values of the society around them. Such differences and hostilities have been accentuated during a period of international clashes between many Western and Muslim countries and between movements in the Muslim world and Western society.

Despite the term "guest workers," these were not guests whose length of stay was determined by their hosts. Whole families migrated and remained to produce offspring. Whatever the legal authority of the host country to terminate their stay, the same political forces which combined to create more open immigration laws remained a political barrier to obstruct any attempt to return the immigrants to their homelands. In short, "guest worker" programs proved to be irreversible and the immigrants and their children became a growing proportion of the population of the host countries, since the immigrants were usually younger than the native-born population and had more children. The second and later generations of these immigrant families were as prone to disaffection as the second generations of some other immigrants have been in other lands around the world.

Although the first generation of immigrants were brought in to become workers, unemployment has tended to be high among the second and later generations. In parts of France, for example, unemployment rates among Muslim young men have been estimated at about 40 percent. One measure of their alienation from the society around them is that they commit not only economic crimes but also gang rapes, for which they seem "not merely unrepentant or unashamed but proud." A shrewd observer of peoples and places around the world described the young Muslim population in and around Paris:

> Where does the increase in crime come from? The geographical answer: from the public housing projects that encircle and increasingly besiege every French city or town of any size, Paris especially. In these housing projects lives an immigrant population numbering several million, from North and West Africa mostly, along with their French-born descendants and a smattering of the least successful members of the French working class. From these projects, the excellence of the French public transport system ensures that the most fashionable *arrondissements* are within easy reach of the most inveterate thief and vandal. . . A kind of anti-society has grown up in them— a population that derives the meaning of its life from the hatred it bears for the other, "official," society in France.

Unappeased by "the people who carelessly toss them the crumbs of Western prosperity," the young men from these alienated immigrant enclaves, with a "them-and-us worldview," needed "to see themselves as warriors in a civil war, not mere ne'er-do-wells and criminals." All this was said *before* the Muslim riots of 2005 which swept through Paris and other French cities, and which shocked many who had no inkling of what bitter enemies now lived within their borders. According to ***The Economist***:

> A month after the riots died down, France is still taking stock. In three weeks of violence across the country, some 10,000 vehicles were burned, 255 schools, 233 public buildings and 51 post offices were attacked, 140 public-transport vehicles were stoned, and 4,770 people were arrested, according to figures obtained by ***Le Monde***.

The ***Washington Post*** reported: "Most of the recent violence in France— the worst civil unrest in the country in nearly 40 years— has occurred in poor suburbs and neighborhoods populated by large numbers of immigrants and their French-born children."

France has not been unique in being shocked to discover the consequences of lowering the barriers to immigration in stage one without considering what could happen in later stages. Britain has been rocked by explosions in London's subway system, set off by British-born Muslims of a second or later generation. Moreover, organized public displays of animosity and contempt toward British society by Muslims in Britain have included death threats on which authorities have refused to take any action, even when these threats have been pointed out to them. In other parts of Europe, threats have been made against people who have exercised what is traditional free speech in their own country by criticizing some aspect of Islamic culture, as they criticize their own culture. A painting that had hung in the British Museum for generations was taken down after complaints that it was offensive to Muslims.

In Germany, two-thirds of the 2.6 million Turks in the country do not have German citizenship and the visiting Turkish prime minister urged them not to assimilate. According to ***The Economist***:

> Just 14.8% of German children but 45.4% of Turks end up in ***Hauptschulen***, which ought to prepare them for simple trades but often fail to do even that. In Neukölln they are a dumping ground. Graduates cannot work out how many square metres of carpet would cover a floor, says the district's education chief, Wolfgang Schimmang.

How did such circumstances come about?

With the rise of attitudes and beliefs hostile to recognition of different endowments of desired characteristics among different groups, culminating in non-judgmental "multiculturalism" in many countries in the latter part of the twentieth century, both the process of selectively choosing the countries from which immigrants would be accepted and the process of assimilating them after their arrival were severely limited. Often the emphasis has shifted from the interests of the receiving country to the plight of those who want to enter from poorer and often less free countries. Along with this philosophical shift, there has been a growing desire of employers to get workers for low-skilled jobs whose pay scales were not always sufficient to attract an adequate supply from the native-born population in prosperous countries with generous welfare-state benefits that made not working at all a viable option.

Cultural assimilation has been held back by the "multicultural" idea of accommodating and perpetuating group differences instead of seeking social cohesion by drawing various segments of the population into the common culture of the country. In Britain, for example, there are more than a hundred ethnic support groups, ranging from an Afro-Caribbean lunch club to a forum for Chinese diabetics, just in Liverpool, and swimming pools in most big towns have "women-only nights, aimed mainly at tempting modest Muslims into the water," according to ***The Economist***. Individually and in the short run, many of these things may be benign but, thinking beyond stage one, this can mean freezing social divisions at the expense of the social cohesion required to sustain a society.

Increasingly, both U.S. government documents and documents from private businesses and other organizations in the United States have been printed in foreign languages. Courts have been asked to either overlook or deal leniently with violations of American law by people whose acts are considered legitimate in their native cultures. In the past, various ethnic organizations in the United States— among the Irish, the Jews, the Lebanese, and among American blacks— put forth sustained efforts over a period of decades to change the behavior of people in these groups to conform to the norms of the larger society around them, in order to advance the group as a whole. In the new, multicultural world, however, ethnic organizations turned their attention to getting the larger society to accept these groups as is, and even stigmatizing those in their groups who tend to assimilate.

All too often, today's ethnic organizations, whether among Muslims in Europe or Mexicans in the United States, seek to keep their constituencies foreign in culture and alienated in attitude from the larger society around them. This is not to say that all, or even most, of the people in the immigrant communities in Europe or the United States share the adversary attitude of many organized immigrant movements or the European or American "multiculturalists" who wish to preserve foreign cultures. For example, when a proposition against teaching foreign school children in their native languages— usually Spanish— was put on the ballot in California in 1998, more than 40 percent of Hispanic voters supported the ending of so-called "bilingual" education.

What proportion of various other immigrant groups in Europe or America want to assimilate, and to what degree, remains largely unknown. What is known is that the organized and vocal portion of these immigrant groups tend to be not only against assimilation but even against the values of the societies in which they now live.

SUMMARY AND IMPLICATIONS

Economics cannot provide "answers" to the immigration "question." What economics can do is provide questions to address to politicians who claim to have answers. Moreover, economic analysis goes beyond stage one, as political proposals seldom do. The political phrase "guest workers," for example, suggests that immigrants brought in to do various work are like guests who come and go as their hosts decide, and that the impact of these immigrants on the existing citizens can be evaluated on the basis of their work alone. That is not true even in narrowly economic terms, given the vast sums of money expended to provide medical care and welfare benefits to immigrants, as well as schooling for their children, not to mention the costs of imprisoning a disproportionate number of immigrants from Mexico living in the United States, both legally and illegally, or the costs created by crime and terrorism by immigrants in Europe, not to mention the diseases being introduced into Western nations by immigrants from poorer countries.

Whether in Europe, the United States, or elsewhere, both the costs and the benefits of immigration can vary enormously with the origins of the immigrants. This is one of many reasons why there is no solution to the problem of immigration in general— because there are no immigrants in general. There are specific immigrants from specific places with specific patterns and specific track records.

History can be either a help or a hindrance to understanding today's immigration issues. A study of the past can show general patterns, many of which can be recognized in today's events as well, such as a growth of disaffection and alienation among the offspring of some immigrants from poor countries, even when the first generation was glad to have improved their lot in life by moving to a more prosperous and freer nation. History can also show what valuable contributions some immigrants have made in some countries during some eras. But what history cannot do is show that to be inevitable for all immigrants in all eras, or even for most immigrants in most eras.

The fact that past critics of particular immigrant groups that were deemed to be inassimilable at some time in the past turned out to be wrong under the conditions of those times does not mean that critics who point out how little assimilation takes place among particular groups today must also be wrong under today's very different conditions. Among these different conditions today are ethnic organizations promoting the perpetuation of foreign cultures and of past or present resentments, in contrast to ethnic organizations of the past that promoted assimilation. Moreover, immigrants to the United States in the past were cut off from reinforcements of their foreign cultures by newcomers from their homelands when the drastic restrictions on immigration in the 1920s stopped so many newcomers from arriving in America. Those who today invoke historical parallels are seeking to keep the flow of cultural reinforcements coming. Things happened in a particular way in the past for particular reasons. Where those factors no longer exist, there is no reason to expect the outcomes to be the same out of sheer historical parallelism.

Among the things that politicians say that economics can challenge is the oft-repeated claim that immigrants take jobs that the citizens of the country will not take. That can be challenged both empirically and analytically. In the United States, for example, there are no major sectors of the economy in which even half the workers are immigrants. A study of 473 job classifications found only 4 in which immigrants were a majority—

stucco masons, tailors, produce sorters and beauty salon workers— and even in those occupations native-born Americans were more than 40 percent of the workers. Agriculture is a sector in which many claim that immigrant labor is essential but half of all agricultural workers in the United States were born in the United States.

The fear that there would be "ten-dollar lettuce" if illegal immigrants were not available to pick it is completely inconsistent with the economics of agricultural prices. A fraction of the price of agricultural produce goes to the farmer and an even smaller fraction to the farm workers. For example, the average American household spent $370 for fruits and vegetables in 2004, of which $65 went to farmers, who in turn paid $22 to farm laborers. Even if farm laborers' pay doubled, that would raise the price of a year's supply of all fruits and vegetables put together by just $22, or less than 10 percent. Ten-dollar lettuce makes a catchy political slogan but it has nothing to do with economic reality.

Like history, economics cannot be invoked thoughtlessly, without regard to the specifics of the time and place. In the abstract, the free movement of people, like the free movement of goods and services, promotes economic benefits when there are willing participants, ready to transact on mutually agreeable terms, unimpeded by a national boundary. But the movement of people from country to country has different consequences from the movement of goods and services. When Americans buy a Toyota from Japan, the Toyota does not demand that the United States accommodate the Japanese language or that Americans adjust themselves to Japanese customs in their own country, much less introduce diseases into the American population. Moreover, Toyotas do not give birth to little Toyotas that can grow up with the problematic attitudes of some second generation immigrants.

In the abstract, all things are the same except for the differences and different except for the similarities. But such truisms do not make policies for people the same as policies for goods and services. Not only do people differ from goods and services, people differ from other people, and any policy— on immigration or anything else— which insists on ignoring such differences among people risks discovering that ideas which sounded good in stage one can turn out to be disastrous in later stages, when those ignored differences produce "unintended consequences." In the case of immigrants, those consequences can be irreversible.

Chapter 7

The Economics of Discrimination

It is painfully obvious that discrimination inflicts economic and other costs on those being discriminated against. What is not so obvious, but is an important causal factor nonetheless, is that discrimination also has a cost to those who do the discriminating. Moreover, the cost of discriminating varies with the circumstances. For an American owner of a professional basketball team to refuse to hire blacks would be to commit financial suicide. But, for the conductor of a symphony orchestra to pass over the relatively few black violinists available would cost practically nothing, in the absence of anti-discrimination laws, since there are far more white violinists available to take their places.

Variations in the costs of discrimination help explain many otherwise puzzling anomalies, such as the fact that blacks were starring on Broadway in the 1920s, at a time when a black man could not enlist in the U. S. Navy nor a black woman be hired as a telephone operator by most phone companies, even in the Northern states. Variations in the cost of discrimination also help explain why black ghettoes in the United States tended to expand with the growth of the black population in the twentieth century, while in centuries past Jewish ghettoes in Europe tended simply to become more overcrowded with the growth of the Jewish population. In countries around the world, employment discrimination has tended to be greatest in the hiring of government employees and employees in government-regulated utilities.

Before getting into the economics behind such things, it is first necessary to be clear as to just what is and is not defined as discrimination, so that we can avoid the common problem of people talking past each other, as happens too often in discussions of discrimination.

PREJUDICE, BIAS, AND DISCRIMINATION

Prejudice, bias, and discrimination are too often confused with one another. Each requires careful definition before discussing substantive issues, if those discussions are not to get hopelessly bogged down in semantics.

Prejudice

Prejudice means prejudgment. Yet the term has been widely used more loosely to refer to adverse opinions in general about particular racial or ethnic groups. Unless we are prepared to accept as dogma that there cannot possibly be anything about the skills, behavior, or performance of any group, anywhere in the world, which reduces their productivity as workers or their desirability as neighbors, we cannot automatically equate adverse opinions or actions with prejudgments. Too much empirical evidence exists to allow any such dogma to survive scrutiny. For example, per capita consumption of alcohol and rates of alcoholism have varied by some multiple among various groups in the United States and in the Soviet Union, among other places—and the adverse effects of alcohol and alcoholism have been too well documented to require elaboration. Rates of crime, disease and other adverse conditions have likewise varied widely among various groups in countries around the world.

Were the organized crime activities of the Chinese tongs in various countries in Southeast Asia mere "perceptions"? Was the Maharashtrian majority in Bombay simply prejudiced against other Maharashtrians when they preferred to buy from businesses run by people from South India, rather than businesses run by their own compatriots? Is it just racial prejudice which causes ***black*** taxi drivers in New York to avoid picking up black male passengers at night?

Adverse judgments and actions cannot be automatically attributed to prejudgment. Often those with the most direct knowledge have the most adverse judgments, while those observing from afar— or not observing at all— attribute these adverse judgements and actions to prejudice. By the same token, particular minority groups may be sought out for particular attributes judged favorably, without this being a matter of prejudgment. During the great era of skyscraper-building in the United States, for example, Mohawk Indians were often sought out to work high up on the steel frameworks while the skyscrapers were being built, because of their demonstrated ability to perform their work undistracted by the dangers.

In centuries past, Germans' reputation in mining caused them to be sought out for this work in England, Spain, Norway, Mexico, and the Balkans. Back in the eighteenth century, when Catherine the Great decided that Russia needed to bring in "some merchant people" from other countries, she informed one of her high officials that merchants in other parts of Europe should be issued passports to Russia "not mentioning their nationality and without enquiring into their confession." This was a way of circumventing the ban on the immigration of Jews into Russia, rather than taking the politically unpopular step of lifting the ban.

In short, whether judgments or actions toward particular groups are favorable or unfavorable, these actions cannot be automatically equated with prejudgments. Indeed, it is a sweeping prejudgment to do so, especially when those who attribute prejudice to others often have less direct knowledge of the groups in question, at the times in question, than those who made the favorable or unfavorable judgments.

Even when favorable or unfavorable judgments about groups are based on knowledge, judgments of particular individuals from within these groups may be made on the basis of prejudice. As W.E.B. Du Bois pointed out about the hiring of blacks in the nineteenth century, "the individual black workman is rated not by his own efficiency, but by the efficiency of a whole group of black fellow workmen which may often be low." Therefore, even if white people were to lose their racial prejudices overnight, he said, this would make very little immediate difference in the economic condition of most blacks. According to Du Bois, writing in 1898, "some few would be promoted, some few would get new places" but "the mass would remain as they are," until the younger generation began to improve in response to greater job opportunities due to reduced racial barriers.

In short, Du Bois saw white employers' adverse judgments of black workers at that time as being generally accurate, though not accurate as regards all individual black workers currently or the potential of black workers in the future. Whatever the empirical validity of his assessments, what is relevant here is that he made the crucial analytical distinction between adverse judgments based on experience and unsubstantiated prejudgments. Moreover, while the lumping together of disparate members of a group can explain why particular individuals from that group earn less than comparable individuals from other groups, such individual disparities cannot explain ***group*** disparities. For that, the generalization about the group's performance as a whole must be erroneous. Seldom is any serious effort made to demonstrate such group-wide errors. More often, the simple fact that an adverse generalization has been made about a group is taken as itself evidence of prejudice and the under-rating of particular individuals from that group is taken as proof.

Racial and ethnic groups are not the only groups subject to prejudice. A women who applies to work in certain fields might encounter employer reluctance to hire her, if the field or the particular job is one requiring long hours and long continuity in the job, especially if the long hours must be worked at unpredictable times, whenever the job demands it. Women in general have tended not to work as long hours as men, nor to work continuously for as many years. The particular woman applying for a particular job might be just as willing to work under these conditions as a man but, like the black worker whose productivity is higher than that of most other black workers, this job applicant may be passed over because of the employer's inability to know the strength of her resolve to remain continuously employed or her willingness to work whatever hours the job requires or her determination to avoid getting pregnant and find herself unable to carry out her resolves.

Here again, as with racial and ethnic groups, gross differences between the pay and employment of women and that of men cannot be fully explained by this prejudice, however much it may explain the lesser employment opportunities of particular women who differ significantly from women as a group. Nor is the employer's use of general patterns among women as a guide when assessing a particular individual simply irrational, given the low probability of the employer's knowing that particular individual well enough to be confident of her own values and resolve. Moreover, the effect of this particular prejudice lessens with age and especially after a woman has passed the usual child-bearing years. Thus women aged 40 to 64 who have never married, have never had children, are college-educated, and who work full-time earn ***higher*** average incomes than men of the same description. The implication of this is that, when women reach these ages, employers no longer fear the effect of pregnancy and child-rearing on a woman's work, so they need no longer rely on general patterns in assessing individuals. Another implication is that, in this case, prejudice does not reflect bias or else women's incomes would continue to be lower than that of men even after passing the child-bearing years.

Among racial and ethnic minorities as well, the use of general group patterns as a means of sorting particular individuals can likewise give way when that pattern no longer applies. Thus employers' reluctance to hire young black men because such a significant proportion of them have prison records gives way among those particular employers who automatically screen all job applicants for prison records. Such employers have been found to employ young black males to a greater extent than other employers do. Such employers no longer have to rely on prejudice, since they have a more accurate (and more costly) sorting device already in use for their job applicants in general. Similar to the situation with women workers, prejudice does not imply bias against the group as a whole; otherwise, knowledge of the presence or absence of individual prison records would not make such a difference. In the case of blacks, there is further evidence of this in the fact that employers who are reluctant to hire young black males are not equally reluctant to hire young black females or older blacks.

In short, prejudice is not simply irrational, nor necessarily a result of antipathy toward particular groups, but reflects the difficulty or higher cost of obtaining more accurate knowledge of particular individuals. What is a prejudgment as regards the individual is an empirical generalization as regards the group. The fact that the prejudgment may be incorrect as regards the individual does not mean that the empirical generalization is necessarily incorrect as regards the group or that incorrect assessments explain income or other differences among groups. Prejudice may be the main reason why particular individuals have lesser career opportunities than similar individuals from different groups, but these prejudices may still be insufficient to explain differences between groups as a whole.

Bias

Biases differ from prejudices and there are at least two kinds of bias which also differ from each other.

The first kind of bias is what might be called cognitive bias. The person making judgments or taking actions may not begin with any specific adverse beliefs about a particular group, nor any hostility toward them, but his mode of judgment may cause individuals of equal ability to be ranked differently when they come from one group rather than another. For example, someone who places great weight on how an applicant for a job or college admissions dresses may pass up many highly qualified members of groups that do not put much emphasis on dress or who have different patterns of dressing from those of the evaluator or of other groups being evaluated.

Even in the absence of any adverse prejudgments or negative feelings toward the group in question, such an evaluator may thus systematically undervalue the achievements or potential of individuals from some groups.

In addition, circumstances may also generate bias, in addition to human bias. As a scholarly study of India noted:

> Aspiring members of previously victimized groups encounter biased expectations, misperceptions of their performance, and cultural bias in selection devices; they suffer from the absence of informal networks to guide them to opportunities, entrenched systems of seniority crystallize and perpetuate the results of earlier discriminatory selections. Thus norms of non-discrimination in present distributions are insufficient to erase or dislodge the cumulative effects of past discrimination.

This kind of situation is sometimes characterized in the United States as "institutional racism," as distinguished from the intentional and overt racial bias of individuals. This kind of cognitive bias can also be present in impersonal criteria drawn up in good faith, and many claims have been made that various mental tests are "culturally biased" in this sense.

Before evaluating such claims, it is necessary to be clear as to what is and is not being alleged. Nor can we simply dismiss criteria which produce adverse results for particular groups as "irrelevant" to the job in question, or substitute plausibility for an empirical test of whatever correlation may or may not exist between particular criteria and subsequent performances. While careful empirical analysis is necessary, that analysis must be preceded by clear definitions of what we do and do not mean by the words being used.

Another and very different kind of bias is based on favoritism for one's own group, which may exist independently of any belief or presumption about inferior abilities in other groups. Indeed, this kind of bias can co-exist with a belief that some other group is not merely equal but superior. This is in fact a phenomenon found in various countries around the world and at various periods of history. For example, an advocate of affirmative action programs for Malays in Malaysia declared: "Whatever the Malays could do, the Chinese could do better and more cheaply." Nor was he the only leader to see his own group as less capable than other groups in the same society. In Nigeria, preferential hiring of people from the northern part of the country was advocated on grounds that otherwise "the less well-educated people of the North will be swamped by the thrusting people of the South." The same has been true of leaders of the Sinhalese in Sri Lanka, Turks in

Cyprus, indigenous Fijians in Fiji, Lulua in Zaire, and Assamese in India's state of Assam.

A political movement organized to ban Japanese immigration to the United States, early in the twentieth century, sought to do so precisely on the ground that these immigrants were of high ability and formidable competitors:

> We have been accustomed to regard the Japanese as an inferior race, but are now suddenly aroused to our danger. They are not window cleaners and house servants. The Japanese can think, can learn, can invent. We have suddenly awakened to the fact that they are gaining a foothold in every skilled industry in our country. They are our equal in intellect; their ability to labor is equal to ours. They are proud, valiant and courageous, but they can underlive us. . . We are here today to prevent that very competition.

The bias of those seeking favoritism for themselves is wholly independent of any claim that others are inferior and is often insisted upon most fervently when others are considered to have superior performance. There may of course also be favoritism for groups who consider themselves superior— whites in the American South during the Jim Crow era, whites in South Africa under apartheid, or Germans under the Nazis— but such a belief is not inherent in programs of favoritism, which are perfectly compatible with the opposite belief that others are too formidable as competitors to be dealt with without some offsetting official advantage. Claims of superiority are in fact inconsistent with demands for preferential treatment, since superiority of performance would make preferential standards unnecessary.

Discrimination

Both bias and prejudice are attitudes. The practical question is how and to what extent such attitudes are translated into acts of discrimination. But before addressing that question, we must first be clear as to what we mean by the word "discrimination."

Policies of treating members of particular groups less favorably than similar members of other groups are usually called "discrimination" when practiced by the group with dominant political power and "reverse discrimination" or "affirmative action" when practiced ***against*** members of the group with dominant political power. Discrimination may also be practiced by private employers, landlords, or institutions. However, if words are to have any fixed meanings— without which discussions are fruitless— the term cannot be extended to all situations in which some groups turn out to have less favorable outcomes than others.

While biases and prejudices are conditions in people's minds, discrimination is an overt act taking place outside their minds in the real world. Nor is there necessarily a one-to-one correlation between the two, as so often assumed by those who make the fight against "racism" or "sexism" their number one priority or by those who claim that opponents of affirmative action must be assuming that prejudice and bias have been eradicated.

It is not only theoretically possible to have more discrimination where there is less bias or prejudice, and less discrimination where there is more bias and prejudice, this has in fact happened in more than one country. The degree to which subjective attitudes are translated into overt acts of discrimination depends on the ***costs*** of doing so. Where those costs are very high, even very prejudiced or biased people may engage in little or no discrimination. The first black football player signed by the Washington Redskins in the 1960s was hired by a man reputed among sports writers who knew him to be deeply racist. Yet he broke a long tradition of all-white football teams in Washington by hiring a star wide receiver who was black— at a time when the Redskins' offensive game was very ineffective.

There is no inherent contradiction in a racist breaking the color line to hire blacks— or in someone who is not a racist failing to do so. The costs they face when making their decisions must be taken into account, along with their predispositions, in any causal analysis. During the last years of the Jim Crow era in the South, there were stories of Southerners like Arkansas'

Senator J. William Fulbright who voted against their consciences to continue racial segregation, because to do otherwise would be to jeopardize their political careers. Personal costs can lead to actions either more adverse or less adverse than the individual's own beliefs and feelings.

VARIATIONS IN COSTS

Where the costs of discrimination are low or non-existent for those making hiring and promotions decisions, then discrimination can become extensive, not only in terms of decisions not to hire or promote members of particular groups, but also in terms of extending such discrimination to a wider range of groups by a wider range of employers. At one time, there were said to be American railroads in which Catholics could rise only so high and others in which this was true of Protestants. Within living memory, there was a time when not a single Ivy League college or university had a Jew among its tenured faculty, despite a large number of Jewish intellectuals and scholars available. This was common in both American and European universities before World War II. Nor was a black allowed in the Marine Corps, at even the lowliest rank, when World War II began. In other parts of the world as well, there has been similarly severe discrimination, sometimes even broader in its scope.

While many discussions of discrimination ignore the *cost* of discrimination to those doing the discriminating, on the most elementary economic principle that more is demanded at a lower price than at a higher price, we should expect to see the severity of discrimination vary with the cost to the discriminator. That is in fact what we find in country after country and in era after era— but only if we look at evidence.

In Poland between the two world wars, for example, an absolute majority of all the physicians in private practice were from the Jewish minority, which was only 10 percent of the population. Yet the Polish government did not hire Jewish physicians, though many other Poles obviously became patients of Jewish physicians in the private sector, or else so many Jewish doctors could not have made a living. What was the difference between the public sector and the private sector in this regard?

In both sectors, there were both financial and medical costs to refusing to use Jewish physicians. To staff a government hospital with all-Gentile physicians, in a country where so many of the physicians were Jews, meant either having to pay more to attract a disproportionate share of the available Gentile physicians or accepting lesser-qualified physicians than some of those available from the Jewish community. In either case, financial or medical costs were entailed, if not both. However, in the case of those who made decisions within the Polish government, there was no cost at all to be paid by them. Financial costs were paid by the taxpayers and the human costs were paid by patients in government hospitals, subject to lower quality medical treatment than was available in the society at the time. Neither of these costs was a deterrent to discrimination by government officials.

In the private sector, however, both kinds of costs were paid by sick people. Concern for one's own personal health, especially in an emergency situation or when confronted with a potentially crippling or fatal disease, could easily overcome whatever anti-Jewish attitudes one might have. Given the respective incentives in the government and in the private sector, the different levels of discrimination against Jews is very much what one might expect, on the basis of the most elementary economic principles.

Poland provides examples of another phenomenon— more discrimination where there was less hostility and less discrimination where there was more hostility. Anti-Jewish feelings tended to be stronger in eastern Poland than in western Poland. Yet Jewish artisans were more prevalent in eastern Poland, just as black artisans once had better job opportunities in the American South, where racism was most rampant. In both cases, organized labor affected the cost of discrimination.

Guilds were stronger in western Poland than in eastern Poland and American labor unions were stronger in the North than in the South during the eras under discussion. To the extent that organized labor succeeds in raising pay levels above where they would be under supply and demand in a free market, they provide incentives for employers to hire fewer workers because labor is now more costly, both absolutely and relative to the cost of capital that may be substituted for it. At the same time, wage rates raised above the level that would prevail under supply and demand attract more workers who apply for jobs that have higher pay. The net effect is that organized labor tends to create a chronic surplus of job applicants. Given that surplus, the cost to the employer of turning away qualified applicants from the "wrong" group is less than it would be if the employer had to be concerned about finding enough similarly qualified replacements for those who have been arbitrarily rejected.

Even in the absence of discrimination by guilds or unions themselves— and there was plenty of that— it would still be cheaper for employers to discriminate on their own than would be the case in a free market. Given this situation, it is not so puzzling that Jewish artisans found it easier to practice their skills in that part of Poland that was more hostile to Jews and that black American artisans found it easier to practice their skills in the Jim Crow South than in the more unionized North. Differences in costs of discrimination outweighed differences in negative predispositions.

The same pattern can be seen in employment statistics over time. Both in the American South during the Jim Crow era and in South Africa under white rule, blacks were a much higher percentage of railroad employees in the early twentieth century than they were at mid-century. In both countries, labor markets were more freely competitive in the earlier era and more controlled in the later era— and in both countries it would be hard to claim that there was less racism in the earlier era.

Not only labor unions, but also government regulation, can reduce the cost of discrimination. Where a public utility with a monopoly has its prices set by a government regulatory agency on the basis of its costs, it has little or no incentive to keep those costs down to a level that would be necessary for its survival in a competitive market. Costs of discrimination, like other costs, can simply be passed on to the customers of a regulated monopoly. When the American telephone industry was a regulated monopoly, blacks were seldom hired for even such routine jobs as telephone operators before the civil rights laws were enacted. As of 1930, for example, there were only 331 black women in the entire country working as telephone operators, out of more than 230,000 women in that occupation. As late as 1950 black women were only one percent of all the women working for phone companies.

Because each local telephone company was a monopoly within its own territory, it could pass on higher costs to everyone who used telephones. Had it not discriminated, its costs would have been lower and its monopoly profits could theoretically have been higher but, because its profit rates were in fact constrained by government regulation, the phone company would never have seen that additional money anyway. Instead, its officials could indulge their racial preferences with no net loss of profits. Meanwhile, blacks were beginning to star on Broadway as early as the 1920s, in an industry with cut-throat competition, where large profits and devastating losses were both common.

The cost of refusing to hire black entertainers who could fill a theater was just too high for this industry to follow the same practices as the telephone industry. The one-to-one correspondence between racism and discrimination that is often assumed cannot explain such differences between sectors of the same economy at the same time. Even less can it explain the persistence of such differences between industries over time, when there is a complete turnover of decision-makers throughout the economy. Even after a given set of decision-makers and their individual predispositions have passed from the scene, the persistence of the same set of incentives tends to reproduce the same end results with a new set of decision-makers in the same respective industries, whatever the individual predispositions of these new decision-makers.

Because major league baseball has operated as a cartel exempted from anti-trust laws, it too had low costs of discrimination and was able to keep black players out— so long as all teams did so. But this situation changed in 1947, when the Brooklyn Dodgers hired Jackie Robinson as the first black major league ballplayer.

Because there was competition ***within*** the cartel among its various teams, once the color barrier was broken by just one team hiring just one black player, the cost to other teams of keeping out other black players rose sharply. The net result was that, in a matter of a relatively few years, large numbers of black players flooded into the major leagues. For a period of seven consecutive years, no white man won the National League's Most Valuable Player award. Had other teams not followed the lead of the Dodgers in hiring black players, all these MVP stars would have become Dodgers, giving Brooklyn a virtual monopoly of National League pennants and perhaps of world championships.

This cost was obviously much too high for the competing teams to pay for continuing racial exclusion in major league baseball. Their racial attitudes may not have changed, but the cost of translating those attitudes into discriminatory exclusions had changed drastically.

Given the influence of the costs of discrimination on the amount of actual discrimination, it is also possible to understand another otherwise puzzling phenomenon— the especially strong reversals of racial policies in sectors of the economy least subject to the pressures of the competitive marketplace. These include the government itself, government-regulated public utilities, and non-profit organizations, such as academic institutions, hospitals, and foundations. Colleges and universities that had never hired blacks for their faculties in pre-World War II America led the way when affirmative action in the 1960s and 1970s meant preferential hiring and promotion of black professors and preferential admissions of black students. There was also a very similar sharp reversal of hiring policies in the telephone industry, among others, at the same time. Between 1966 and 1968, not only did the hiring of blacks increase by more than 10,000 workers, blacks constituted one third of all new employees. As of 2007, A.T.&T. was ranked number one in the country in promoting "diversity" or "multicultural business opportunities" among its suppliers.

Sudden radical changes from especially discriminatory policies against a particular group to preferential policies toward the very same group are hard to explain by predispositions, since many of the same decision-makers were in control during the transition period. It is much easier to understand in terms of the incentives and constraints of the circumstances in which they operated. More specifically, neither discrimination nor "reverse discrimination" cost them as much as either policy would have cost decision-makers in those sectors of the economy where institutional survival depends on keeping costs within narrow limits, in order to meet competition in a free market. Once the political and social climate changed, government, government-regulated utilities, and non-profit organizations could change most quickly with the least cost to themselves.

The power of the free market was perhaps best demonstrated in white-ruled South Africa during the era of apartheid. Here we need not wonder about racial predispositions or about the fact that the vast majority of employers in industry, agriculture, and government were white. Yet, even in a country which became a worldwide symbol of racial oppression, white employers in competitive industries violated official government policy on a massive scale by hiring more black workers and in higher positions than the law allowed. There is no compelling evidence that these particular white employers had different racial predispositions than the white people who administered the apartheid government. What they had were very different costs of discrimination.

While government agencies and government-regulated railroads, for example, could maintain apartheid policies at virtually zero cost to themselves, it was a wholly different economic situation for people spending their own money. Home-building was a typical example:

> To build a house in Johannesburg meant either waiting for months for a white, expensive, legal building gang, or finding a black gang, perhaps with a white nominally in charge in case an official came inquiring. Most customers opted for the quicker, cheaper service.

Such practices became so widespread in South Africa that the white-run apartheid government cracked down in the 1970s, fining hundreds of building construction companies. Moreover, this was by no means the only industry that hired more blacks than they were allowed to by law. In the clothing industry, no blacks at all were allowed to work in certain categories of jobs, under the apartheid laws. Yet, as of 1970, blacks were an absolute majority of the workers in those job categories. There were also residential areas in South Africa set aside by law for whites only— and yet there were not only many non-whites living in these areas (including black American economist Walter Williams), at least one such area had an absolute majority of non-whites. Competition in a free market simply made discrimination too expensive for many, even though violating the apartheid laws also cost money.[1]

The expansion of black residential areas into white residential areas has been even more common in the United States. However, this more or less continuous expansion of black ghettoes has been in contrast to the history of the original ghettoes— those of the Jews in Europe in centuries past. Jewish ghettoes in Europe in centuries past tended to become more overcrowded as the Jewish population grew, though there were particular times and places where Jews were allowed to expand an existing ghetto or to set up a new ghetto to accommodate their growing populations. Here again, the difference has been in the economic costs of discrimination.

Black ghettoes have expanded through the marketplace because of the costs of excluding black renters and home buyers. This is not to say that there was no resistance by whites. Often there was organized, bitter, and even violent resistance. The key question, however, is: What was the end result? The usual end result was that black ghettoes expanded in cities across the country. Moreover, where this expansion was stopped by laws or government policies, by restrictive covenants, or by violence or the threat of violence, that reinforces the point that the costs of discrimination were too great for the expansion of black ghettoes to be stopped in the marketplace. By and large, black ghettoes continued expanding with the growth of the black population.

The boundaries of Jewish ghettoes in Europe were not determined by the marketplace but were established by the dictates of those with political power. Only when these political leaders found it expedient did these boundaries expand. That is why Jewish ghettoes tended simply to become more crowded with the passage of time and population growth. There was usually no cost to political leaders for discriminating against Jews. In

---

[1] One of the reasons for the weakening of apartheid, even before the end of white-minority rule in South Africa, was that many of the white Afrikaners, the principal supporters of apartheid, rose over the years into the ranks of business owners and now had to pay the costs of discrimination, which before had been paid by British and Jewish business owners. Faced with these costs, many Afrikaners began to lose their enthusiasm for apartheid and some even spoke out against it, despite the authoritarian and repressive South African government.

particular circumstances— when there was a war on, for example, and the rulers needed the help of Jewish financiers— various proscriptions might be eased and more ghettoes allowed to be founded to relieve overcrowding. During the Thirty Years War (1618-1648), for example, new Jewish communities were permitted to be established and new occupations and markets opened up to Jews, while a synagogue was permitted to be built in Vienna for the first time in more than 200 years and a synagogue was permitted in Denmark for the first time ever.

In short, costs of discrimination are not only a fact of life, they are a potent force in actual decision-making, even in countries with strong racial, ethnic, or religious predispositions. How much of a force depends on the economic incentives and constraints in particular sectors. What this means is that not only is the assumed one-to-one correlation between racism and discrimination false, but also that those who wish to reduce discrimination need to pay attention to the economic conditions which make it more expensive or less expensive for decision-makers to discriminate. Too often, however, those opposed to discrimination are also opposed to free competitive markets that make discrimination more costly. They do not think beyond stage one.

Even a given market— such as the market for housing or the labor market, for example— can have more discrimination or less discrimination according to whether its prices are determined by supply and demand or are imposed by external agencies such as government, labor unions, or a cartel. For example, when a landlord refuses to rent an apartment to people from the "wrong" group, that can mean leaving the apartment vacant longer. Clearly, that represents a loss of rent— if this is a free market. However, if there is rent control, with a surplus of applicants, then such discrimination may cost the landlord nothing.

Similar principles apply in job markets. An employer who refuses to hire qualified individuals from the "wrong" groups risks leaving his jobs unfilled longer in a free market. This means that he must either leave some work undone and some orders unfilled or else pay overtime to existing employees to get it done, losing money either way. However, in a market where wages are set artificially above the level that would exist through supply and demand, the resulting surplus of applicants can mean that discrimination costs the employer nothing. Whether these artificially higher wages are set by a labor union or by a minimum wage law does not change the principle.

In all these cases, the crucial factors in the cost of discrimination have been the presence or absence of competition and whether those making the decisions have been spending their own money or someone else's money. When one's own money is at stake, groups hostile to each other may not only fail to discriminate, they may in fact seek each other out. A landmark study of Polish immigrants and Jewish immigrants from Poland in early twentieth-century Chicago reported:

> . . . the Poles and the Jews in Chicago . . . have a profound feeling of disrespect and contempt for each other, bred by their contiguity and by historical friction in the pale; but they trade with each other on Milwaukee Avenue and on Maxwell Street. A study of numerous cases shows that not only do many Jews open their businesses on Milwaukee Avenue and Division Street because they know that the Poles are the predominant population in these neighborhoods, but the Poles come from all over the city to trade on Maxwell Street because they know that there they can find the familiar street-stands owned by Jews.

EMPIRICAL EVIDENCE

Those who equate discrimination with differences in life chances confound highly disparate reasons for differences in outcomes among groups. Even if one regards differences in life chances as more important than discrimination, any serious attempt to deal with either social phenomenon must distinguish them from one another.

Life Chances

In one sense, life chances are easier to determine than discrimination. For the past, the probabilities that a black child would become a physician or a member of Congress can be determined mathematically from statistics on the size of the black population and the numbers of blacks who ended up in those occupations. Even in this simplest case, however, there are complications.

Do we mean by life chances mere statistical probabilities in general or do we mean the likelihood that a given attempt, with a given effort, will succeed? What if very few black boys want to become ballet dancers or are prepared to endure peer disapproval if they persist in their efforts in this direction? In short, even the apparently simple issue of determining life chances raises complicating questions as to the ***source*** of the differences in probabilities and outcomes among groups. Whether that source is internal or external becomes even more of a complication when seeking to determine the existence and magnitude of discrimination.

Where discrimination is distinguished from differences in life chances, the empirical question is whether individuals of similar qualifications have similar prospects of employment, college admission, and other benefits when they come from different groups. Where there are substantial differences in qualifying characteristics among groups, as there often are, the question then becomes: What of those particular individuals who have the same qualifying characteristics as members of other groups? Do they have the same prospects or results?

Comparability

Gross comparisons between groups may tell a radically different story than comparisons of comparable individuals. For example, black income has never been as high as white income in the United States and, in years past, the disparities were even greater than they are today. Yet, as far back as 1969, young black males who came from homes where there were newspapers, magazines, and library cards earned the same incomes as young white males with the same things in their homes and with the same education. As of 1989, black, white, and Hispanic Americans of the same age (29) and with the same IQ (100) all averaged between $25,000 and $26,000 in income when they worked year around.

American women's incomes have never been as high as the incomes of American men but, as early as 1971, women in their thirties who had never married and who had worked continuously since school earned slightly ***higher*** incomes than men of the same description. In Canada, women who never married have earned more than 99 percent of the income of men who never married. Among college faculty members, American women who had never married earned slightly ***higher*** incomes than men who had never married, as far back as 1969.

None of this says anything about life chances, however relevant it may be to questions about employer discrimination. The percentage of black males who came from the kinds of homes described was very different from the percentage of white males who came from such homes. IQ scores are likewise distributed very differently among American blacks, whites, and Hispanics. It is not uncommon, both in the United States and in other countries, for one racial or ethnic group to differ in age from another by a decade or more— and age makes a large difference in income. So does marriage. While married men tend to earn more than single men and married men with children still more, the exact opposite is the case for women. Nor are the reasons particularly obscure, since marriage and parenthood create very different incentives and constraints for women than for men.

The justice or social desirability of traditional sex roles in marriage can be debated. But that debate is not about employer discrimination, much less about the presumed predispositions of employers. Questions about the existence or magnitude of employer discrimination are questions about whether individuals who show up at the workplace with the same developed capabilities and liabilities are treated the same there. It is not a question about whether life has been fair to them before they reached the employer, however important that question might be when dealing with other issues. Yet, increasingly, laws and policies have defined as employer discrimination a failure to pay the extra costs associated with those workers who are pregnant, suffering from mental illness, or are more of a risk because of a prison record or the health problems associated with old age. When hiring, employers have incentives to think beyond stage one, even if those who make or advocate laws and government policies do not.

Whatever the merits or demerits of having such additional costs paid by the employer or by the government or by others, a failure to do so is not the same thing as treating equally valuable workers differently because they happen to come from different groups. When workers whose net value to the enterprise is in fact different are hired, paid and promoted according to those differences, that is not employer discrimination, whatever else it might be. This is not even a question about desirable social policy. It is a question about using words that have some specific meaning, rather than as mere sounds used to evoke particular emotions. Only when terms have some specific meaning, understood by those on both sides of an issue, can we at least engage in rational discussions of our differences of opinion about what is or is not desirable social policy. Otherwise, we are simply talking past each other.

While isolated data can demonstrate graphically the distinction between differing life chances, on the one hand, and discrimination on the other, the more general problem of determining which phenomenon exists in particular situations requires more complex and often uncertain methods. For example, it is common to "control" statistically for certain factors and then see if individuals from different groups have similar results when those factors have been taken into consideration. Yet this is much easier to accept in principle than to apply in practice.

Nothing is easier than to imagine that one has taken all relevant factors into account, when in reality there may be other factors which have influence, even if no data have been collected on them or they are not quantifiable. Where there are very significant differences in known factors between one group and another, it would be reckless to assume that all remaining unknown factors are the same. Yet that is done again and again in discussions of discrimination.

A scholar in India, for example, attempted to compare Bombay medical school students with such comparable social characteristics as father's income and occupation, but later discovered in the course of interviewing these students that those who were the same in these respects, but who were also untouchables, were not comparable on other variables, such as the quality of the schools they had come from, the number of books in the homes in which they had grown up, and the literacy rates among their fathers and grandfathers.

Similarly, a study of black and white faculty members in the United States found that those who were comparable on some variables were nevertheless very different on other variables. Even black professors with Ph.D.s usually received those Ph.D.s at a later age, from institutions with lower rankings in their respective fields, and these professors had published fewer articles. When such variables as published articles, the ranking of the institutions from which Ph.D.s were earned, and years of academic experience were all held constant, black professors with Ph.D.s earned *more* than comparable white professors with Ph.D.s, as far back as 1970— a year before affirmative action policies were mandated by the federal government.

None of this is unusual. It is commonplace in countries around the world for groups who differ in the quantity of their education to differ also in the quality of their education. This means that comparisons of individuals with ostensibly the "same" education from different groups can amount to comparisons of apples and oranges. Therefore equating differences in pay between members of different groups who have the "same" education with discrimination is a non sequitur.

Educational quality may differ along many dimensions, including institutional ranking, individual performance, or fields of specialization. Such differences have existed between the Chinese and the Malays in Malaysia, Tamils and Sinhalese in Sri Lanka, and European and American Jews versus Middle Eastern Jews in Israel, as well as between caste Hindus and untouchables in India and among blacks, whites, and Hispanics in the United States. The education of American college-educated women and men likewise differs in fields of specialization and in the postgraduate education added on to that of these women and men whose education is considered the "same" because they have all graduated from college.

Education is not unique in having such differences among apparently similar individuals from different groups. A highly publicized study, from which many in the media concluded that there was racial discrimination between minority and white applicants for mortgage loans in the United States, failed to note that the minority applicants had larger debts, poorer credit histories, sought loans covering a higher percentage of the value of the properties in question, and were also more likely to seek to finance multiple dwelling units rather than single-family homes.

When these factors were taken into account, the differences in mortgage loan approval rates shrank dramatically, though the remaining difference of 6 percentage points was nevertheless attributed to discrimination, as if there could not possibly be any other differences in the remaining unstudied factors, despite large differences in the variables that were already studied. For example, other data from the U.S. Census show that blacks and whites with the same incomes average very different net worths— and net worth is also a major consideration in decisions to approve or disapprove mortgage loan applications. Perhaps even more revealing was that, just as blacks and whites differed on qualifications variables, just as they differed in loan application approvals, so whites and Asian Americans differed— with whites having lower qualifications than Asian Americans and Pacific Islanders, and being denied conventional loans a higher percentage of the time.

Much statistical data do not permit such a fine breakdown as the data comparing black and white faculty members in 1970 or the follow-up study on mortgage lending. For much of the media— and often even in academia— it is sufficient to find intergroup differences in outcomes to conclude that there has been discrimination. This happens, however, only when the conclusion fits existing preconceptions. Statistics showing whites with lower incomes, higher infant mortality rates, and higher rates of denial of mortgage loan applications than Asian Americans are never taken to show discrimination against whites, even though identical data— often from the same studies— are taken as proof of discrimination against blacks.

Gross statistical differences between the "representation" of different groups in particular occupations, institutions, or income levels are likewise usually considered sufficient for concluding that the "under-represented" groups were "excluded" by discriminatory policies or by individual or institutional biases or prejudices, however subtle, covert or unconscious these might be. Yet nothing is more common, in countries around the world, than huge differences in representation between groups, even when the more fortunate group is in no position to discriminate against the less fortunate group. These include situations where the more fortunate group is a minority with no institutional or political power over the majority.

In Malaysia, for example, for the entire decade of the 1960s, members of the Chinese minority in Malaysia received more than 400 degrees in engineering, while members of the Malay majority received just four. This was in a country where the universities were controlled by the Malays, who also controlled the government that controlled the universities. Nor was this situation unique. In czarist Russia, the German minority— about one percent of the population— was an absolute majority in the St. Petersburg Academy of Sciences. Southern Nigerians were an absolute majority of the people in a number of professions in northern Nigeria when that country gained its independence. The list could go on and on, filling a book much larger than this one.

None of this disproves the existence of discrimination or minimizes its magnitude. It simply asks that those who assert its existence ***demonstrate*** its existence— by some evidence that will stand up to scrutiny.

ANTI-DISCRIMINATION LAWS

Both discrimination and affirmative action involve costs. It could hardly be otherwise, since they are both essentially preferential policies, though the preferences are for different groups. Whatever the rationales or goals of these policies, the economic question is: What are the actual consequences of such policies— and not just in stage one? In principle, anti-discrimination laws preclude preferential treatment of either a majority or minority. But this policy cannot be defined by its intentions, goals or rationales. The real question is: What are its specific characteristics and their consequences— and, again, not just in stage one?

The likely consequences of laws and policies against discrimination depend on how discrimination is defined and determined by those with the power to enforce such laws and policies. The incentives and constraints created by these definitions and methods of determining whether or not discrimination exists provide more clues as to what to expect than do the goals or rationales. What is then decisive is the empirical evidence as to what actually happens.

Legal Definitions

In the United States, "discrimination" had a very simple and straightforward legal meaning at the beginning of the federal civil rights legislation of the 1960s. It meant treating individuals differently according to the racial or ethnic group in which they were classified. Even the term "affirmative action," as used initially in President John F. Kennedy's Executive Order in 1961, meant that an employer must be active, rather than passive, to make sure that job applicants and employees were treated the same, "without regard to their race, creed, color, or national origin." Anti-discrimination laws, such as the Civil Rights Act of 1964, were likewise designed to prevent differential treatment in employment, in access to public accommodations, and in various other contexts. However, even before the Civil Rights Act of 1964 was passed, a competing definition of discrimination had already begun to emerge.

Earlier that year, a state Fair Employment Practices Commission in Illinois ruled that the Motorola company had discriminated against a black job applicant by requiring him to take the same test that other applicants took. This was considered to be discriminatory because blacks usually did not have either as much or as good an education as whites, and so were less likely to do well on tests. As one of the Commission's examiners put it, the test was unfair to "culturally deprived and disadvantaged groups." This implicitly shifted the operational definition of discrimination from a denial of equal treatment to a denial of equal prospects of success.

Critics of the federal civil rights legislation being considered in Congress pointed to the Motorola case as an example of what to expect if the Civil Rights Act of 1964 became law, while the Act's advocates and defenders vehemently denied it. Although nothing in the Act itself authorized any such definition of discrimination, subsequent interpretations by the federal courts, including the Supreme Court, established the broader definition of discrimination as the use of criteria which have a "disparate impact" on the prospects of success by minority groups. In other words, a failure to have a workforce reflecting the demographic profile of the local community was now taken as presumptive evidence of discrimination, with the burden of proof to the contrary falling on the employer.

The issues revolving around such policies have already been amply— or perhaps more than amply— debated by many advocates and critics from political, moral, legal, and sociological perspectives. The economic question, however, is: What incentives and constraints does this definition of discrimination create and what are the likely consequences of those incentives and constraints?

Economic Consequences

The most obvious and most immediate consequence is that those employers who were discriminating against minorities now had an incentive to stop doing so, in order to avoid the costs arising from legal action under anti-discrimination laws. However, the empirical evidence suggests that the extent of discrimination in the sense of treating equally capable individuals differently because of race, may have been considerably less than that assumed by those who equate discrimination with different outcomes for different groups. Nevertheless, whether the amount of discrimination is large or small, the immediate, stage-one effect of anti-discrimination laws is to reduce it.

What about other consequences unfolding over time? The ease with which private parties or government agencies can make a charge of discrimination against an employer who is in fact ***not*** discriminating, but whose work force does not reflect the local population profile, now makes locating near concentrations of minority populations legally more risky. Those employers in these risky locations may not be able to do much about it in the short run. However, as time goes on, new businesses that arise have a choice of where to locate, and even old businesses with branches in more than one location can shift their operations away from minority population centers, in order to reduce their legal risks. Eventually, even the employer with only one plant or office can find an opportunity to move elsewhere.

Whether minority workers gain more jobs through the effect of anti-discrimination laws in reducing discrimination or lose more jobs through the incentives that such laws provide for employers to relocate away from places with substantial minority populations is an empirical question. But it is a question that is seldom asked, much less answered. Yet studies of the location of new plants set up in the United States by Japanese companies have found statistical evidence that these plants were usually located away from communities with substantial black populations. Nor was this practice limited to foreign companies. American companies often did the same things when selecting sites for new plants, according to the ***New York Times***:

> A number of companies automatically eliminated from consideration counties in which blacks were 30 percent or more of the population. . . Some industrial development officials said they were also advised in advance that companies had no interest in such areas.

While there may be other factors behind such patterns, it should be noted that in earlier generations blacks had higher labor force participation rates than whites before various government interventions made it more costly or more risky to hire blacks.

For employers, another way of avoiding charges of discrimination by minority employees or job applicants may be to hire in such a way as to have a racially representative sample of the local population. However, this can risk charges of "reverse discrimination" by white job applicants who were not hired, or white employees who were passed over for promotion. Since racial or ethnic groups tend to differ in their particular skills and experience, it is unlikely that the qualifications of members of different groups in a given location will be the same— the only way to have both non-discriminatory hiring and a demographically representative workforce at the same time.

One way out of this dilemma for many employers is to hire in such a way as to create demographic representation, and at the same time escape charges of "reverse discrimination," by justifying preferential hiring on grounds of affirmative action based on a need for "diversity." This way of avoiding lawsuits from both minority and majority individuals, or from government agencies, works only in so far as courts accept such arguments. Therefore, when affirmative action has been challenged in the Supreme Court, even when it is challenged in cases involving college admissions, many corporations have filed briefs in favor of the colleges with racial preferences in admissions standards. The "diversity" defense is a legal safe haven for employers, and one which they do not want to lose.

The net effect of anti-discrimination laws and "affirmative action" policies on individuals and groups who have historically been discriminated against is by no means clear in the light of empirical evidence. For example, while preferential admissions policies get more black students on academic campuses than before, and more than would be admitted under normal standards, studies of various colleges and universities indicate that ***graduation*** rates of black students are highest on campuses where their test scores are similar to those of other students on those campuses and lowest where there are the greatest disparities in test scores. Since the purpose of being in college in the first place is not simply to provide the institution with an ethnically diverse student body, but to get an education and graduate, what matters is how well that purpose is served by admitting minority students who do not meet the same standards as the other students around them.

The students who fail to graduate need not be "unqualified" to be in college. Often they are fully qualified to meet the standards of some other institutions, rather than the ones which admitted them. When elite colleges and universities admit minority students who would normally qualify to be at second-tier institutions, that leaves second-tier institutions with fewer minority students, which in turn leads these institutions to admit students who would ordinarily qualify at lower-ranked colleges and universities. Such systematic mismatching of minority students in both elite and non-elite institutions can then lead to lower graduation rates up and down the academic ladder. After preferential admissions policies were banned in the University of California system and in the University of Texas system, the total number of black students in these systems as a whole did not go down. Instead, they were redistributed within each system, with fewer going to the flagship university— at Berkeley and Austin, respectively— and more going to other campuses within each system, where their qualifications were more similar to that of other students on those campuses.[2]

Law schools are a special case, since there is an external qualification test— the bar exam— to be met after graduation, and which has to be passed in order to have a career as a lawyer. Here, too, those black students admitted preferentially failed the bar exam more often than those who met the normal standards of the law schools to which they were admitted. Because of the difficulties of keeping up in an educational environment where the pace is geared to students with higher academic qualifications, it is by no means clear that going to a "better" school means getting a better education, whether in law schools or in colleges and universities. A study published in the ***Stanford Law Review*** in 2004 found that black students admitted under preferential policies failed the bar exam more often than those admitted by meeting the normal standards at the law schools they attended. In short, on net balance there may be ***fewer*** black lawyers under preferential admissions to law schools than if black students were admitted wherever they met the same standards as other students.

---

[2] Much confusion has been spread by a study showing that black students succeed better at universities with higher average test scores (***The Shape of the River*** by William G. Bowen and Derek Bok, p. 259). What this leaves out is that the ***differential*** between the scores of black and white students is less at such schools— and it is the differential that matters. For example, the difference in average composite SAT scores between black and white students at Harvard was 95 points, compared to 184 points at Duke and 271 points at Rice. See ***Backfire*** by Bob Zelnick, p. 132.

SUMMARY AND IMPLICATIONS

Much discussion of discrimination fails to allow people with opposing views to confront their substantive differences— much less confront evidence— because so many of the words used have ambiguous and shifting meanings. In particular, these discussions abound in terms which confuse differences in internal personal qualities— such as skills, education, and experience— with externally imposed barriers to employment, college admissions, and other goals. Thus those who fail to qualify for particular benefits are often said to be denied "access" or "opportunity," when in fact they may have had as much access or opportunity as anyone else, but simply did not have the developed capabilities required. The facts may of course vary from individual to individual or from group to group, but we do not even know what facts to look for when considering issues revolving around discrimination, if our terms make no such distinctions.

Similarly, a mental test may be characterized as "culturally biased" if one group scores higher than another, as if it is impossible for different groups to have different interest, experience, upbringing, education, or other factors that would lead to a real difference being registered, rather than a biased assessment being made.[3] Would anyone consider basketball to be a culturally biased game because blacks generally play it better than whites? It might well be that, if whites took as much interest in the game and played it as often as blacks, they would be just as good at it. But measuring what people actually do in the real world is very different from assessing what they would do under other, hypothetical circumstances.

The owner of a professional basketball team is not engaging in racial discrimination when he hires more blacks than whites in a country where

---

[3] A complicating factor here is a history of controversies over whether there are innate racial differences in intelligence. But that explosive emotional issue has little or no relevance to questions about discrimination. Innate potential exists at the moment of conception but no one applies for a job or for college admissions at the moment of conception. By the time any such application is made, numerous personal and social factors have had an influence over the years— and these factors have seldom been the same for every individual or for every group. Moreover, employers are far more likely to be interested in the developed capabilities that have emerged, rather than the innate potential with which someone began life.

the population has more whites than blacks. If cultural bias means only that a given test has some predictive power only within a given culture— that people who score well on that test will probably perform well in that particular culture but not necessarily perform well in a very different culture— then such a conclusion is both trivial and misleading because everyone, everywhere, performs within some particular culture. A "culture-free" test would have predictive validity only in a culture-free society, and there is no such society anywhere.

None of this says anything about how much discrimination there is. What it says is that a vocabulary has come into being that makes it virtually impossible to determine how much discrimination there is, since the results of both discrimination and numerous other factors are lumped together under the same words.

Those who do not think beyond stage one may assume that, whatever the level of discrimination, anti-discrimination laws reduce it. Yet the incentives and constraints created by such laws can either increase or reduce the employment or other opportunities of minority groups, on net balance. There may be honest differences of opinion on what the net balance turns out to be, but even the question itself does not arise until we look beyond stage one. More precise definitions of terms or finer breakdowns of statistics might yield very different estimates of the amount of discrimination, but the crucial point here is that the vocabulary actually in use is not adapted to discovering how much discrimination exists, however well adapted it may be for political purposes.

Chapter 8

The Economic Development of Nations

International differences in economic production are extreme. As measured by purchasing power, Japan has a larger Gross Domestic Product than Russia and Great Britain combined. The United States has a larger Gross Domestic Product than Japan, India, and Germany combined. Indeed, some American states have larger Gross Domestic Products than many nations. New Jersey has a higher GDP than Egypt, for example, and California has a higher GDP than Canada or Mexico. However, a country's Gross Domestic Product— the total value of its annual output— is not necessarily a reliable guide to its standard of living. Much depends on how many people have to share that output. China has the second highest GDP in the world, as measured by purchasing power, but its output is shared among more than a billion people, and its GDP per capita is not even among the top 70 countries in the world.

Nations differ not only in the total value of their output and the standard of living indicated by GDP per capita, but also in how rapidly or how slowly their economies are growing. Despite the widespread use of the euphemism "developing countries" for poor countries, many poor countries are not developing as fast as richer countries, and some so-called "developing countries" are not developing at all, but retrogressing. In most of the modern industrialized world, economic growth is more or less taken for granted, with only the rate of growth being a matter of concern. Yet economic growth is by no means universal, even today. In addition to such short-run setbacks as depressions, there have been countries and whole regions, such as sub-Saharan Africa, where output per capita is lower than it was two generations ago.

In the long millennia of history, economic growth has usually not been something that could be taken for granted. Moreover, ***growth***— an increase in output— is not the same as ***development***, an improvement in the ways and means of producing output, whether through technological advances or improved management or organization. Economic growth is possible when the population grows and more people produce a larger total of goods and services, even if they produce them in the same ways as a smaller population produced them before and continue to have the same standard of living as before.

Of all the technological advances in history, none was more profound and far-reaching in its impact than agriculture. Without agriculture, it would be impossible to have cities, and without cities civilization is virtually inconceivable. Societies of hunters and gatherers must be spread very thinly on the land, in order for the spontaneous produce of nature to provide enough food for people to survive. Concentrations of people require concentrations of food, which agriculture provides. Agriculture also requires people to think beyond stage one— to plant in the spring, in order to reap in the fall, and store enough food to last through the winter. Time, work, and risk became inescapable concerns for all in agricultural societies, as distinguished from societies in which most people are employees, with the management of time and risk left to others. The farther from the tropics an agricultural society is, the more keenly the people must be aware of time and of the necessity of beginning planting soon after the snow and ice are gone in the spring, so as to be able to produce a crop during the shorter growing seasons of climates farther away from the equator. Farmers cannot simply drift along from day to day, as hunter-gatherers might in some tropical land with abundant food spontaneously supplied by nature the year round. Farming demands that particular things be done in particular seasons— which is to say, that people are constantly forced to think beyond whatever stage they are in currently.

Concentrations of populations gave agricultural societies decisive advantages over hunter-gatherer societies when they contended for the same land. Even more important for economic and cultural development, concentrations of population made cities possible, with all their potential for economies of scale and for making costly investments in both economic, social, and cultural institutions achievable, when the high costs of these institutions could be spread over large numbers of people living within a relatively small area of land. Because cities were usually established on navigable waterways, they had access and communication with other cities and ultimately to the seaports of distant lands. The cultural universe of a city was thus much larger than the cultural universe of land-locked villages, isolated mountain communities, or that of nomadic hunter-gatherers constantly on the lookout for food.

Not only the products of other places, but also the ideas and the technologies of other places, have been available to cities. With a lag, these imports from other places and cultures could be diffused into the surrounding countrysides and especially into other urban communities.

In much of the world, especially where agriculture has been the principal economic activity, people followed the practices of their forebears for centuries before modern agricultural practices began to emerge and spread. Economic development has by no means been automatic. In some parts of the world, even today, farmers have continued to farm and fishermen have continued to fish in much the same way as their ancestors did centuries earlier, leading to standards of living not very different from what they had been in ancient times. Advances in technology and wealth have been greater in some regions of the world than in others, and greater during some periods of history than in others. However, there have also been periods of stagnation and periods of retrogression, sometimes brought on by the disruptions and destruction of war, sometimes by plagues or other natural disasters, and sometimes by ill-conceived economic policies.

At the beginning of the twentieth century, Argentina was one of the ten richest countries in the world, ahead of France and Germany. But, at the beginning of the twenty-first century, no one would even compare the troubled and chaotic Argentine economy with that of France or Germany. Many ill-conceived policies in between led to this falling behind in a country blessed with natural resources and spared the wars which ravaged other countries in the twentieth century. Between 1998 and 2002, income per person in Argentina dropped by two-thirds.

Sharp changes in countries' relative positions have taken place in much shorter periods than a century. As of 1991, India and China had very similar output per capita. But, a decade later, China's output per capita was double that of India. China had begun the process of moving away from a government-run economy to more of a market economy. When India began making the same kinds of changes in the 1990s, its economic development became more rapid as well. Over a span of centuries, changes have been even more dramatic. It has been estimated that in 1700 more than half the output of the entire world was produced in Asia and less than one-fourth in Europe. But, by 1890, Europe had surpassed Asia and, with the addition of the United States, Western countries were producing more than half the world's output.

Why development has been greater in some places than in others, and at some times rather than others, is a question of great practical importance for the economic fate of billions of human beings today, though it is a question for which no single answer is likely to explain everything. Technology has had much to do with it, though not everything. Similarly for geography, natural resources, and other factors, including the human factor. As in other areas of economics, attempts to understand certain basic realities are made more difficult by the distractions of popular myths and misconceptions.

DIFFERENCES IN DEVELOPMENT

The striking and even shocking differences in economic development seen in many parts of the contemporary world have led many to develop, or be drawn to, sweeping and often melodramatic theories that claim to explain such economic contrasts. Yet such economic contrasts have been common throughout history. Ancient China was so far in advance of Europe that, while there was a great demand among Europeans for silk, chinaware (the name is significant) and other exotic products, the Europeans produced little or nothing comparable to trade, and so had to pay in gold for what they bought from China. Within Europe, the contrasts have been equally great.

When the ancient Greeks had monumental architecture that is still imitated today and landmark intellectual figures like Plato and Aristotle, illiteracy was common across much of northern Europe and there was not a single building in all of Britain when the Romans invaded in the first century A.D., nor had a single Briton's name yet entered the pages of history. The contrast today between the wealth of Western countries and the poverty of the Third World is nothing new. World leadership in various fields— the arts, science, literature, economic development— has changed many times over the centuries, suggesting an equality of human potential, but at no given time in recorded history has there been equality of achievement.

While differences in economic development have long been common, the particular advantages of one society over another during a particular era have not been permanent. Europe eventually overtook China, after many centuries. So did Japan. More important, the advances achieved in one society have often diffused outward to other societies. What was perhaps the most consequential economic advance in the history of the human race— agriculture— began in the Middle East and spread outward, first to nearby regions such as the eastern Mediterranean countries.

One society was not always more advanced in all things, so different advances came from different places, even at a given time. For example, the numbering system in use around the world today originated centuries ago among the Hindus of India, and displaced Roman numerals in the West, as well as every other numbering system that it competed with in every other country. Because Europeans first became aware of this numbering system when they encountered it in use among the Arabs, they called such numbers "Arabic numerals." But that was not the origin of these numbers.

Innumerable borrowings from one culture to another have taken place almost continuously over thousands of years. However, the pace of these borrowings and the opportunities to borrow have varied greatly in different parts of the world and in different periods of time. People living in remote mountain valleys or on isolated islands in the middle of a vast sea have usually not been able to keep up with the advances of technology and other developments in other societies. When the Spaniards discovered the Canary Islands in the fifteenth century, they found people of a Caucasian race living at a stone age level. So were the Australian aborigines when the British discovered them. In both cases, isolation meant deprivation of the advances of the human race around the world.

While such things as technology and natural resources are obvious factors in economic development, less obvious factors may be of equal or greater importance. The role of government can be crucial. After the Roman Empire collapsed in the fifth century A.D., the institutions it had maintained collapsed with it. What had once been an inter-connected economy and legal system, stretching from Britain to North Africa, now fragmented into many independent local jurisdictions, often separated by areas of varying sizes that were not effectively controlled by any government and were unsafe for travel or trade.

As trade declined and the advantages of specialization disappeared for lack of markets, cities also declined, roads fell into disrepair, educational institutions declined or disappeared, and law and order broke down. It has been estimated that it was a thousand years after the collapse of the Roman Empire before the standard of living in Europe rose again to where it had been in Roman times. The presence or absence of effective government can be a major factor in economic development or economic retrogression.

Establishing law and order over a wide area not only enables producers to find large markets, and therefore take advantage of economies of scale in production, it also encourages people as well as products to move to where they are most in demand. When the British established control over vast areas of West Africa formerly controlled by a variety of tribes and rulers, this enabled the Ibos from southern Nigeria to migrate to northern Nigeria in safety, setting up enterprises and pursuing careers in places where they would never have dared to locate before, among alien peoples. In various other parts of the world as well, during the period of European imperialism, vast numbers of immigrants from China, India, and Lebanon migrated to lands under the protection of imperial law, establishing many enterprises and creating whole industries that helped bring these societies into the modern world.

Another of the functions of government that affects economic development is its role in providing property rights. But many Third World countries suffer from the fact that, while property rights may exist, they are not realistically available to vast numbers of people. In some of these countries, a majority of the economic activity takes place "off the books" in the underground economy. For example, most of the housing in Egypt and Peru has been built illegally, whether because of numerous restrictions and red tape that impede building housing legally, or because of costly legal processes which poor people are unable to afford. In Egypt, where 4.7 million homes have been built illegally, legally registering a lot on state-owned desert land requires 77 bureaucratic procedures at 31 agencies— and these procedures can take five years or more. In Haiti, it can take 19 years to acquire property rights. In some countries, bribes are necessary to get officials to expedite legal processes, and often the poor are unable to offer a sufficient bribe.

In these circumstances, much of a country's total wealth may not be covered by property rights. In Peru, the value of real estate that is outside the legal system— that is, not covered by property rights— has been estimated to be more than a dozen times larger in value than all the foreign investment that has ever been put into the country throughout its entire history. Even in a desperately poor country like Haiti, the value of illegal real estate holdings has been estimated as four times the value of all the legally operating businesses in the country, nine times the value of all assets owned by the government and more than 150 times the value of all foreign investments in Haiti in its entire history. For the Third World as a whole and the former Communist countries as well, the estimated value of all the real estate that is not legally owned is more than 90 times the value of all the foreign aid to all Third World countries over a period of three decades.

What this means economically is that these vast, but legally unrecognized, assets cannot be used the way property is used in industrially advanced countries to promote further economic expansion. Many Americans have created their own businesses— some of which later grew into giant corporations— by borrowing money to get started, using their homes, farms, or other real estate as collateral to get the initial capital required.[1] But an Egyptian or a Peruvian or other Third World individual who wants to do the same thing cannot get a loan on a home that is not legally recognized as property, because banks and other financial institutions avoid lending money on assets whose ownership is unknown or unclear, and which therefore cannot be taken over in case of default. Lenders must think beyond stage one, not only to determine what their prospects of being repaid are, but also what their recourse will be if they are not repaid. By making property rights difficult to establish, a country's legal system has, in effect, frozen its own assets and thereby blocked its own economic development.

Real estate is just one of many economic assets lacking property rights in Third World countries. In many of these countries, unauthorized buses and taxis provide most of the public transportation, and unauthorized vendors supply most of the food sold in the markets and on the streets. According to the British magazine ***The Economist***: "In a typical African country, barely one person in ten lives in a formal house"— that is, a house with property rights— "and only one worker in ten holds a formal job." While these economic activities can go on without property rights, such assets cannot be used as building blocks for creating new corporations or venture capital, as they are in countries like the United States or the industrial nations of Western Europe. Legally, it is the same as if these assets did not exist— which in turn means that their potential use for further economic development is thwarted.

Those who do not think beyond stage one often think of property rights as simply benefits to those individuals fortunate enough to own property. This ignores the role of property rights as a key link in a chain of events

[1] During its early struggling years, McDonald's was saved from financial ruin by real estate deals involving the land on which its franchised restaurants were located. But, without property rights on that land, McDonald's might well have disappeared into bankruptcy, long before it became an international corporate giant. See John F. Love, ***McDonald's: Behind the Arches***, revised edition, pp. 152-155.

which enable people without property to generate wealth for themselves and for the whole society.

One implication of this is that some Third World countries could gain the use of more capital by making property rights more accessible within their own borders than by a ten-fold increase in the amount of foreign aid they receive. Moreover, the increased capital would be in the hands of millions of ordinary people, while foreign aid goes into the hands of the political elite. In short, although property rights are often thought of as things that are important primarily to the affluent and the rich, these legal recognitions of existing assets may be especially needed by poor individuals in poor countries, if they do not wish to continue to be poor. Millions of Third World people have already demonstrated their ability to create, in the aggregate, vast amounts of wealth, even if their tangled legal systems have not yet demonstrated an ability to let that wealth readily become property that can be used for further expansion and development. As Peruvian economist Hernando de Soto concluded, after a worldwide study of this phenomenon:

> The lack of legal property thus explains why citizens in developing and former communist nations cannot make profitable contracts with strangers, cannot get credit, insurance, or utilities services: They have no property to lose. Because they have no property to lose, they are taken seriously as contracting parties only by their immediate family and neighbors. People with nothing to lose are trapped in the grubby basement of the precapitalist world.

Put differently, what property rights provide, in countries where these rights are readily accessible, is the ability of people to convert physical assets into financial assets, which in turn enables them to create additional wealth, whether individually or in combination with others. Property rights enable strangers to cooperate in economic ventures, some of which are large enough to be beyond the means of any particular individual, and so must be undertaken by corporations which can mobilize the wealth of thousands or even millions of people, who cannot possibly all know each other. Moreover, property rights provide incentives for people to monitor their own economic activities more closely than government officials can— and protect them from the over-reaching caprices or corruption of such officials. In short, property rights are an integral part of a price-coordinated economy, without which that economy cannot function as efficiently. This in turn means that its people in general— not just property owners— cannot prosper as much as if the economy did operate more efficiently.

GEOGRAPHY

While the influence of the geographical settings in which peoples evolve has been widely recognized to one degree or another, the nature of that influence can vary greatly. It is relatively easy to understand the economic implications of the vast deposits of petroleum in the Middle East, the iron ore deposits of Western Europe, the tin in Malaysia, or the gold in South Africa. What may not be so obvious, but of equal or greater importance, is the crucial role of navigable waterways for transporting these and other natural resources, and the products resulting from them, to different regions of the Earth— creating wider cultural interactions in the process.

It is not simply that some people may be economically more fortunate because of the geographical setting in which they happen to live at a given time. More fundamentally, they themselves can become enduringly different people, partly as a result of their broader cultural contacts and the expanded universe of human experience on which they can draw. For example, when British settlers first confronted the Iroquois on the east coast of North America in centuries past, there was a clash, not simply between the culture developed within the British isles versus the culture developed within the regions controlled by the Iroquois. There was a clash between cultural universes of very different sizes. The British were able to cross the Atlantic, in the first place, only by using trigonometry developed in Egypt, the compass invented in China, utilizing knowledge of astronomy developed in the Middle East, making calculations with numbers created in India, and drawing on other knowledge written in letters created by the Romans. Once ashore, the British had the advantage of weapons using gunpowder, which originated in Asia, and horses whose military uses had been developed in Central Asia and the Middle East, but which did not exist in the Western Hemisphere before the European invasion.

Meanwhile, the Iroquois were geographically cut off from the civilizations of the Aztecs and the Incas, and had no way of knowing of their existence, much less drawing upon their economic, cultural, and military developments. Moreover, two vast oceans cut off the entire Western Hemisphere from developments in the rest of the world. The peoples of the Western Hemisphere were not as isolated as the people living in the Canary Islands or the Australian aborigines, since they had a certain amount of interaction among regions of their hemisphere, but their range of cultural access was nowhere near as great as that of people living on the vast Eurasian land mass, where the majority of the human race has lived throughout recorded history.

Navigable Waterways

Access to the outside world is facilitated by navigable waterways— and access to these waterways is radically different in different parts of the world. Although Africa is more than twice the size of Europe, its coastline is shorter than the European coastline. That is because the coastline of Europe twists and turns innumerable times, creating harbors where ships can anchor, protected from the rough waters of the open sea, while the African coastline is much smoother and has far fewer harbors. The enormous importance of rivers and harbors to economic and cultural development is indicated by the fact that nearly all the world's great cities developed on rivers or harbors, at least during the millennia before railroads and automobiles lowered the cost of land transport.

The fact that so many cities around the world arose on navigable waterways reflects in part vast differences in costs between transporting goods by water and transporting them by land. For example, in mid-nineteenth century America, before the transcontinental railroad was built, San Francisco could be reached both faster and cheaper from a port in China than it could be reached over land from the banks of the Missouri.

In the city of Tiflis in the Caucasus, it was cheaper to import kerosene from America, across 8,000 miles of water, than to get it over land from Baku, less than 400 miles away. Similarly huge disparities between land transport and water transport costs have been common in Africa, in Japan, and in England before the railroad era. In the Ottoman Empire, the estimated cost of shipping wheat just 100 kilometers exceeded the value of the wheat itself.

Even after the development of roads and of motorized transport, trains, and planes, water transport has generally remained much cheaper than land transport. For example, in the United States transporting oil by ship costs about one-fourth of the cost of transporting it by pipeline, less than 5 percent of the cost of transporting it by railroad and little more than one percent of the cost of shipping it by truck.

The vast amounts of food and other products needed continuously to supply a city's population, and the vast amounts of raw material and finished merchandise to be moved in and out of a city to earn the money to pay for that population's consumption, have all been carried more cheaply by water. It is therefore hardly surprising that so many cities are on rivers— London on the Thames, Cairo on the Nile, Paris on the Seine, New York on the Hudson. Many other cities like Singapore, Sydney, and Stockholm are on harbors and still others are on huge lakes like Chicago or on inland seas like Odessa or Sevastopol. Nor should it be surprising that Western Europe, heavily criss-crossed by rivers, is one of the most densely urbanized regions of the world, while tropical Africa— where navigable waterways are much more scarce— has long remained one of the least urbanized regions in the world.

The relatively few cities that have arisen independently of waterways have usually had other transportation advantages. In the great desert regions, for example, the distances between sources of drinking water— compared to the distance that a camel can travel without water— determine which routes across the trackless sands or dry steppes are feasible and which are not. In turn, these routes and their traffic determine which of the oases have enough economic activity passing through them to become permanent settlements. Settlements at the crossroads of several routes through the desert— Samarkand in Central Asia, for example — could grow to be large cities, much as river and harbor ports grew into urban centers in other parts of the world. The development of railroads and, later, automobiles and trucks, brought a revolution in land transport that made water transport unnecessary to create major cities, which could now be based on railroad junctions (Atlanta[2]) or based on the automobile (Los Angeles).

The railroad revolution was particularly important in sub-Saharan Africa, which was largely lacking in both waterways and draft animals— the latter being victims of disease borne by the tsetse fly. Prior to the building of railroads by European colonial powers, Africans often carried freight on their heads. While this made for colorful caravans of porters, it was also a very expensive form of transport. In British West Africa, for example, it took 37 men to carry a ton of cocoa for a day's journey. A thousand times as much could be carried ten times as far by train, using half a dozen men. Nor was Africa unique in being very profoundly affected by the modern transportation revolution:

> In 1830 it cost more than thirty dollars to move a ton of cargo three hundred miles overland— from central Pennsylvania to New York, Berlin to Bonn, or Lyons to Paris— and another ten dollars to ship it across the Atlantic. This was a prohibitive expense for such heavy goods as wheat. . . By 1900 the railroad had reduced the cost of land transportation by more than four-fifths, the steamship by more than two-thirds. To ship a ton of cargo the same three hundred miles overland now cost five dollars instead of thirty, across the Atlantic three dollars instead of ten.

Despite the importance of these modern developments, for most of history in most of the world, waterways have been crucial. During the European industrialization of the nineteenth century, every one of the early industrial regions had the benefit of navigable waterways. Where that advantage was lacking— as in parts of Eastern Europe and Mediterranean Europe, and especially in the Balkans— economic development lagged far behind that in such countries as Britain, France, and Germany. The standard of living in the geographically less favored parts of Europe was

[2] An old Southern expression says: "Whether you are going to Heaven or Hell, you have to change in Atlanta."

much more like the standards of living in non-European countries than like those in the more advanced parts of the continent. The fossil fuels which were largely lacking in southern Europe, for example, often could not be brought into the interior by water— the only economically feasible way of delivering them.

Although urban growth was dramatic in much of nineteenth century Europe, few towns developed in the Balkans. As roads and railroads developed and were improved in the more developed parts of Europe, they remained virtually unknown in the Balkans, so that people living in Balkan villages were isolated from people in other villages less than 20 miles away. The Balkan mountains fractured the peninsula culturally as well as isolating it economically, thereby contributing to the tribalistic divisions and lethal hatreds which have long marked the region. Although the Balkans were rich in natural harbors, there were few rivers to connect these harbors to the hinterlands, which were often cut off by mountains. While much of nineteenth century Europe not only grew economically but became interconnected with other nations within the continent and overseas, much of Eastern and Southeastern Europe lived close to "self-sufficiency"— which is to say, it was isolated, poor, and backward.

To have a large economic or cultural universe, it is not enough that there be waterways. How ***navigable*** those waterways are is crucial. Africa has the Nile and other great rivers, but these other rivers have serious impediments to navigation, and have seldom produced either cities or civilizations comparable to those of Egypt. Because most of sub-Saharan Africa is more than a thousand feet above sea level, its rivers must come down from that altitude on their way to the sea. The resulting rapids, cascades, and waterfalls prevent even the greatest of sub-Saharan rivers from providing access to and from the sea, in the way that the Hudson, the Yangtze, the Danube, or other great commercial waterways of the world can. Although Africa's Zaire River carries more water than any of these three other rivers just mentioned, its waterfalls alone are enough to preclude it from having the same significance as an artery of trade or as a site for cities. Even African rivers that are navigable may be navigable for some limited distances between cascades or waterfalls, or by boats of limited size, or for some limited times during the rainy seasons. However, the dry season often severely reduces or eliminates their navigability.

Nor is Africa's geographic situation any better as regards harbors. Not only does the smooth African coastline provide few harbors, its coastal waters are often too shallow for large, ocean-going ships to approach closely to the land. The net result was that, even during centuries when much of the international trade of the world went around Africa on its way between Europe and Asia, relatively seldom did these ships attempt to stop and trade with Africans. They could stop in those relatively few places where there were harbors or they could anchor offshore and have cargo loaded onto smaller craft that were able to make their way to land through the shallow coastal waters. Still, the higher costs of taking much longer to unload a given amount of cargo meant that there were severe constraints against international trade with even the coastal peoples of Africa, much less those in the vast interior hinterlands or at higher elevations. Moreover, the coastal plains of Africa average only 20 miles in width, often with steep escarpments behind them.

In short, with harbors as with rivers, Africa seldom had the geographic essentials for developing cities. Where cities or large-scale political units did develop in tropical Africa, it was typically where these geographical hindrances were not as great.

Disparities between the costs of land transport and water transport translate into similar disparities in the reach of trade and in the range of goods which are feasible to trade by nations and peoples with and without navigable waterways. Huge transportation costs shrink the economic universe, severely limiting how far given goods can be carried, and severely limiting which goods have sufficient value condensed into a small size and weight (gold or diamonds, for example) to be feasible to transport over land for substantial distances. These same high transportation costs shrink the cultural universe as well, handicapping not only economic development but, more importantly, the development of the people themselves, who lack access to as wide a range of other people's knowledge, skills, and technologies as do people who are situated in port cities and other cultural crossroads.

The significance of particular geographic features— mountains, rivers, climate, soil, etc.— is even greater when these features are viewed in combination. For example, the effect of rainfall on agriculture depends not only on how much rainfall there is but also on the ability of the soil to hold it. Thus a modest amount of rainfall may be sufficient for a flourishing agriculture on the absorbent loess soils of northern China, while rain falling on the limestone soils of the Balkans may drain off rapidly underground. Similarly, the economic value of navigable waterways depends on the lands adjacent to them. Navigable rivers which go through land without the resources for either industry or agriculture— the Amazon for example— are of little economic value,[3] even though navigable waterways in general have been crucial to the economic and cultural development of other regions more fully endowed with other resources.

In Russia as well, waterways isolated from the major natural resources of the country, as well as from each other, cannot match the economic role of rivers which flow into one another and then into the sea, after passing through agriculturally or industrially productive regions, as in Western Europe. The Volga is Russia's premier river for shipping, even though there are other Russian rivers which have more than twice as much water flow, because the Volga passes through areas containing most of the resources and people of the country. Larger rivers in Siberia, which drain northward into the Arctic Ocean— when they are not frozen and cannot flow at all— have no such economic significance as the Volga.

Similarly, harbors that are not as deep, not as wide, nor as well-sheltered as other harbors, may nevertheless become busy ports if they represent the only outlets for productive regions in the vicinity, as has been the case of

---

[3] The Amazon, for example, is by far the world's greatest river but the soils in its region have been characterized as "startlingly poor" and it has led to no great cities being established along its banks. See Jonathan B. Tourtellot, "The Amazon: Sailing a Jungle Sea," ***Great Rivers of the World***, edited by Margaret Sedeen (Washington: National Geographic Society, 1984), p. 302.

Genoa in northwestern Italy or Mombasa in East Africa. Similarly, the port of Dubrovnik on the Dalmatian coast, strategically located for the international trade routes of the Middle Ages, flourished despite a harbor that was not particularly impressive in itself. While the historic role of London as a world port has depended on the Thames, this river is also not especially impressive in itself, but has simply provided an outlet for impressive industrial and commercial facilities nearby.

The presence or absence of draft animals can facilitate or limit the benefits of navigable waterways. Where large, ocean-going ships unloaded vast cargoes in port cities in centuries past, horses or oxen were crucial to the economical land transportation of those cargoes that needed to be dispersed to markets in those cities and in their hinterlands. In North Africa, camels could be used. But none of these draft animals existed in the Western Hemisphere before Europeans arrived, so there was no such economic payoff to building large ocean-going ships, and none were developed. This in turn limited the cultural universes of the indigenous Western Hemisphere peoples, even in places where there were rivers and harbors comparable to those in Europe. Much of sub-Saharan Africa lacked both the navigable waterways and the draft animals, and so had even smaller cultural universes.

Sometimes a variety of favorable geographical features exist in combination within a given region, as in northwestern Europe, and sometimes virtually all are lacking, as in much of tropical Africa, while still other parts of the world have some of these favorable features but not others. The consequences include not only large variations in economic wellbeing but, more fundamentally, large variations in the skills and experience— the human capital— of the people themselves. Given the enormous range of combinations of geographical features, the peoples from different regions of the earth have had highly disparate opportunities to develop particular skills and economic experience or to acquire them from others. International migrations then put these peoples with disparate skills, aptitudes, and outlooks in proximity to one another and in competition with one another in other lands, often producing very different economic and social outcomes.

Among the more geographically fortunate parts of the world, in terms of having the natural resources needed for the development of a modern industrial economy, as well as the navigable waterways to carry both these resources and the products resulting from them, have been Northern and Western Europe. Iron ore and coal deposits, the key ingredients of steel manufacturing and the heavy industry dependent on it, are concentrated in the Ruhr valley, in Wales, and in the region so bitterly fought over by France and Germany, Alsace-Lorraine. In addition to the broad coastal plains which have provided the peoples of Western Europe with much prime agricultural land and with navigable rivers, Europe in general has many peninsulas, islands, and numerous harbors that give the continent excellent access to the sea— and therefore to the commerce and cultures of the world.

Climate

Favorable climate is also a factor. The Western European climate is greatly benefitted by the flow of the Gulf Stream, cutting through the North Atlantic, just as other streams flow through land. This stream of warm water, originating in the Gulf of Mexico, warms Western Europe to give it milder winters than places at similar latitudes in the Western Hemisphere or in Asia. London, for example, is farther north than any place in the 48 contiguous United States, yet it has milder winters than New York City, much less cities in Minnesota or Wisconsin.

Eastern, Central, and Mediterranean Europe do not share all these advantages. The Gulf Stream's influence on the climate of European nations on the Atlantic coast becomes progressively less in the more distant central and eastern portions of the continent, where rivers are frozen for more days of the year and where winters are longer and more bitterly cold. The natural resources required for modern industry are also less abundant and, in many places, virtually non-existent in Central and Eastern Europe. The broad coastal plains of Northern Europe have no counterparts in the Balkans, where hills and mountains come down close to the sea and the coastal harbors often have no navigable rivers to link them to the hinterlands. Spain has likewise been lacking in navigable rivers and Sicily lacking in both rivers and rainfall.

These sharp differences in geographical advantages have been reflected not only in great disparities in wealth among the different regions of Europe, but also in similarly large differences in skills, industrial experience, and whole ways of life among the peoples of these regions. Thus, when the peoples of the Mediterranean migrated to the United States or to Australia, for example, they did not bring with them the industrial skills or the whole modern way of life found among German or English immigrants. What they did bring with them was a frugality born of centuries of struggle for survival in the less productive lands and waters of the Mediterranean, and a power of endurance and persistence born of the same circumstances. The ability of Italian immigrants to endure poor and cramped living conditions and to save out of very low wages, which caused comment among those around them, whether in other European countries or in the Western Hemisphere or Australia, had both geographical and historical roots. Similar characteristics have marked various other Mediterranean peoples, but the Italians are a particularly revealing example, because they include not only the Mediterranean people of the south but also people from the industrial world of the Po River valley in the north, whose geographical, economic, and cultural characteristics are much more similar to those found among Northern and Western Europeans. Northern and southern Italians have long differed economically and socially, not only in Italy, but also in Australia, the United States, and Argentina.

The enduring consequences of the different skills and experiences possessed by people from different parts of Europe can be seen in the fact that the average income of immigrants from Southern and Eastern Europe to the United States in the early twentieth century was equal to what was earned by the bottom 15 percent among immigrants from England, Scotland, Holland, or Norway. Illiteracy was higher among immigrants from Southern and Eastern Europe. In school, their children tended to lag behind the children of either native-born Americans or the children of immigrants from Northern and Western Europe, while their I.Q. scores were often very similar to those of American blacks, and were sometimes lower.

Nor was all this peculiar to American society. In pre-World War II Australia, immigrants from southern Italy, Dalmatia, Macedonia, and the Greek countryside were typically illiterate and spoke primarily their local dialects, rather than the official languages of their respective home countries. More than three quarters of these Southern European immigrants to Australia were from the rugged hills or mountains, the steep coastlines or islands of the region, rather than from the urban areas or plains. Although these remote areas were eventually drawn into the modern world, the skills of their peoples continued to lag behind the skills of peoples in other parts of Europe that were more industrially advanced and this was reflected in their earnings in Australia, as in the United States. As late as the 1970s, the median earnings of immigrants to Australia from Greece, Italy, or Yugoslavia fell below the earnings of immigrants from West Germany or from English-speaking countries. Southern Europeans in Australia remained under-represented in professional and technical occupations, and from nearly half among the Italian immigrants to an absolute majority among the Greek and Yugoslavian immigrants were unskilled laborers. These patterns were not simply a result of such subjective factors as others' stereotypes, perceptions, or racism, but in fact reflected historical realities, however much additional penumbra of prejudice may have developed around those realities, or remained resistant to change after the realities themselves began to change with the assimilation and rising skill levels of the newcomers.

In addition to the effect of climate on the flow of water— freezing rivers in Russia during the winter and the drying up of rivers in tropical Africa after the rainy season is over— it has long had a major direct effect on agriculture. Moreover, agriculture has been the place where the vast majority of the peoples of the world have worked throughout almost all of history. Even countries that are heavily industrial and commercial today were primarily agricultural until recent centuries. In the United States, for example, it was 1920 before more than half the American population lived in cities.

Temperature and rainfall determine what crops can be grown where. In extreme cases, they determine that no crops at all can be grown, as in deserts and in places where the land is frozen year around, such as in parts of Siberia. In places where moisture-laden air blows across a mountain range, it is not uncommon for the rainfall on the side where the moisture originates to be several times as great as in the "rain shadow" on the other side of the mountains, where the air goes after it has lost most of its moisture while rising over the crests. On some western slopes of southern Italy's Apennine Mountains, for example, the annual rainfall reaches 2,000 millimeters while parts of the eastern slopes get as little as 300-500 millimeters. Similarly, in the American Pacific Northwest, precipitation on parts of the west side of the Cascade Mountains averages up to ten times as much as on parts of the Columbia Plateau to the east. Obviously the agricultural possibilities presented to the people living on one side of the mountain range differ greatly from those presented to people living on the other side. They must grow different crops and acquire different skills and experiences while doing so.

Climate also affects the diffusion of knowledge and experience. Because climate tends to vary less from east to west than it does from north to south, knowledge of particular crops and animals that flourish in a particular climate likewise spread more readily from east to west than from north to south. Thus the cultivation of rice spread from China all the way across the Eurasian land mass into Europe, while the cultivation of bananas could not spread from Central America into Canada, even though that is a shorter distance, because the climate differs so much between Central America and Canada. The same goes for the domestication or hunting of animals peculiar to a particular climate. The knowledge of such things likewise spreads more readily from east to west, than it does from north to south. Nor could knowledge of the crops, flora and fauna in the temperate zone of South America diffuse smoothly to the temperate zone of North America, because many of the techniques and practices could not spread through the vast tropical regions between these two temperate zones. Very different plants and animals existed in the tropics, so that much of the knowledge and many of the techniques from the temperate zones could not be applied in the tropics, and therefore could not be transmitted through the tropics to temperate zones on the other side.

Temperature is, of course, not the only aspect of climate. Rainfall is another. Knowledge and techniques of agriculture that apply in a wet climate may not all be usable in arid regions. Therefore differences in rainfall patterns can produce cultural isolation as regards agricultural techniques, just as natural barriers like mountains or deserts can produce cultural isolation in general. Those isolated climatically have likewise been unable to draw upon the knowledge and experience of peoples in similar climates elsewhere, when there have been hundreds or thousands of miles of very different climate patterns in between.

During the many centuries when ships were moved on the seas by the power of the wind in their sails, knowledge of particular wind patterns and ocean currents in particular regions of the world was crucial to the ability to carry on trade among different societies. Much of this knowledge was as localized as knowledge of the plants and animals peculiar to particular geographic settings. Knowledge of sailing in general was not enough when trying to sail off the west coast of Africa, for example, in places where it was easy for Europeans to use the wind and currents in that region to get in but hard to use them to get back out again. Conversely, sailors familiar with the monsoon winds of Asia could sail westward as far as Africa during the times of the year when those winds were blowing in that direction, and then return home later, after the time came for the winds to shift direction and begin blowing eastward.

Like other special knowledge of local or regional conditions, knowledge of wind patterns and ocean currents, and the techniques developed to deal with these localized patterns, tended to be confined to those living in the area. Put differently, various regions tended to develop different knowledge and techniques. Thus, for example, those countries which became leading seafaring nations and naval powers in the Mediterranean during the Middle Ages were not able to play the same role in the later era of trade and warfare in the Atlantic, where the waters were much rougher, and the wind and weather conditions more severe. Those nations which had been the leading naval powers in Europe in the earlier era, when the Mediterranean was the principal avenue of waterborne commerce and naval warfare, were unable to match the upstart Atlantic naval powers when the central theater of trade and warfare shifted to the Atlantic after the Europeans discovered the Western Hemisphere.

POPULATION

Some of the worst poverty in the world today can be found in thinly-populated regions like sub-Saharan Africa. Meanwhile, population density is several times higher in much more prosperous Japan. There are also densely populated poor countries, such as Bangladesh, but Singapore is even more densely populated and has a far higher standard of living. The United States and Tanzania have very similar population densities, but radically different economic levels. Clearly, there are other factors that have much more to do with prosperity than population does. Indeed, a case can be made for many regions of the world that it is precisely the thinly spread population which makes it so expensive to provide electricity, sewage lines, and medical care that many of these people are often without such things.

In some ultimate sense, there must of course be a limit to the earth's capacity to sustain human life. But there are ultimate limits to many things— perhaps all things— and yet that provides little or no practical guidance as to how close we are to those limits or what the consequences are of various alternatives today. There are ultimate limits to how fast a given automobile will go, and yet we may drive it for years without ever reaching even half of that ultimate speed, because there are much narrower limits to how fast we can drive safely through city streets or even on highways. As a young man, John Stuart Mill brooded over the fact that there was an ultimate limit to the amount of music that could be produced by using the eight notes of the musical scale. But, at that time, Brahms and Tchaikovsky had not yet been born nor jazz yet conceived, and rock music was more than a century away. Ultimate limits alone tell us virtually nothing useful about whether there is or is not a practical problem.

If we were in fact approaching those ultimate limits, whether in food supply, natural resources, or other necessities of life, their rising prices would not only inform us, but force us to change course, without public exhortations or politically-imposed limitations. Indeed, many political solutions are as inconsistent as they are counterproductive. For example, there are restrictions on the use of water by the general public, imposed by the same political authorities who supply water below cost to farmers. These farmers consequently grow crops requiring huge amounts of water from costly government irrigation projects in the California desert, instead of leaving such crops to be grown in the rainy regions of the world, where ample water is supplied free from the clouds. Although the water is costly to the government— which is to say, the taxpayers— it is cheap to the farmers, and is used as if it were abundant.

Food shortages and famines have sometimes been used as evidence that population has outgrown the food supply. But hunger and starvation in modern times have almost always reflected local problems such as crop failures in a given area, combined with difficulties in getting enough food into the stricken region fast enough to prevent death from either malnutrition or diseases to which the people have been made vulnerable by malnutrition.

In some very poor countries, the roads and other infrastructure are not sufficiently developed to carry vast amounts of food to widely scattered people with the urgency that is needed. All too often, in both poor and more affluent countries, the famines have resulted from human error or malice or military operations that disrupt food distribution systems. During the First World War, for example, the Allied naval blockade prevented food from reaching many in central Europe:

> Germans were forced to eat their dogs and cats (the latter came to be known as "roof rabbits") as well as bread made from potato peels and sawdust. Civilian deaths by starvation climbed to hundreds of thousands per year.

None of this had anything to do with overpopulation. Neither did the man-made famine in the Ukraine in the 1930s, which took millions of lives, and which Josef Stalin used to break the back of resistance to his regime.

"Overpopulation" theories do not stand up well to empirical scrutiny. But they do not have to. They have in fact remained popular for more than two centuries, in the face of large and growing evidence of their falsity. Even within Malthus' own lifetime, his prediction that growing numbers of people tended to cause their standard of living to be reduced was falsified by empirical evidence of rising population and rising living standards occurring simultaneously. That has continued to be the general pattern ever since. Wars, natural disasters, and other local disruptions of food supplies have caused famines from time to time in various places around the world, though less so than in centuries past, when the world's population was a fraction of what it is today. Indeed, obesity and a search for export markets for agricultural surpluses are problems for a growing number of countries today.

Even in a poverty-stricken country like India, the number of people has been nowhere close to what the land could support. A twentieth century study found:

> Half the population of India lives on less than a quarter of the total available land, and one-third is concentrated on less than 6 percent of the land. At the other extreme, vast areas continue to be almost uninhabited.

In centuries past, similar conditions were found in Eastern Europe, where Western observers often commented on the emptiness of the land and its fertility, even though the people of Eastern Europe were typically much poorer than the people of Western Europe, where population densities were greater. These circumstances led many Eastern European rulers to recruit German farmers to come settle in their domains and even to allow them to live under German law in the places where they settled. Clearly the poverty of Eastern Europe was not due to "overpopulation."

Photographs of crowded cities in Third World countries may create the impression that there is not enough room for the populations of these countries and that this somehow accounts for their poverty. However, crowding is what cities are all about, whether in poor countries or in rich countries. Park Avenue has more people per square mile than in many Third World villages or urban slums. Crowding lowers the cost per person of supplying everything from electricity to running water to sewage lines, movie theaters and ambulance services. That is why there have been crowded cities in countries with vast amounts of open space, whether in twentieth century India or nineteenth century America.

FOREIGN INVESTMENT

Thus far we have been considering factors which promote or retard the economic development of a given country or region from within that country or region. Much economic development, however, has been created in particular places and times by foreigners investing their money, technology or skills. This has been done in a variety of ways, through private investors, financial institutions or business enterprises, and the recipient countries have ranged from sovereign states to colonies of imperial powers.

Private Investment

Although Britain led the world into the age of the industrial revolution, in earlier centuries Britain was one of the more technologically backward nations of Western Europe. An influx of immigrants, often refugees from religious or other persecutions but sometimes just immigrants seeking greater freedom or economic opportunity, brought to the British Isles valuable skills in industry, commerce, or finance.

These included Huguenots who created a watch industry that had never existed in Britain before, Germans who built the first pianos in Britain, and Lombards and Jews who at one time were the principal groups running London's financial institutions. The reliability and impartiality of British law also attracted investments from continental Europe. All of this developed not only the British economy but also the British people, who eventually became by the nineteenth century the leading industrial, commercial, and financial people in the world. Now Britain was exporting capital, on net balance, instead of importing it. By the end of the nineteenth century and the early years of the twentieth half of all international investments in the world came from London. Britain now exported more than half its capital in the years immediately before the First World War.

The United States was likewise transformed from a predominantly agricultural nation to an industrial power with the aid of skills, talents, and technologies brought to the country by massive inflows of immigrants from Europe, and with vast amounts of foreign investments which helped build such infrastructure as canals and railroads in the nineteenth century. Moreover, the United States continued to be the world's leading recipient of foreign investment on into the twenty-first century. Nor was the United States unique in being developed with the help of overseas investors. On the eve of the First World War, foreigners owned one-fifth of the Australian economy and one-half of the economy of Argentina.

None of this meant that these nations were passively dependent on foreigners. The internal circumstances of these nations were crucial in determining whether foreign investment poured in. At a minimum, foreign investors had to be able to rely on having their investments remain their private property, rather than being subject to confiscation or "nationalization" as it is phrased politically. The local economy also had to have whatever was needed to complement the investors' capital, whether that was natural resources, suitable labor, technology or infrastructure. Differences among nations in all these respects have led to highly disparate amounts of foreign investments coming into different countries.

How the native-born population responded to the influx of foreign-born people with skills that they lacked was also a crucial factor. Nineteenth century Japanese, for example, not only welcomed but recruited these foreigners with the skills and experience to industrialize Japan, while they sent many of their own young people to more industrially advanced countries as students to acquire such skills themselves. But twentieth century Malays remained largely spectators as Europeans, Chinese, and people from India created a modern industrial and commercial economy in colonial Malaya and then in an independent Malaysia. Indeed, Malays resented all three and, after independence, greatly restricted the economic activities and educational opportunities of the Chinese and Indian minorities. Among nations lagging in economic development, what happened in nineteenth century Japan was the exception and what happened with the Malays has been the rule. Accordingly, the dramatic rise of Japan from a poor and backward nation in the nineteenth century to one of the most advanced and prosperous nations in the world during the twentieth century has likewise been the exception rather than the rule.

In short, it has not been simply a lack of financial or human capital which has retarded the economic development of many poorer countries but the active suppression of both. Sometimes this has been simply a political expression of popular resentments of foreigners or domestic minorities visibly more prosperous and more industrially or commercially advanced than the indigenous people. This pattern has been widespread, from the resentments of the Indians and Pakistanis by indigenous populations in East Africa to the resentments of the Lebanese in West Africa, the British in Argentina, the Jews in Eastern Europe, the Armenians in the Ottoman Empire, the Chinese throughout Southeast Asia, and many indigenous minorities such as the Marwaris in India's state of Assam and the Ibos in northern Nigeria.

Sometimes the resistance to foreign capital has been ideological, based on Marxist-Leninist theories of international exploitation, "dependency" theory in Latin America, or a more amorphous belief that foreigners could prosper only at the expense of the local population. The magnitude of the self-inflicted economic losses from rejection and suppression of foreign financial and human capital can be estimated from the dramatic increases in economic development in both China and India after such restrictive policies were eased in both countries toward the end of the twentieth century. Economic growth rates rose rapidly in China and India after such restrictions were greatly reduced, and tens of millions of people in both countries rose out of poverty.

Foreign Aid

Another source of foreign financial and human capital— transfers of wealth to governments in poorer countries from governments in more prosperous countries or from international agencies— does not have nearly as good a track record. While these kinds of transfers have been called "foreign aid," it is an open question whether or how much this process has in fact aided poorer countries to rise out of their poverty. Moreover, the amount of private capital going to Third World nations is many times the amount of foreign aid, even though most private capital goes to prosperous nations rather than poor nations. Indeed, the amount of remittances from Third World citizens living abroad exceeds all the foreign aid in the world.

Not only are there countries where massive amounts of foreign aid have failed to increase the output per capita, on which a rising standard of living depends, South Korea is a country whose rise from abysmal poverty to one of the more prosperous nations in the world began right after the United States drastically ***reduced*** foreign aid. As of 1960, South Korea's real per capita income was below that of Haiti, which has long been one of the most poverty-stricken nations on earth. Massive American aid during the 1950s— amounting to 10 percent of South Korea's total output— failed to change that. The change came after that aid began to disappear:

> But aid peaked in 1957, and by the early 1960s Korea could no longer count on it to sustain what was a relatively low rate of investment. Nevertheless, by the mid-1960s, Korea had turned itself around and achieved an unprecedented near-double-digit growth rate. And by the mid-1980s, it had acquired the status of an upper-middle-income country.

All of this was contrary to prevailing opinions among "experts" on development. As of 1951, the "consensus view in the United States was that whereas the East Asian countries, such as the Republic of Korea, were likely to turn into basket cases, India and Africa would quickly grow out of poverty." This view "was shared by the scholarly community, which flocked to study India as the model of economic development." The passage of time revealed how painfully, and even tragically, mistaken this view of the prospects of India and Africa was, as India grew very slowly and many sub-

Saharan African nations were poorer, decades after independence, than they had been during the colonial era. Not only were the predictions of development "experts" wrong as regards which countries were more likely to grow out of poverty, more fundamentally they were mistaken as to the causes and cures of Third World poverty.

If subjugation to imperialist and industrialized nations was the cause of Third World poverty, as was widely assumed, then obviously the achievement of independence should have led to rising standards of living and rising economic growth rates in the formerly subjugated nations in Africa and Asia. If economic dependence on foreign investors, as in much of Latin America, was the reason for the countries in that region lagging behind the rest of the Western world economically, then policies to keep out foreign investors and depend on internal development were the obvious remedies— and the remedies adopted both in much of Latin American and initially in South Korea. In both places, there were policies restricting foreign trade and foreign investment, and policies aimed at producing domestically the things that had formerly been imported. It took years in South Korea, and decades in Latin America, for the repeated failures of these policies to eventually bring about a change in policies.

Economic growth rose in both places when they opened their economies to the world market, as well as freeing their economies from many domestic regulations. India and China likewise had large increases in their economic growth rates after their markets were freed from many government restrictions that had previously applied both domestically and internationally.

SUMMARY AND IMPLICATIONS

Many of the most popular explanations of vast differences in economic development among nations are also among the most readily refutable. "Overpopulation" theories can seldom survive the process of definition, much less the test of empirical evidence. Neither do most "exploitation" theories. It might seem that natural resources would be a major factor in a country's prosperity or poverty but there are too many high-income countries with meager natural resources— Switzerland and Japan, for example— and too many low-income countries with rich resources, such as Chile and South Africa. Technology can be important but much technology from advanced industrial nations has been transferred to sub-Saharan Africa and failed to become economically viable without the complementary factors of skills and experience, or even attention to maintenance.

In another sense, however, less economically developed nations have been able to "leap-frog" over some stages of development which more economically advanced nations went through to reach their current levels of technology. For example, most modern industrialized nations went through a stage when they had to invest vast sums of wealth in the creation of telephone networks of wires and conduits— a cost beyond the means of poor, thinly populated countries such as those in sub-Saharan Africa, where the cost per person would be prohibitive. However, the development of cellular telephones in the late twentieth century enabled many Africans to have phone service without such massive investments in infrastructure. In 2008, *The Economist* magazine reported, "in Africa, people who live in mud huts use mobile phones to pay bills or to check fish prices and find the best market for their catch."

The ultimate economic factor is the human factor. Even such a major factor as geography exerts much, if not most, of its effects through its expanding or restricting the cultural universe from which given peoples can draw on other peoples, near and far. As already noted, when Europeans first crossed the Atlantic to settle in the Western Hemisphere, they were able to find their way where only water could be seen from horizon to horizon by using astronomy, compasses and a numbering system all first developed outside of Europe. People cut off from such sources of foreign knowledge by geographic barriers would have had a far more daunting task. People kept out of touch with most of the rest of the human race by geographic barriers would likewise find it difficult to match the progress of people able to draw on many cultures. Narrow, inbred cultures have often been impoverished cultures, and impoverished cultures have usually meant economically impoverished people.

The massive transplantations of people from one part of the world to another, made possible by the transportation revolutions of the past few centuries, have meant that people with a given culture often settle in a very different environment from that in which their culture evolved and among other peoples with very different cultures. The most dramatic examples may be the Europeans who settled the Western Hemisphere but there have at one time or other been more people from India living in Fiji than there were indigenous Fijians and in medieval times there were often more Germans than Slavs living in the cities of Slavic Eastern Europe, even though Slavs predominated in the surrounding countrysides.

Even cultures fortunate enough to be exposed to other cultures may be exposed to different cross-currents of cultures, depending on where a particular culture is located and what their own geographic setting and historic influences have created— as well as how receptive or resistant they are to outside cultures. Spain and the Western Hemisphere nations formed by the culture brought by Spanish conquerors have been different from Britain and the Western Hemisphere nations formed by the culture brought by British conquerors. Both political and military events have added their influence as history unfolded. In short, peoples and their cultures have differed greatly at a given time and these differences sometimes change over time.

As already noted, Argentina went from one of the richest nations on earth at the beginning of the twentieth century to a nation in dire economic crisis at the end. Yet, just a few years later, Argentina and much of the rest of Latin America had, through changed economic and political policies, begun to have a robust rate of economic growth, lifting millions of the poorest people out of poverty. One study found that, for Latin America as a whole, about 15 million households rose out of poverty between 2002 and 2006. Yet other nations, in Latin America and elsewhere, continued to stagnate or even to deteriorate economically. With nations, as with individuals, not all have had the same opportunities and not all have taken equal advantages of what opportunities they did have.

All the numerous and interacting factors behind economic development make it virtually impossible that different parts of the world would all have equal development, and therefore equal standards of living, at any given time. Yet the puzzlement, unease and dissatisfaction caused by seeing large economic disparities between societies have created demands for explanations— usually without creating an equal demand for years of study of the historical, geographic, and economic factors behind these disparities. Instead, there has been a demand for simple and emotionally satisfying explanations, especially melodramatic explanations with ideological overtones, such as "exploitation" theories. "Overpopulation" is also a simple explanation that lends itself to melodrama and to solutions favored by those inclined toward controlling other people's lives.

Exploitation theories explain the wealth of some by the poverty of others, whether comparing nations or classes within a given nation. Sadly, however, many of those who are said to be exploited have had very little to exploit and many of those described as "dispossessed" have never possessed very much in the first place. Moreover, the actual behavior of those described as exploiters often shows them shunning those that they are said to exploit, in favor of dealing with more prosperous people, from whom they expect to earn more money. Thus, most American international trade and investment goes to high-income nations like those in Western Europe or the more prosperous regions of Asia, such as Japan or Singapore, with only a minute fraction of that trade or investment going to Africa or to the more poverty stricken regions of Asia or the Middle East. Conversely, the United States is itself the largest recipient of investments by foreigners. Similarly, within the United States, capitalists are far more anxious to establish businesses in middle class or wealthy communities, rather than businesses in blighted ghettos or on poverty-stricken Indian reservations.

At particular times and places in history, conquerors have indeed extracted wealth from the conquered peoples, but the real question is: How much of today's economic differences between nations and peoples does that explain? Spain, for example, extracted vast amounts of gold and silver from its conquered lands and peoples in the Western Hemisphere, at great economic and human costs to those who were subjugated. But much of this wealth was quickly spent, buying imported goods from other countries, rather than developing Spain itself, which has remained one of the poorer nations in Western Europe. Meanwhile, Germany— lacking colonies of any serious economic consequence for the German economy, for most of its history— became one of the most prosperous nations in Europe. Switzerland and Sweden have had no colonies at all and yet have been among the most prosperous countries in Europe and the world.

In Asia, Japan embarked on an ambitious campaign of conquest in the twentieth century and its behavior toward its conquered fellow Asians was as brutal and ruthless as that of Spain toward those whom it had subjugated in the Western Hemisphere. Moreover, Japan used its own lack of natural resources as a justification for its actions. Yet, after Japan's defeat in World War II led to the loss of all its colonies and conquered lands, the Japanese economy not only recovered from the devastations of war, it rose to new heights. The natural resources that it lacked could be bought in international markets for less than the cost of conquering other countries and maintaining armies there to keep them subjugated.

Exploitation theories are sometimes based on assumptions of ignorance and naivete on the part of some groups, such as Third World peoples, as well as wily and unscrupulous outsiders who are able to make high profits from paying the indigenous people less than their goods are really worth in the world market. Obviously, everyone is ignorant of things they have not encountered before and those living in isolated parts of the world place whatever value they do on new products, based in part on their novelty. But the question is: How long can such a situation last? More specifically, can it last long enough to explain international differences in income and wealth that go on for centuries? An observer writing about West Africa, early in the twentieth century, reported that the ability of foreign traders to obtain much gold and ivory in that region for a little inexpensive colored cloth and cheap knives had already been ended by the growth of competition, and that consequently "the margin of profit was diminished." This is what anyone should have expected on the basis of elementary economic principles. Dated anecdotes from the earlier period might continue to be repeated for many years afterward, but the only current exploitation they demonstrate is exploitation of the gullibility of those who are led to believe that this represents a serious explanation of international economic differences.

Exploitation theories are part of a larger and more general category of external explanations of differences in income and wealth among peoples and nations. Strictly geographical explanations which explain such differences simply in terms of the presence or absence of valuable natural resources or of favorable climate or fertile soil are likewise external explanations. Internal explanations would include the cultures of the people themselves, even if these cultures have historically been influenced by geographical factors. However these cultures have come about and whatever the influence of geography, history, religion, or politics, these cultures are at any given place and time a fact of life, as each group trails the long shadow of its cultural heritage. As a noted historian once said: "We do not live in the past, but the past in us."

As each social, ethnic or other group, and each nation, has had a different past they almost inevitably have a different present and face different prospects for the future. Cultures in which females are seldom educated to the same level as males have forfeited much of the potential of half their populations. Cultures in which books and computers are far more widespread, and attract far more interest, than in other cultures have far more options and outlets for the development of their people's native talents. Demographic differences among groups and nations are among the other internal factors which can have major influences on their economic fate. A nation where the average age is under twenty, as in Yemen or Afghanistan, cannot have accumulated as much human capital— skills, experience, education— per person as a nation where the average age is around forty, as in Germany or Italy.

The difference between internal and external explanations of economic disparities is more than academic. These different kinds of explanations point in radically different directions when it comes to choices of what to do about these disparities. Exploitation theories, for example, point toward liberation from the exploiters, or at least withdrawal from transactions with them, as the way to prosper more in the future than in the past. Cultural explanations, however, would suggest more contact with more successful cultures and perhaps emulation of them in some respects. External explanations in general tend to be more psychologically acceptable and more politically attractive than internal explanations which can sound like "blaming the victim." But which kinds of explanations actually apply to given peoples at a given time is another question entirely.

No single factor can account for the large disparities in economic development among the countries of the world. Nor is the relative influence of any particular factor likely to remain the same over time. Although various geographic factors have played a major role in the economic opportunities available to various peoples, economic development also affects the influence of geography. The invention of railroads and trucks has made available low-cost transport for the first time in regions lacking in navigable waterways and draft animals, such as much of West Africa. Production and sales of cocoa, cotton, and tin began to flourish on a large scale in that part of the world after railroads replaced the costly use of human porters, who were very limited in the size of the loads they could carry. Even mountains became less formidable barriers after techniques of tunneling and blasting through them developed, while airplanes have flown over these mountains and shrunk the role of distance in general. Portable radios and cellular telephones made long-distance communications possible for the first time in many poor and isolated areas, and the Internet has put the peoples of the whole world in instant communication with one another. In short, economic development has reduced the role of geographic factors, which had played such a major role in both advancing and retarding economic development.

SOURCES

CHAPTER 1: POLITICS VERSUS ECONOMICS

The epigraph is from page 47 of the January/February 2007 issue of *Stanford* magazine in an article titled "A Capital Thinker." The quote about the California electorate and electricity prices is from page 101 of ***Culture and Prosperity*** by John Kay. The quote from Congressman Dick Armey is from page 183 of his book, ***Armey's Axioms***. The disastrous effects of price controls in Zimbabwe were described on pages A1 and A8 of an article titled "Caps on Prices Only Deepen Zimbabweans' Misery" in the *New York Times* of August 2, 2007. Herbert Stein's statement about the adverse effects of the Nixon price controls is from page 186 of his book ***Presidential Economics***, second revised edition, and his comment that these controls were not expected to reduce inflation is from page 161 of the same book. Richard Nixon's remarks about his price controls and Milton Friedman's comments on those policies are from a column titled "The Politics of Economics" on page 92 of the October 16, 1978 issue of *Newsweek*. Herbert Stein's comment on the political reasons why price controls on oil were not lifted is from page 193 of ***Presidential Economics***. The economic effects of President Reagan's removal of oil price controls are discussed on page 74 of the Summer 1986 issue of ***Policy Review*** in an article titled "Snake Oil Salesmen." Franklin D. Roosevelt's explanation about his experimental approach to dealing with the Depression is from page 76 of ***The Idea Brokers: Think Tanks and the Rise of the New Policy Elite*** by James A. Smith. The fact that many policy interventions begun by President Herbert Hoover were later expanded by FDR is mentioned on pages 148–149 of ***The Forgotten Man*** by Amity Shlaes. Examples of Hoover's interventions are discussed on pages 91–100 of the same book. Peter Temin's comments on the stock market crash of 1987 are from page 43 of his book ***Lessons from the Great Depression***. Additional remarks about the 1987 stock market crash are from page 27 of the book ***The Stock Market*** by Rik W. Hafer and Scott E. Hein. Criticisms of President Reagan following the 1987 stock market crash are from "A Capital City Out of Sync" on page A2 of the November 6, 1987 issue of the ***Washington Post***, and also in a column titled "It's Morning Again" from page A35 of the *New York Times* of October 22,

1987. Karl Marx's comment is from a letter to Friedrich Engels dated February 3, 1851 and reprinted on page 275 of Volume 38 of their ***Collected Works*** in the edition published in Moscow in 1982. William E. Simon's remarks about testifying before Congress are quoted from page 61 of ***A Gift of Freedom*** by John J. Miller. The comment by Professor N. Gregory Mankiw is from an op-ed column of his titled "How to Avoid Recession? Let the Fed Work" on page 4 of the business section of the ***New York Times*** of December 23, 2007. Job and profit losses in steel-using industries in the wake of policies to protect the steel-producing industry are discussed in an article titled "Sparks Fly over Steel" on pages 57–58 of the November 15, 2003 issue of ***The Economist***. Results of the effect of the Americans with Disabilities Act on the employment of the disabled are cited on page 18 of the ***New York Times Magazine*** of January 20, 2008, in an article titled "Unintended Consequences: Why Do Well-Meaning Laws Backfire?" Data on spending and taxing in New York City are from pages 27–35 of the Winter 2003 issue of ***City Journal***, in an article titled "Bloomberg to City: Drop Dead." The fact that 17 million Americans lost their jobs in the years 1990–1995 was reported on page 7 of an article titled "The Upside of Downsizing" from the November/December 1996 issue of ***The Southwest Economy***, published by the Federal Reserve Bank of Dallas. Adam Smith's comments on the neglect of infrastructure in 18th century France are on pages 687 and 688 of his ***The Wealth of Nations***, 1937 Modern Library edition.

CHAPTER 2: FREE AND UNFREE LABOR

Information on debt peonage in India is from pages 80–88 of the April 2002 issue of ***Scientific American***, in an article titled "The Social Psychology of Modern Slavery." The fact that some slaves in ancient Greece lived and worked apart from their owners is mentioned on page 12 of ***The Slave Systems of Greek and Roman Antiquity*** by William L. Westermann. Data on the number of hours worked by the top and bottom 20 percent of American families is from page 27 of ***Income and Wealth*** by Alan Reynolds. The experiences of Paul Williams are from ***Paul R. Williams, Architect: A Legacy of Style*** by Karen E. Hudson, published in 1993 by Rizzoli International Publications. The experiences of F. W. Woolworth are from ***Remembering Woolworth's*** by Karen Plunkett-Powell, especially from pages 19–20, 30–33, and 83–86. The high rate of job turnover at McDonald's is from an article titled "You Want a Career With That?" on page 10 of the November 2005 issue of ***Incentive***. Data on the income mobility of the top one percent and bottom 20 percent of U.S. households in the years 1996 to 2005 are from page A24 of the November 13, 2007 issue of the ***Wall Street Journal***, under the title "Movin' On Up." A fuller account can be found in the report "Income Mobility in the U.S. from 1996 to 2005," published by the Department of the Treasury on November 13, 2007. Data on the upward movement of individuals in the labor force who were in the bottom 20 percent in income in 1975 are from page 8 of a publication titled ***By Our Own Bootstraps: Economic Opportunity & the Dynamics of Income Distribution***, an excerpt from the 1995 Annual Report of the Federal Reserve Bank of Dallas. Data on the high rate of turnover among the 400 individual taxpayers with the highest incomes are from "The 400 Individual Income Tax Returns Reporting the Highest Adjusted Gross Incomes Each Year, 1992–2000," Internal Revenue Service, Statistics of Income Bulletin, Spring 2003, Publication 1136 (Revised 6–03). Statistics on the high proportion of crimes committed by a small percentage of the youth population are from page 492 of ***Crime***, edited by James Q. Wilson and Joan Petersilia. Similar data on adult criminals are found on page 43. Similar data on youth offenders in Britain can be found on pages 199–200 of ***A Land Fit for Criminals*** by David Fraser. Information on the IQs of criminals is from page 243 of ***The Bell Curve*** by Richard J. Herrnstein and Charles Murray. The comparison of British and American burglary rates is from page 165 of ***Guns and Violence*** by Joyce Lee Malcolm. The leniency shown toward burglars in the United Kingdom is discussed on pages 82, 279, 294, 295, and 297 of ***A Land Fit for Criminals*** by David Fraser. The data on burglaries in occupied and unoccupied homes in the United States, Britain, Canada, and the Netherlands are from page 140 of ***Point Blank*** by Gary Kleck, and the dramatic decline in burglaries in Kennesaw, Georgia, after each household was required to have a firearm is reported on page 136 of the same book. Data on the sharp rise in murder rates in the United States after the legal reforms of the 1960s is from page 409 of ***Crime and Human Nature*** by James Q. Wilson and Richard J. Herrnstein. Data on the increased risk of becoming a victim of a violent crime is from page 4 of ***Criminal Violence, Criminal Justice*** by Charles E. Silberman. Data and graphs showing crime rates and incarceration rates in the United Kingdom, Australia, New Zealand, and the United States are from pages 3–8 of an article titled "Does Prison Work?" in the Summer 2002–2003 issue of the Australian Publication ***Policy***, published by the Centre for Independent Studies in St. Leonards, New South Wales. See also page 97 of ***A Land Fit for Criminals*** by David Fraser. The effect of the bail bond system in the United States is discussed on pages A1 and A16 of the January 29, 2008 issue of the ***New York Times*** in an article titled "World Spurns Bail for Profit, But It's a Pillar of U.S. Justice." Criminals in Britain searching each other for weapons prior to committing robberies are mentioned on page 32 of ***The Abolition of Britain*** by Peter Hitchens. The history of firearms laws and murder rates in London and New York is from pages 141–144, 223, and especially page 225 of ***Guns and Violence*** by Joyce Lee Malcolm. The increase of violent crime in England as gun restrictions were tightened in the latter part of the twentieth century is described on pages 164–166 and 168 of the same book, and also on page 151 of ***A Brief History of Crime*** by Peter Hitchens. The statement about the American Mafia's reluctance to commit acts of violence against law enforcement officials for fear of increased scrutiny of their illegal activities is from page B2 of the October 26, 2007 issue of the ***New York Times***, in an article titled "'80's Plot to Hit Giuliani? Mob Experts Doubt It." The episode involving taking a shopper into custody, to be forced to serve as a juror, is from a front-page story in the August 20, 2002 issue of the ***Wall Street Journal***, under the title, "When the Jury Box Runs Low, Deputies Hit the Wal-Mart." The estimate of a million or more Europeans enslaved on the Barbary Coast from 1530 to 1780 is from page 23 of ***Christian Slaves, Muslim Masters*** by Robert C. Davis. The treatment of European galley slaves by their North African masters is described in Chapter 3 of the same book. The use of Irish immigrants, instead of black slaves, for hazardous work in the antebellum South is mentioned on pages 70 and 215 of ***The Cotton Kingdom*** (Modern Library edition) by Frederick Law Olmsted; on pages 186–187 of ***Life and Labor in the Old South*** by U. B. Phillips; on page 394 of ***The Americans*** (Putnam edition) by J. C. Furnas; on page 101 of the second volume of ***The Americans*** by Daniel Boorstin; pages 301–302 of ***American Negro Slavery***, by U. B. Phillips; and page 520 of the first volume of ***History of Agriculture in the Southern United States to 1860*** by Lewis C. Gray. Information on the economics of the Soviet Gulags is from Chapter 2 of ***Labor Camp Socialism*** by Galina M. Ivanova. The superfluous railroads built at the cost of Gulag prisoners' lives were discussed on pages 123 to 124 of ***Behind the Facade of Stalin's Command Economy***, edited by Paul R. Gregory. The estimate of a million or more Europeans enslaved on the Barbary Coast from 1530 to 1780 is from page 23 of ***Christian Slaves, Muslim Masters*** by Robert C. Davis, while figures for the number of Africans brought in bondage as slaves to the United States are from pages 72, 75 and 87 of ***The Atlantic Slave Trade: A Census*** by Philip D. Curtin. The various roles played by slaves in countries around the world and a capsule history of slavery around the world can be found in Chapter 7 of my book ***Race and Culture***. The use of slaves as human sacrifices was discussed on page 26 of ***Human Bondage in Southeast Asia*** by Bruno Lasker; on page 191 of ***Slavery and Social Death*** by Orlando Patterson; and on page 325 of ***Indians of North America***, second edition, by Harold E. Driver. The better treatment accorded slaves in occupations requiring individual initiative, such as divers in the Carolina swamps or in tobacco processing, was described on pages 114–116, 119–120 of ***The Cotton Kingdom*** by Frederick Law Olmsted; on page 188 of ***Slavery in the Americas*** (1967 edition) by Herbert S. Klein; and on page 127 of ***A Journey in the Seaboard Slave States*** (1969 edition) by Frederick Law Olmsted. The case of the slave who was a river boat captain over a crew that included both black and white sailors is from the December 1962 issue of the ***Mississippi Valley Historical Review***, pages 472–484, in an article titled, "Simon Gray, Riverman: A Slave Who Was Almost Free." Frederick Douglass' comment on urban slaves was quoted from page 110 of ***Slavery in the Cities*** by Richard C. Wade. Books on white indentured servants in colonial America include ***White Servitude in Colonial***

America: An Economic Analysis by David Galenson and *Colonists in Bondage* by Abbot Emerson Smith. The estimate that more than half of the white population outside of New England arrived in colonial America as indentured servants is from pages 3–4 of the latter. The history of coerced Chinese indentured laborers shipped to the Western Hemisphere in the nineteenth century is discussed on pages 35, 46, 50, 73–75, 95–98, and 124 of *Chinese Bondage in Peru* by Watt Stewart and pages 18–19, 27–29, 80, and page 117 of *A Study of the Chinese in Cuba* by Duvon Clough Corbitt. The unscrupulous methods used to gather indentured labor in Britain to be shipped to its Western Hemisphere colonies are discussed in Chapter 4 of *Colonists in Bondage* by Abbot Emerson Smith. Data comparing the slave population in the United States with slave societies in other parts of the Western Hemisphere is from Chapter 4 of the book *The Comparative Histories of Slavery in Brazil, Cuba, and the United States* by Laird W. Bergad, and page 87 of *The Atlantic Slave Trade: A Census* by Philip D. Curtin. Lincoln's remark about every drop of blood drawn with the lash being repaid in blood drawn by the sword is from his second inaugural address. See pages 17 to 19 of *Lincoln's Greatest Speech: The Second Inaugural* by Ronald C. White, Jr. The purchase of freedom in ancient times was mentioned on pages 25 and 83 of *The Slave Systems of Greek and Roman Antiquity* by William L. Westermann. Purchase of freedom later in the Western Hemisphere is mentioned on pages 7–8, 24–26, 31–34, 63, 86, 88, 90, 91, 96, 125, and 225–226 of *Neither Slave Nor Free*, edited by David W. Cohen and Jack P. Greene.

CHAPTER 3: THE ECONOMICS OF MEDICAL CARE

The statement that American health care costs consume about one-sixth of the nation's economic output is from page A13 of the January 9, 2007 issue of the *New York Times* in an article titled "In '05, Medical Bills Grew at Slowest Pace in 6 Years." Data on how much of American medical bills are paid for out of pocket and by other means is from page 11 of *The iii Insurance Fact Book: 2008*, published by the Insurance Information

Institute. Information on the Soviet Union's medical care system is from a front-page story in the ***Wall Street Journal*** of August 18, 1987, titled "Soviet Health System, Despite Early Claims, Is Riddled by Failures." Japan's shorter and more numerous patient visits to doctor's offices, compared to such visits in the United States, are reported on page 350 of ***American Health Care***, edited by Roger D. Feldman. Similar experiences in Korea and in Canada's Quebec province are from page 352 of the same book. Information on Britain's government-run medical system is from page 52 of an essay titled "Will Money Cure the NHS?" in ***The World in 2003***, published by ***The Economist*** magazine. The bleak conditions in British hospitals and the 90 patient deaths due to infections picked up in the hospital are reported on page 4 of the October 19, 2007 issue of the ***Christian Science Monitor*** in an article titled "British Healthcare in Crisis Despite Massive Investment." The decline in standards of patient care and the increased sloppiness and rate of infection in English hospitals are described in London's ***Daily Mail*** of December 8, 2003, in an article from page 10 titled "Mops and Buckets, Not Memos and More Bureaucrats." The London hospital administrator who spent more time on cleaning and maintenance than on her patients is mentioned on page A13 of the December 8, 2003 issue of the ***Evening Standard***, in an article titled "You're Wrong Again, Mr. Reid." The pompous language used by England's Chief Medical Officer in referring to soap and water is quoted from the ***Daily Mail*** of December 8, 2003 in an article from page 10 titled "Mops and Buckets, Not Memos and More Bureaucrats." Information on the waiting times for elective surgeries in Australia, New Zealand, Canada, the United Kingdom, and the United States are from page 12 of a study by Jeremy Hurst and Luigi Siciliani titled ***Tackling Excessive Waiting Times for Elective Surgery: A Comparison of Policies in Twelve OECD Countries***, published in 2003 by the OECD. The role of waiting times for elective surgery in equilibrating supply and demand is from page 13 of the same study, and the fact that cataract, hip replacement, and coronary artery bypass surgeries are all considered to be elective is from page 10 of the study. The thousands of patients in England waiting more than six months for audiology and colonoscopy tests are mentioned on page 365 of the August 25, 2007 issue of the *British Medical Journal*, in an article titled "Thousands of Patients Wait More Than 26 Weeks for Tests." The statement that 90 percent of Canadian patients in Ontario wait 336 days for hip replacement surgery is from page A01 of the June 17, 2006 issue of the *Toronto Star*, in an article titled "India Offers Surgery in a Hurry." The year-long waiting time for hip replacement surgery in Britain was reported on page 154 of the July 2006 issue of the *Action for Victims of Medical Accidents Medical & Legal Journal*, in an article titled "Delay and Treatment Overseas: *Watts v Bedford* Revisited." The higher number of CT scanners and MRI units in the United States per million population compared to other OECD countries is shown on page 67 of the study *Health at a Glance 2007: OECD Indicators*, published by the Organisation for Economic Co-operation and Development. The quoted material about France's health-care system is from page 28 of the September 18, 1998 issue of the British magazine, *New Statesman*, in an article titled "A Hypochondriac's Paradise." Canada's medical system's problems were discussed on page 36 of the August 31, 1998 issue of *BusinessWeek* magazine, in an article titled "Canada's Health-Care System Isn't a Model Anymore." London's newspaper *The Guardian* reported the story of the British girl who received a breast implant in its November 9, 1998 issue, page 6, under the title, "Girl, 12, to Get Breast Implant." China's medical problems were reported on page 71 in the November 7, 1998 issue of *The Economist*, in an article titled "Pharmaceuticals in China: Overdosed." The Redding, California, cardiologist who ordered unneeded bypass surgery was discussed on pages A1 and A14 of the *San Francisco Chronicle* of November 2, 2002 under the headline: "Claims of Unneeded Surgeries Go Back 5 Years." The 10,000 people in Britain who had waited 15 months or more for surgery were reported on page 55 of the April 13, 2002 issue of *The Economist*, in an article titled "The NHS: Condition Still Critical." The lengthy wait times in Canada for patients seeking treatment from specialists in ophthalmology and orthopaedic surgery are shown in a chart on page 25 of the study *Waiting Your Turn: Hospital Waiting Lists in Canada*, 14th edition, written by Nadeem Esmail and Michael Walker, and published by the Fraser Institute. The wait times in different provinces just to get a referral to a specialist from a general practitioner are shown on a chart on page 24 of the same study. The British woman whose cancer surgery was postponed until it had to be cancelled because the cancer had become inoperable during the long delays was mentioned in ***The Economist*** of November 24, 2001, on page 52 of an article titled "Walking Wounded." The higher per capita costs of medical treatment in the United States in relation to other countries are shown on page 11 of the May/June 2004 issue of ***Health Affairs*** in an article titled "U.S. Health Care Spending in an International Context," which began on page 10. The description of black market medical care in China is from page 49 of ***The China Business Review*** of November-December 1998, in an article titled "Medical Investment Alternatives," which began on page 47. Bribes in Tokyo hospitals are mentioned on page 351 of ***American Health Care***, edited by Roger D. Feldman. The rising costs of vaccines and the resulting decline in immunizations are described on page C1 of the ***New York Times*** of March 24, 2007 in an article titled "In Need of a Booster Shot." The increase in American citizens with private health insurance from 10 percent to 50 percent during the decade from 1940 to 1950 is from page 9 of the June 23, 1994 issue of ***Policy Analysis***, No. 211, in an article titled "Why Health Care Costs Too Much." The story about the woman who bought several pairs of eyeglasses with her husband's medical savings account is from pages D1 and D2 of the November 5, 2002 issue of the ***Wall Street Journal*** in a story titled "Getting Uncle Sam to Cover Your Massage— Rush to Use Up Medical Savings Accounts Prompts Creative Reading of Rules." The proportion of uninsured people in various age brackets is from a chart on the front page of the ***Wall Street Journal*** of March 17, 2003, under the title, "A Young Woman, an Appendectomy, and a $19,000 Debt." The high range in medical malpractice insurance rates paid by doctors in different states is from page C3 of the March 5, 2003 issue of the ***New York Times*** in an article titled "Malpractice Insurance: No Clear or Easy Answers," which began on page C1. The malpractice premiums in excess of $200,000 paid by obstetricians in Florida are mentioned on page 240 of the article "Effects of the Medical Liability System in Australia, the UK, and the USA," published in ***The Lancet*** dated July 15, 2006. The fact that the state of Pennsylvania lost one-third of its surgeons between 1995 and 2002 is reported on page 30 of the December 17, 2005 issue of ***The Economist*** in an article titled "Scalpel, Scissors, Lawyer." The quotation from the medical study of the causes of infant brain damage and cerebral palsy was from page A12 of the February 27, 2003 issue of the ***Wall Street Journal***, under the title "Delivering Justice." The increased use of C-sections over the past three decades with no resulting decrease in the incidence of cerebral palsy is noted on page 32 of the December 17, 2005 issue of ***The Economist*** in the previously mentioned article "Scalpel, Scissors, Lawyer," while the fact that 76 percent of American obstetricians have been sued at least once is from page 30 of the same article. The statement that the average damage award in a jury trial is $4.7 million is from page 30 of the same article, "Scalpel, Scissors, Lawyer." The frequency with which obstetricians in Pennsylvania perform unnecessary sonograms and biopsies is noted on page 116 of the article "Moore's Law" from the November 28, 2005 issue of ***Forbes***. The Las Vegas woman who was turned down by 28 obstetricians was mentioned on page A8 of the June 24, 2002 issue of the ***Wall Street Journal*** in an article beginning on the front page titled "Assigning Liability." The estimate that the direct costs of medical malpractice lawsuits account for less than one percent of total health spending in the United States is from page 241 of the July 15, 2006 issue of ***The Lancet*** in an article titled "Effects of the Medical Liability System in Australia, the UK, and the USA." The statement that spending on prescription drugs in the United States represents about one-tenth of total health care spending in the country is from page A13 of the January 9, 2007 issue of the ***New York Times*** in an article titled "In '05, Medical Bills Grew at Slowest Pace in 6 Years." The quotation from the official of Pfizer is from page 68 of the January 20, 2003 issue of ***Fortune*** magazine, under the title "The $10 Billion Pill" which began on page 58. The fact that generic equivalents are not identical to the brand name drug being copied is mentioned on page D1 of the April 22, 2008 issue of the ***Wall Street Journal***, under the title "Inexact Copies: How Generics Differ from Brand Names." That American consumers pay for half of the pharmaceutical industry's research efforts is from page 38 of the October 13, 2003 issue of ***BusinessWeek*** in an article titled "Drug R&D: Must Americans Always Pay?" The reduction in the share of the world pharmaceutical drug market held by the European pharmaceutical industry since 1990 is mentioned on page 40 of the same article. The decline in sales of the drug Ceclor after the introduction of generic drugs in the marketplace is mentioned on pages A1 and A10 of an article titled "Hard to Swallow" in the ***Wall Street Journal*** of November 18, 1998. The Food and Drug Administration's ban on advertising the uses of aspirin as a heart-attack preventative is discussed on pages 285–286 of ***American Health Care***, edited by Roger D. Feldman. The prohibition of doctors at the Stanford, Yale and University of Pennsylvania medical schools from receiving free drug samples is discussed on pages 1220–1222 of the March 5, 2007 issue of the ***Journal of the American College of Cardiology*** under the title "Your Soul for a Pen?" The estimated $16 billion value of free drug samples is from page 730 of the March 3, 2007 issue of ***The Lancet***, under the title "US Campaign Tackles Drug Company Influence Over Doctors." The fact that some clinical trials of new drugs add an additional eight years to the approval process is reported on pages 6 and 7 of the February 2003 issue of ***Fraser Forum*** under the title "Using Our Heads on Head-to-Head Trials." The comment from the former Commissioner of the FDA is quoted from the article "Questioning the US FDA's Drug Approval Process," published in the June 2007 issue of ***Fraser Forum***, page 32. The delay in the approval of new drugs in Canada and the European Union is from pages 4–5 of the article "Patients Waiting Too Long for Government Permission to Use New Drugs in Canada," also published in the June 2007 issue of ***Fraser Forum***. Information on the withdrawal of the arthritis drug Vioxx from the market is from page D1 of the October 5, 2004 issue of the ***Wall Street Journal***, under the title "Putting Side Effects in Perspective." Data on the shortage of organ transplants in relation to the growing number of patients on organ waiting lists is from pages 40, 41, 44, and 85 of ***Black Markets: The Supply and Demand of Body Parts*** by Michele Goodwin, and page 10 of the article "How to Save Thousands of Lives Each Year" from the July 2002 issue of ***Consumers' Research***. The kidney shortage in Western Europe and the 700,000 worldwide dialysis patients were noted on page 137 of the June 2003 issue of the ***Journal of Medical Ethics*** in an article titled "An Ethical Market in Human Organs." The quote about the benefits of lifesaving organs is from page 2 of ***The U.S. Organ Procurement System: A Prescription for Reform*** by David L. Kaserman and A.H. Barnett. Information on the increasing wait time for kidney and heart transplants is from page 33 of the same book, and also page 44 of ***Black Markets: The Supply and Demand of Body Parts*** by Michele Goodwin. Data on the ratio of cadaveric to living donor transplants is from pages 11–12 of the previously mentioned article "How to Save Thousands of Lives Each Year" from the July 2002 issue of ***Consumers' Research***. The number of living donor transplants in the United States in 2006 is given on page A12 of the March 23, 2007 issue of the ***Chronicle of Higher Education*** in an article titled "The True Price of a Human Organ." The dangers to both buyer and seller in black market organ transactions are described in an article titled "Psst, Wanna Buy a Kidney?" in the November 18, 2006 issue of ***The Economist***, page 15. The high markups charged by Internet organ brokers are noted on page 74 of the January 29, 2007 issue of ***Forbes***, under the title "Desperate Arrangements," which began on page 72. The $3,000–$4,000 fee paid to a living kidney donor in Iran is from page 60 of the article "Your Part or Mine?" from ***The Economist*** dated November 18, 2006. The high prices charged by Internet organ transplant brokers in California and Taiwan were reported on page 72 of the previously mentioned article "Desperate Arrangements," from the January 29, 2007 issue of ***Forbes***. The low medical risks for donors and increased health and financial benefits to recipients of a kidney are from pages 60 and 62 of the above mentioned article "Your Part or Mine?" from ***The Economist*** dated November 18, 2006. ***The Economist***'s estimate that the country's wait list for kidneys would be eliminated if less than 1 percent of Americans aged 19–65 donated a kidney is from page 15 of the article "Psst, Wanna Buy a Kidney?" from the November 18, 2006 issue. The transplant surgeries of Governor Robert Casey and Mickey Mantle are mentioned on pages 1–2 of ***Black Markets: The Supply and Demand of Body Parts*** by Michele Goodwin, and page 2 of ***The U.S. Organ Procurement System: A Prescription for Reform*** by David L. Kaserman and A.H. Barnett. The criticisms of new guidelines established by the United Network for Organ Sharing appeared on pages D1 and D6 of the September 13, 2007 issue of the ***Wall Street Journal*** in an article titled "New Limits Debated for Organ

Donation." The use of financial incentives to increase the supply of organs, and the estimated payments to kidney and liver donors are from pages 3, 11, and 13 of "Introducing Incentives in the Market for Live and Cadaveric Organ Donations" by Gary S. Becker and Julio Jorge Elías, from the Summer 2007 issue of the ***Journal of Economic Perspectives***. The high annual costs of dialysis are mentioned on page 67 of the August/September 2007 issue of ***Policy Review*** in an article titled "Supply, Demand & Kidney Transplants," which began on page 59. The cost estimates of the whole organ transplant process are arrived at by adding the organ procurement costs to the other costs cited on page 12 of the Becker and Elías study, "Introducing Incentives in the Market for Live and Cadaveric Organ Donations" in the Summer 2007 issue of the ***Journal of Economic Perspectives***. The estimate that organ transplants could significantly reduce government expenditures is from page 11 of "Organ Sales and Moral Travails: Lessons from the Living Kidney Vendor Program in Iran," published by the Cato Institute as the March 20, 2008 issue of ***Policy Analysis***, No. 614. The experience in Iran is cited on page 4. The concern among critics over the poor and desperate selling their organs is quoted from page A22 of the ***Wall Street Journal*** of November 13, 2007, in a story beginning on the front page titled "Kidney Shortage Inspires a Radical Idea: Organ Sales." The difference between health care and medical care is pointed out by Dr. Dana Goldman in an article titled "Sending Back the Doctor's Bill" from the July 29, 2007 issue of the ***New York Times***, section 4, page 3. Data on differences in the levels of prenatal care and infant mortality rates among American women from various ethnic groups are from pages 9, 11, and 41 of ***Health, United States, 1990***, published by the Public Health Service of the U.S. Department of Health and Human Services. That the United States ranked among the top 3 countries with low death rates from "mortality amenable to health care" is shown on page 61 of the January 1, 2008 issue of ***Annals of Internal Medicine*** in an article titled "Achieving a High-Performance Health Care System with Universal Access: What the United States Can Learn from Other Countries." The multi-tiered pricing employed by hospitals is detailed on page A7 of a story beginning on the front page of the ***Wall Street Journal*** of March 17, 2003 titled "A Young Woman, an Appendectomy, and a $19,000 Debt."

CHAPTER 4: THE ECONOMICS OF HOUSING

The 28 million American families spending more than 30 percent of their incomes on housing were reported on page B7 of the June 9, 2002 issue of the ***Washington Post*** in a story titled "Housing on the Back Burner." The quotation about the gap in pricing between expensive communities and average ones is from page 1 of the National Bureau of Economic Research's Working Paper 12355 titled "Superstar Cities," written by Joseph Gyourko, Christopher Mayer, and Todd Sinai. The wide disparity in housing prices in Houston, Texas, and San Jose, California, is noted on page 8 of a study by Randal O'Toole titled "Do You Know the Way to L.A.?: San Jose Shows How to Turn an Urban Area into Los Angeles in Three Stressful Decades," from the October 17, 2007 issue of ***Policy Analysis***, No. 602. The nearly four-fold rise of home prices in Palo Alto during the 1970s, the closing of several schools there as enrollments declined, and a decline in the city's population in general, were mentioned on pages 10, 85, 89, and 90 of a 1982 study by the Stanford Environmental Law Society titled ***Land Use and Housing on the San Francisco Peninsula***, edited by Thomas M. Hagler. The fact that the rate of increase in California incomes was below the national average during the time when California housing prices skyrocketed is from page 238 of a 1995 book by William A. Fischel titled ***Regulatory Takings: Law, Economics, and Politics***. The fact that a median-priced home in the San Francisco Bay Area in 2005 cost more than three times the national median was reported on page A11 of the ***San Francisco Chronicle*** of October 16, 2005 in a story beginning on the front page under the title "Making Ends Meet: Struggling in Middle Class." The fact that the median price of a home in San Mateo County, California, exceeded one million dollars in 2007 is from a front-page story of the August 16, 2007 issue of the ***San Mateo County Times*** under the title "Median Home Cost over $1M." The fact that Utah, Maryland, Virginia, Colorado, and Minnesota lead the nation in percentage of homes with four or more bedrooms is from a front-page story from the June 4, 2007 issue of ***USA Today*** titled "Not-so-humble Abodes," and also from a wire report in the Associated Press dated May 23, 2007 under the title "Appetite for Big Houses Keeps Growing." The increase in the ratio between home prices and income in San Jose, California, from 1969 to 2005 is from page 8 of the previously mentioned study by Randal O'Toole titled "Do You Know the Way to L.A.?: San Jose Shows How to Turn an Urban Area into Los Angeles in Three Stressful Decades," from the October 17, 2007 issue of ***Policy Analysis***, No. 602. The lower rates of homeownership in California compared to the rest of the country are shown on a graph on page A1 of the ***San Francisco Chronicle*** of August 18, 2005, under the title "How Do They Afford It?" The effects of zoning restrictions on housing costs are discussed on pages 4, 15–16, and 21 of a study by Edward L. Glaeser and Joseph Gyourko titled "The Impact of Zoning on Housing Affordability," Working Paper 8835, published in March 2002 by the National Bureau of Economic Research. The efforts to prevent development on the site of Bay Meadows racetrack in San Mateo, California, by a woman who never once attended a race there are mentioned on pages A13 and A17 of the July 1, 2003 issue of the ***San Francisco Chronicle*** under the title "Racing Against Time; Group Wants to Preserve Bay Meadows." The purchase of 17,000 acres of Coastside property in the San Francisco Bay Area to be preserved for farming was discussed on pages 1 and 13 of the news section of the September 5, 2007 issue of the ***San Mateo County Times***, in an article titled "Coastside Farmland Will Remain That Way." Nantucket's distinction of being the first large community where the average home price exceeded a million dollars was mentioned on page 192 of ***Sprawl*** by Robert Bruegmann, where its severe land use restrictions are also mentioned. Land use restrictions in Loudoun County, Virginia, were described in the ***Washington Post*** of July 24, 2001, in a story from pages B1 and B4 titled "Loudoun Adopts Strict Controls on Development." The affordability in fast-growing regions of the United States with few restrictions on land supply compared with the low affordability and slow growth of heavily regulated areas is from page 134 of ***The Best-Laid Plans*** by Randal O'Toole. The fact that the real median housing price in Las Vegas did not change between 1980 and 2000 while the city's population nearly tripled is from page 332 of the October 2005 issue of the ***Journal of Law and Economics***, in an article titled "Why is Manhattan So Expensive?: Regulation and the Rise in Housing Prices," by Edward L. Glaeser, et al. The recent rise in home prices in Las Vegas, due to the increased resistance of environmental groups to land development, is discussed on page 125 of ***The Best-Laid Plans*** by Randal O'Toole. The quote about the success of inclusionary housing policies is from page 3 of the Local section of the August 15, 2007 issue of the ***San Mateo County Times***, in an article titled "Affordable Housing Quotas Working." The fact that only 7 percent of the Palo Alto police force live in Palo Alto is from page 7 of the August 1, 2007 issue of the ***Palo Alto Weekly***, in an article titled "Police Headquarters Faces Design Choice About Oak Tree." The proportion of income spent on housing by Americans in 1901 and 2002–2003 is from pages 6 and 63 of ***100 Years of U.S. Consumer Spending: Data for the Nation, New York City, and Boston***, Report 991 of the U.S. Department of Labor. The higher proportion of income spent on housing by New Yorkers in 2003 compared to 1901 is from a front-page story in the May 20, 2006 issue of the ***New York Times*** in an article titled "After Century, Room and Board in City Still Sting." The fact that the real income of New Yorkers had quadrupled during the century is mentioned on the same page. The fact that nearly one-fourth of Palo Alto's police live across the San Francisco Bay is from page 7 of the August 1, 2007 issue of the ***Palo Alto Weekly***, in an article titled "Police Headquarters Faces Design Choice About Oak Tree." The affordability of a two-bedroom apartment on a nurse's salary in various cities was reported on page 34 of the December 7, 2002 issue of ***The Economist*** under the title "The Roof That Costs Too Much." The dramatic decrease from 2002–2005 in the number of apartments in New York City that would be affordable to starting firefighters and police officers was reported on page 1 of Section 4 of the July 23, 2006 issue of the ***New York Times***, in an article titled "Cities Shed Middle Class, and Are Richer and Poorer for It." Statistics on the decline of the black population in various California communities between the 1990 and 2000 censuses are from the following U.S. Bureau of the Census publications: ***1990 Census of***

Population: General Population Characteristics California, 1990 CP–1–6, Section 1 of 3, pages 29, 31, 76, 82, 100, 250, 620; ***Profiles of General Demographic Characteristics 2000*** (2000 Census of Population and Housing: California), Table DP–1, pages 22, 42, 619, 689, 903 (from the website of the U.S. Census Bureau: http://www.census.gov/prod/cen2000/dp1/2kh06.pdf). The 70-minute daily commute of a worker at a water filtration plant in Alameda County is from page G1 of the ***San Francisco Chronicle*** dated February 16, 2003 under the title "Eastward ho." The increase in the number of commuters into the San Francisco Bay Area from outlying counties was reported in the March 6, 2003 issue of the ***San Francisco Chronicle*** on page A15 under the title "Census Sees Long Ride to Work." The early morning commute from Contra Costa County into the San Francisco Bay Area was reported on page 10 of the Local section of the ***San Mateo County Times*** of September 15, 2005, under the title "Bay Area Traffic Problem Second-Worst in Nation." The quote, "driving 'til you qualify" is from page 54 of the May 1, 2006 issue of ***Newsweek***, in an article titled "The Long and Grinding Road," which began on page 53. The fact that the median home price in San Francisco was $790,000 in 2005 is from page C1 of the ***San Francisco Chronicle*** of September 15, 2005 under the title "Still Red Hot, But Slowing." The Bay Area residents moving to the inland valleys to purchase 2,000-square-foot homes for less than $300,000 were reported on page G8 of the ***San Francisco Chronicle*** dated February 16, 2003 in an article titled "Eastward ho." The dramatic increase in home prices in Merced County from 1997–2002 is shown on page G7 of the ***San Francisco Chronicle*** of February 16, 2003 in a story titled "Bay Area Paychecks Price Out the Locals." The decrease in the black population in the city of San Francisco and subsequent increase in the black population in outlying communities is from pages A1 and A6 of the April 9, 2007 issue of the ***San Francisco Chronicle*** under the title "S.F. Moves to Stem African American Exodus." Additional information on black population shifts in the Bay Area between the years 1990–2006 is from pages A1 and A11 of the January 14, 2008 issue of the ***San Francisco Chronicle*** under the title "Bayview's Black Exodus." The projected decrease in the white population in the Central Valley of California is from page G8 of the previously mentioned article

"Eastward ho," from the ***San Francisco Chronicle*** dated February 16, 2003. The effects of rent control, and of price controls in general are discussed in Chapter 3 of my ***Basic Economics***, 3rd edition. The fact that nearly half the rent-controlled apartments in San Francisco had only one tenant is from page 21 of ***San Francisco Housing DataBook***, a study commissioned by the city in 2001 and published in 2002 by consultants called Bay Area Economics, while information on the age of rent-controlled housing in the city is from page 56. The lack of construction in post World War II Melbourne because of rent control laws is from page 125 of ***Rent Control: Costs and Consequences*** edited by Robert Albon. That construction of apartments resumed in communities in Massachusetts for the first time in 25 years after the state banned rent control in 1994 is noted on page 4 of William Tucker's study, "How Rent Control Drives Out Affordable Housing," published in the May 21, 1997 issue of ***Policy Analysis***, No. 274. This study is also the source for the statement that cities with rent control tend to have ***higher*** rents than cities without rent control (see pages 1 and 6). The quote about the investment in luxury housing in Europe is from page 69 of the study ***Rent Control in North America and Four European Countries*** by Joel F. Brenner and Herbert M. Franklin. The rent control exemption granted to vacant New York apartments that rent for $2,000 a month or more was mentioned on page 62 of the article "Is There a New York Housing Crisis?" from the Summer 2006 issue of ***City Journal***. The withdrawal of rental units in Toronto after the imposition of rent control in that Canadian city is mentioned on page 21 of ***Zoning, Rent Control and Affordable Housing*** by William Tucker. The decline in London's rental advertisements after rent control was enacted in that city is from page 11 of the January 24, 1975 issue of ***The Times*** of London, in an article titled "The Doors Have Closed on Furnished Accommodation." The thousands of abandoned buildings taken over by the city of New York are mentioned on page 99 of ***The Homeless*** by Christopher Jencks. The fact that the number of abandoned housing units in New York City is more than sufficient to house the number of homeless people there is from page 123 of ***Rude Awakenings*** by Richard W. White, Jr. The fact that more than one-fourth of households living in rent-controlled apartments in San Francisco had incomes of $100,000 or more is from page 24 of the previously mentioned study ***San Francisco Housing DataBook.*** The fluctuations in the interest rates of conventional thirty-year mortgages from 1973–2005 are shown on page 7 of the October 2006 issue of ***Monthly Labor Review***, in an article titled "Recent Employment Trends in Residential and Nonresidential Construction." The fact that home prices in San Mateo County rose an average of $2,000 a day in March 2005 was reported on the front page of the ***San Mateo County Times*** of April 15, 2005, under the title "County's Home Prices Bust Record." Data on the growth of interest-only mortgage loans are from pages A1 and A16 of the May 20, 2005 issue of the ***San Francisco Chronicle***, in an article titled "High Interest in Interest-Only Home Loans"; and also from an article titled "Keep Eyes Fixed on Variable Mortgages," from the July 15, 2006 issue of the ***New York Times***, pages C1 and C6. The fact that home prices in the United States declined for the first time in more than a decade in 2006 was reported on page D1 of the October 26, 2006 issue of the ***Wall Street Journal***, under the title "Home Prices Keep Sliding; Buyers Sit Tight." Soaring foreclosure rates among several California counties were reported on page C1 of the October 14, 2006 issue of the ***San Francisco Chronicle***, in an article titled "Foreclosure Activity Skyrockets in East Bay." The report on adjustable-rate mortgages and the $40,000 cost to banks to foreclose on a loan is from pages C1 and C6 of the March 31, 2007 issue of the ***New York Times*** in an article titled "Lenders May Prove Adjustable." The 800 percent increase in the number of California homes reverting to bank ownership in 2007 was reported on pages C1 and C2 of the ***San Francisco Chronicle*** from July 25, 2007 under the title "Foreclosures Go Through the Roof." The 87 percent increase in foreclosures filed nationally in June 2007, as well as the near tripling of foreclosures in the Bay Area are reported on pages C1 and C2 of the July 12, 2007 issue of the ***San Francisco Chronicle*** in an article titled "Foreclosure Activity Rises Dramatically." The $7.9 billion in losses related to mortgage transactions sustained by Merrill Lynch were reported in the October 28, 2007 issue of the ***New York Times***, in an article titled "Guesstimates Won't Cut It Any More," in Section 3, pages 1 and 8. The bailout of Germany's IKB Deutsche Industriebank AG was reported on page A18 of the ***Wall***

Street Journal of October 31, 2007 in an article beginning on the front page titled "Bernanke, in First Crisis, Rewrites Fed Playbook." The increase in the number of Californians resorting to risky no-down-payment mortgages was reported on pages C1 and C8 of the February 7, 2007 issue of the *San Francisco Chronicle*, under the title "Home Buyers Going Deeper into Debt." The phrase "pretty funky financing" was quoted on page C1 of the July 25, 2007 issue of the *San Francisco Chronicle*, in an article titled "Foreclosures Go Through the Roof." The statements from the mayor of South San Francisco were quoted on pages 1 and 11 of the September 9, 2007 issue of the *San Mateo County Times*, in an article titled "Homeowners Seek Help on Loan Issues." The decline in apartment occupancy rates in the San Francisco Bay Area in the early twenty-first century when low interest rates boosted home sales was reported on page F1 of the September 16, 2007 issue of the *San Francisco Chronicle* in an article titled "Competition Heats Up." The decline in the annual rent/price ratio between the years 1996–2006 was reported on page A2 of the January 3, 2008 issue of the *Wall Street Journal* under the title "Home Prices Must Fall Far to Be in Sync with Rents." The decline in rents along the San Francisco peninsula after 2001 was reported on page F1 of the September 16, 2007 issue of the *San Francisco Chronicle*, in an article titled, "Competition Heats Up." The subsequent rise in both rents and occupancy rates in San Jose and other Bay Area communities since 2006 is from the same page of the same article. The steep increase in rent prices for apartments of all sizes in San Francisco was observed on pages F1 and F4 of the September 16, 2007 issue of the *San Francisco Chronicle* under the title "Squeeze Hits Landlords." The reference to these apartments as "exorbitantly priced hovels" is from page F1 of the same article. The 12 percent increase in the average rent in San Jose in just one year is reported on page C1 of the article "Renters Pay the Price for Crisis" from the October 18, 2007 issue of the *San Francisco Chronicle*. The higher risks incurred in the development of condominiums, as compared to houses, are mentioned on page A1 of the August 25, 2007 issue of the *Wall Street Journal*, under the title "Condo Troubles Further Squeeze Property Lenders." The auctioning of Bay Area townhouses/condominiums by builders at reduced rates is from pages C1 and C8 of the October 18, 2007 issue of the ***San Francisco Chronicle*** in an article titled "Is Builders' Profit Going, Going, Gone?" The increase in the value of bank loans for the development of condominiums was shown in a chart on page A1 of the August 25, 2007 issue of the ***Wall Street Journal***, in an article titled "Condo Troubles Further Squeeze Property Lenders." The sharp rise in the amount of Corus Bankshares' nonperforming assets over the course of a single year is from page A4 of the same article. The fact that in 2007 condo "reversions" exceeded condo conversions for the first time since the 1980s was reported on page W10 of the September 21, 2007 issue of the ***Wall Street Journal***, in an article titled "The Invasion of the Renters." The fact that "urban renewal" destroyed more housing than it created has been noted in many places, perhaps first in ***The Federal Bulldozer***, 1964 edition, pages 62, 64–67, 221 and 229, by Martin Anderson, which also found that two-thirds of the people displaced by Urban Renewal were blacks or Puerto Ricans at that time. The efforts to save money by Jewish immigrants on New York's lower east side during the nineteenth century are noted on pages 71–72, 83–84 of ***How the Other Half Lives***, by Jacob Riis. The statement that most Jewish immigrants to America in the late nineteenth and early twentieth centuries had their passage to America paid for by family members already living there is from page 113 of ***Perspectives in American History***, Volume IX (1975), in an article titled "Immigration of Russian Jews to the United States: Background and Structure." Information on the prepaid passage of Irish immigrants is from pages 394–395 of ***Perspectives in American History***, Volume X (1976), in an essay titled "The Irish Famine Emigration to the United States." Overcrowding on the lower east side of New York when it was a predominantly Jewish neighborhood was discussed on page 128 of an article by Irving Kristol in the September 11, 1966 issue of the ***New York Times Magazine*** titled "The Negro Today is Like the Immigrant Yesterday," which began on page 50. Living conditions for the Jews in this slum are detailed on page 148 of ***World of Our Fathers*** by Irving Howe, and page 30 of ***Government and Slum Housing*** by Lawrence M. Freidman. Improvements in the housing of Southern blacks in the nineteenth century are discussed on pages 108–109, 111 of ***Competition and Coercion*** by Robert Higgs. Data on the continuing segregation of the descendants of northern and southern Europeans in the United States are from page 154 of *Affirmative Discrimination* by Nathan Glazer. The spread of cholera through nineteenth century Irish neighborhoods was discussed on page 114 of ***Boston's Immigrants*** by Oscar Handlin and page 181 of ***To the Golden Door*** by George Potter. Violence in Irish neighborhoods in various cities is discussed on page 238 of ***To the Golden Door*** by George Potter; on pages 126 and 142 of ***Immigrant Milwaukee, 1836–1860*** by Kathleen Neils Conzen; and on pages 30, 46–48 of ***The Irish in America*** by Carl Wittke. Official government policies promoting racial segregation are discussed on pages 24–25 of a 1978 book titled ***The Builders*** by Martin Mayer. The high costs paid by California home-buyers due to planning laws are quoted from page 13 of the Cato Institute's ***Policy Analysis***, No. 602, an October 17, 2007 study by Randal O'Toole titled "Do You Know the Way to L.A.?: San Jose Shows How to Turn an Urban Area into Los Angeles in Three Stressful Decades."

CHAPTER 5: RISKY BUSINESS

The increase in the number of vehicles receiving the highest safety rating in 2007 was reported in an article beginning on page D1 of the November 15, 2007 issue of the ***Wall Street Journal*** under the title "Number of Safest Vehicles Nearly Triples." Information on low-income residents doing their shopping and banking in higher-income neighborhoods is from pages 10 and 28 of ***The Thin Red Line: How the Poor Still Pay More***, written by David Dante Troutt and published in San Francisco in 1993 by the West Coast Regional Office of Consumers Union. The subtitle refers to an earlier study, ***The Poor Pay More*** by David Caplovitz. Neither study explains the systemic economic causes behind the things they describe but this was done by economics professor Walter E. Williams in an article titled "Why the Poor Pay More: An Alternative Explanation" which appeared in ***Social Science Quarterly*** in September 1973, pages 375–379. The commissions charged by Banco Popular and the risks assumed by check-cashing agencies are mentioned on pages B1 and B4 of the March 6, 2001 issue of the ***Wall***

Street Journal in an article titled "Big Bank Targets Immigrant Group, Many Illegal." The problems encountered by banks lending in "subprime" markets were reported in the ***Wall Street Journal*** of August 16, 2001 in a front-page story titled "As Economy Slows, 'Subprime' Lending Looks Even Riskier," which continued on page A2. The Federal Housing Authority's higher delinquency rates on loans to lower income buyers can be found on page E2 of the November 9, 2002 issue of ***The Washington Post*** under the title "Stuck under a Load of Debt," which began on page E1. The statements about government licensing of motorists and the insurance industry's lack of incentive to guarantee that drivers purchase adequate levels of insurance are quoted from page A6 of the September 1–2, 2007 issue of the ***Wall Street Journal*** in an article titled "On the Road." The damage amounts covered by auto insurers in Arizona are from the same article. Automobile fatality rates by drivers of different ages are shown in Figure 3–19, "Fatality Rate per 100 Million VMT by Age: 1996," from page 3–22 of the publication ***The Changing Face of Transportation***, published in 2000 by the U.S. Department of Transportation. The quote about families riding on scooters in India is from page C4 of the October 12, 2007 ***New York Times***, in a story beginning on page C1 under the title "In India, a $2,500 Pace Car." Ralph Nader's comments about automobile safety are from his book ***Unsafe at Any Speed***, pages vii, viii, ix, x, 14, 18, 26, 42. Automobile fatality rates are from pages 719 and 720 of the U. S. Bureau of the Census' 1975 publication ***Historical Statistics of the United States: Colonial Times to 1970***, Part 2. The results of the government study of the safety of the Corvair were reported in the ***Congressional Record–Senate***, March 27, 1973, pages 9748 to 9774. Its conclusion about the Corvair's performance is quoted from page 9749. The new precautions required of homeowners by insurance companies were discussed on page D1 of the June 7, 2007 issue of the ***Wall Street Journal*** in an article titled "Bracing for Disaster." The growing reliance on insurers of last resort in coastal areas prone to hurricanes and storms was reported on pages A1 and A18 of the June 7, 2007 issue of the ***Wall Street Journal*** in an article titled "As Insurers Flee Coast, States Face New Threat." The quote about re-insurance from the London magazine, ***The Economist*** is from its June 30, 2001 issue, page 66, in an article titled "Filling a Gap." The fact that American life insurance companies transfer risk through reinsurance is discussed on page 55 of ***Life Insurers Fact Book 2007***, published by the American Council of Life Insurers. The charge that the government of India was reluctant to accept international help in response to the cyclone which struck the country in 1999, for political reasons, was made in India's own media and was reported on page 46 of ***Liberty and Hard Cases*** edited by Tibor R. Machan. The Russian government's similar reluctance, for political reasons, to accept international help in rescuing men trapped in one of its submarines— and its later acceptance of such aid with a second submarine in the wake of outcries from the Russian public over the deaths of the men in the first submarine— was reported in a story beginning on the front page of the *New York Times* of August 7, 2005 under the headline: "All 7 Men Alive as Russian Submarine Is Raised." Information on the Swiss Reinsurance Company is from ***An Introduction to Reinsurance***, a brochure published by Swiss Re. The insurance industry practice of denying coverage to homeowners who own certain breeds of dogs, and the efforts by homeowners and lawmakers to prevent this practice, are described in the article "Canine Mutiny: Dog Owners Fight Insurers," from the ***Wall Street Journal*** dated June 1, 2006, pages D1 and D2. Information on New Jersey's experience under state regulation of automobile insurance is from page 24 of ***The Economics of Life*** by Gary Becker and Guity Nashat Becker. The increase in the amount of money paid out by Britain's Motor Insurers Bureau from 1988–2000 due to accidents caused by uninsured motorists was noted on page 76 of the December 21, 2002 issue of ***The Economist***, under the title "Blame Culture." The debate over whether or not insurance companies should have access to patient genetic data was reported on page 70 of the August 25, 2007 issue of ***The Economist***, in an article titled "Do Not Ask or Do Not Answer?" which began on page 69. The issue of "genetic discrimination" in the United States was discussed on page A1 of the May 2, 2008 issue of the ***New York Times*** in an article titled "Congress Clears Bill to Bar Bias Based on Genes." The quotes from the Japanese pilot about the risks of wearing parachutes in aerial combat are from page 176 of ***Samurai!*** by Saburo Sakai, 1957 edition published by E.P. Dutton and Company, Inc. The comment on higher death rates from natural disasters in poorer countries was made on page 39 of an essay by Indian economist Barun S. Mitra titled "Dealing with Natural Disaster: Role of the Market" from the book ***Liberty and Hard Cases***, edited by Tibor R. Machan. Information on the deaths caused by the hurricane that struck Galveston, Texas, in 1900 is from page 38 of the same book, while information on the number of deaths caused when Hurricane Andrew devastated southern Florida in 1992 is from pages 38–39. Barun Mitra's quote about the drought that struck India in 2000 is from page 41 of the same book. Data on deaths from Hurricane Katrina in the United States and earthquakes in India and Pakistan are from page 98 of the March 4, 2006 issue of ***The Economist***, in an article titled "Emerging-Market Indicators," under the heading "Catastrophes." The fact that bank failures in the 1930s were concentrated in unit banks is from page 55 of ***FDR's Folly*** by Jim Powell. The bailout of savings and loan associations in the 1980s at a cost of more than half a trillion dollars is noted on page 57 of the same book. The quotation from Paul Samuelson in defense of social insurance schemes and the economic and demographic data on their problems are from an article titled "Snares and Delusions" on pages 5 and 6 of a special section within the February 16, 2002 issue of ***The Economist***. The special section is titled "Time to Grow Up."

CHAPTER 6: THE ECONOMICS OF IMMIGRATION

The epigraph is from page ix of ***Sustainable Immigration and Cultural Integration*** by Wolfgang Kasper, published by the Centre for Independent Studies in Australia. The estimate of 200 million immigrants worldwide is from page 4 of a special report on migration, titled "Open Up," in the January 5, 2008 issue of ***The Economist***. The migration of highly skilled people from poorer countries to more prosperous nations is discussed on pages 4 and 5 of the same article. The number of international migrants living in the United States was reported on page 21 of ***Pocket World in Figures***, 2007 Edition, published by ***The Economist***. The changes in the country origins of European immigrants in various decades of the 19th century are from page 13 of the US Census Bureau's ***Current Population Reports***, P23–206 published in 2001. The prominence of Italians originating from the cities of Messina and Molfetta among fishermen in the Australian port of Freemantle was noted on page 30 of ***Southern Europeans in Australia*** by Charles A. Price. That Lebanese immigrants from particular towns often settled together in particular towns in Colombia was mentioned on page 368 of ***The Lebanese in the World***, edited by Albert Hourani and Nadim Shehadi. Differences in geographic origin and culture among those who settled in New England and in the colonies of the South are discussed on pages 298–299, 626, 628–629, 634–635, 721–726 of ***Albion's Seed*** by David Hackett Fischer, and on pages 16 to 18, and in Chapters VI and VIII of ***Cracker Culture*** by Grady McWhiney. The use of prepaid tickets by emigrants from Scandinavia during the late nineteenth and early twentieth centuries was noted on page 14 of ***The Age of Mass Migration: Causes and Economic Impact*** by Timothy Hatton and Jeffrey G. Williamson. Information on the prepaid passage of Irish immigrants is from pages 394–395 of ***Perspectives in American History***, Vol. X (1976), in an article titled "The Irish Famine Emigration to the United States." The statement that most Jewish immigrants to America in the early twentieth century had their passage to America paid for by family members already living in the U.S. is from page 113 of the same publication, Vol. IX (1975), in an article titled "Immigration of Russian Jews to the United States: Background and Structure." The chain migration patterns of the Lebanese in West Africa, Indians in East Africa, and Chinese in Southeast Asia were noted, respectively, on pages 242 to 243 of ***The Lebanese Traders in Sierra Leone*** by H. L. van der Laan; pages 73–75 of ***The Indian Minority of Zambia, Rhodesia, and Malawi*** by Floyd Dotson and Lillian O. Dotson; page 300 of ***South Asians in East Africa: An Economic and Social History, 1890–1980*** by Robert G. Gregory; page 172 of ***The Chinese in Philippine Life: 1850–1898*** by Edgar Wickberg; and page 15 of ***The Chinese in New Zealand: A Study in Assimilation*** by Ng Bickleen Fong. The high percentage of immigrants that settled in Australia via the chain migration process is from page 109 of ***Southern Europeans in Australia*** by Charles A. Price. The quote about how the affordability of modern communications and travel facilitates family ties across international borders is from pages 3–4 of a special supplement titled "The Longest Journey," in the November 2, 2002 issue of *The Economist.* The estimated $318 billion in immigrant remittances worldwide in 2007 was reported on page 106 of the December 15, 2007 issue of *The Economist* under the heading "Remittances." The value of worldwide immigrant remittances as a proportion of the GDP of poorer countries was noted on page 116 of the November 26, 2005 issue of *The Economist* under the heading "Remittances." The African doctors sending a substantial proportion of their income home even after 20 years abroad were mentioned on page 11 of a special supplement to the January 5, 2008 issue of *The Economist,* this supplement being titled, "Open Up." The extent of Japanese ownership of land in Brazil was mentioned on page 91 of *The Japanese Immigrant in Brazil* by Teiiti Suzuki. The growing ratio of immigrants to the United States from Asia in the years between 1965–1998 is shown on page 15 of *The First Measured Century: An Illustrated Guide to Trends in America, 1900–2000,* by Theodore Caplow, et al. The estimated 55 million Europeans who migrated to the Western Hemisphere and Australia between the years 1850–1914 are noted on page 3 of *The Age of Mass Migration* by Timothy Hatton and Jeffrey G. Williamson. The differing assimilation patterns of Lebanese immigrants in various countries where they settled is discussed on page 9 of *The Lebanese in the World,* edited by Albert Hourani and Nadim Shehadi. The high rate of savings among Italians living in Argentina was noted on page 50 of *Immigration and Nationalism: Argentina and Chile, 1890–1914,* by Carl Solberg. The cultural differences between Japanese immigrants in Brazil and Japanese immigrants in the United States are mentioned on page 465 of *Perspectives in American History,* Vol. XII (1979), in an article titled, "Japanese Emigration to the United States, 1866–1924." The booing of the *Marseillaise* by the descendants of North African immigrants to France was quoted from page 307 of *Our Culture, What's Left of It: The Mandarins and the Masses* by Theodore Dalrymple. The rioting in France that left more than one hundred police officers wounded in 2007 was discussed on page A1 of the November 28, 2007 issue of the *New York Times,* under the title "In French Suburbs, Same Rage, but New Tactics." The increased levels of crime among the children of Mexican immigrants to the United States was reported on page 68 of ***The Immigration Solution*** by Heather Mac Donald, Victor Davis Hanson, and Steven Malanga. The booing of the American national anthem before a soccer match against Mexico was noted on page A20 of the April 6, 2002 issue of the ***Washington Post*** under the title "Immigrant Invasions." The fact that a 2007 poll in the United States showed that suicide bombing was accepted by one in four Muslim respondents under the age of thirty was reported on page A16 of the ***Wall Street Journal*** dated June 4, 2007 in an article titled "Muslim Melting Pot." The thousands of people of Indian and Chinese descent who returned to their native countries between 2005 and 2006 were noted on page 88 of the July 23, 2007 issue of ***Forbes*** magazine, in an article titled "Back to India." The return of 8.5 million emigrants to Italy between the years 1905–1976 was noted on page 399 of ***Perspectives in American History***, New Series, Volume I (1984), in an article titled "Italian Mass Emigration to the United States, 1876–1930: A Historical Survey." The estimates for Indian migration during the century between the mid 1830s and the late 1930s are from page 99 of ***The Population of India and Pakistan*** by Kingsley Davis. Variations in the rate of return migration among various immigrant groups are from page 9 of ***The Age of Mass Migration*** by Timothy Hatton and Jeffrey G. Williamson. The large financial costs of treating immigrants in Britain's National Health Service were reported on page 20 of the May 23, 2003 issue of the ***Daily Telegraph***, in an article titled "The World's Sick Are Flocking to the NHS— and We're Paying." The high percentage of tuberculosis cases attributed to immigrants in Loudoun and Fairfax Counties in Virginia was reported on page B1 of the August 26, 2005 issue of the ***Washington Times*** under the title "TB Cases Rooted in Foreign Countries; Immigrants, Visitors Carry Disease to Area." The higher rate of Hepatitis A in the Hispanic population of Texas compared to the black and white populations of the state was shown on page 53S of the October 2005 issue of the ***American Journal of Medicine***, in an article titled "United States Epidemiology of Hepatitis A: Influenced by Immigrants Visiting Friends and Relatives in Mexico?" The prevalence of hepatitis A, B and C among African immigrants in Minneapolis was reported on page 84 of the January

11, 1999 issue of ***Archives of Internal Medicine***, in an article titled "Communicable Disease in African Immigrants in Minneapolis." The statement that both the increase in tropical diseases and resurgence of tuberculosis and viral hepatitis in Western countries are the results of the growing migration from less developed nations is from page 115 of the July 2003 issue of ***American Journal of Tropical Medicine and Hygiene***, in an article titled "Infectious Diseases in Immigrants from the Perspective of a Tropical Medicine Referral Unit." The respective educational attainments of immigrants from Asia and Mexico are shown on page 37 of the Census Bureau's ***Current Population Reports***, P23–206. The fact that many Scottish highlanders of the nineteenth century did not speak English and were illiterate and unskilled is noted on page 768 of ***The Australian People: An Encyclopedia of the Nation, Its People and Their Origins***, edited by James Jupp, 1988 edition. The fact that Scottish highlanders settled in separate communities from lowlanders in America is noted on page 118 of ***The Highland Scots of North Carolina, 1732–1776*** by Duane Meyer, and page 621 of ***Albion's Seed*** by David Hackett Fischer. The settlement patterns of urban Scottish lowlanders in Australia were mentioned on page 764 of ***The Australian People***, edited by James Jupp, 1988 edition. The advanced nature of Scottish agricultural methods was noted on page 762 of the same publication and the decline in the proportion of Scottish highlanders immigrating to Australia after the 1850s was noted on page 764. That immigrants in Britain take jobs that unemployed Britons will not take was mentioned on page 14 of a special supplement section of the November 2, 2002 issue of ***The Economist***, this supplement being titled "The Longest Journey." The role of real wages in influencing emigration from the United Kingdom is discussed on page 66 of ***The Age of Mass Migration*** by Timothy Hatton and Jeffrey G. Williamson, where the role of mass migration in bringing about wage convergence is discussed on page 29 and where the rise in wages in Ireland and the decline in both rents and the return on capital during the age of mass migration are noted on page 188, while the decline in Irish emigration is noted on pages 78–80 and 184 of the same book. The surge in emigration among poor southern Italians in the wake of higher wage levels brought on by earlier migrations is discussed on pages 98–100 and the rising wage levels in Sweden during the decades from 1870–1910 are noted on page 198, while the decline in the real wage gap between the Old World and the New World during the late nineteenth and early twentieth centuries is discussed on page 211 of the same book. Estimates for the number of immigrants arriving in the United States from various parts of Europe during different eras are from pages 7 and 40 of ***Heaven's Door*** by George J. Borjas. Changes in the geographic origins of immigrants to the United States after 1965 are reported on pages 11 and 12 of the US Census Bureau's ***Current Population Reports***, P23–206. The fact that the average immigrant earned more than the average native-born American in 1960 is reported on pages 21–22 of ***Heaven's Door: Immigration Policy and the American Economy*** by George J. Borjas. The widening gap in educational attainment between native-born Americans and immigrants after the 1960s is described on the same pages. The fact that the average pay of immigrants from Mexico was 40 percent less than that of the average American is noted on page 44 of the same book. Canada's immigration policy is discussed on pages 58–59 of the same book. The differing views of elite opinion leaders and the general public on the issue of immigration are shown on page 3 of the December 2002 issue of ***Backgrounder***, published by the Center for Immigration Studies, in an article titled "Elite vs. Public Opinion." The quote about "the white Western majority" having to do some assimilating to the immigrants is from pages 31–32 of ***Heaven's Door*** by George J. Borjas. Dismissive reports of growing concerns among European voters about immigrants appeared on page 56 of the November 24, 2007 issue of ***The Economist***, in an article titled "The Trouble with Migrants." Changing public opinion on the issue of immigration in Australia over the last decades of the 20th century was reported on page xi of ***Sustainable Immigration and Cultural Integration***, by Wolfgang Kasper. The fact that one-fourth of the Australian population was foreign-born in 1998 is mentioned on page 6 of the same publication and the reluctance of immigrants to assimilate into the Western culture is mentioned on page viii, while the discussion of the debates on immigration policy in Australia are mentioned on page xvi. Immigration's impact on the economy of Britain was discussed on pages 53–54 of the June 29, 2002 issue of ***The Economist*** under the title "Who Gains from Immigration?" According to the Government Accountability Office, 27 percent of all federal prisoners are criminal aliens. See pages 2, 7, 9, and 19 of the Government Accountability Office's publication ***Information on Criminal Aliens Incarcerated in Federal and State Prisons and Local Jails***, GAO–05–337R. That Mexico is the country of origin of most of these criminal aliens is shown on pages 10, 20, and 25 of the same publication. The varying conclusions reached by different studies of the net costs and benefits of immigration in the United States are mentioned on page 121 of ***Heaven's Door*** by George J. Borjas, and the impact of immigration on the American labor market is the focus of Chapter 4 of that book, while the widening wage gap between native-born American men and immigrant men since the 1960s is discussed on pages 21–22. The 40 percent unemployment rate among young Muslim men in France was reported on page B13 of the April 11, 2006 issue of the ***Los Angeles Times*** in an op-ed column titled "... It's a Major Mistake." Increased crime among the Muslim population in France and a growing hostility toward French society among them is discussed on pages 299–301, 303–304, and 305 of ***Our Culture, What's Left of It*** by Theodore Dalrymple. Damages caused during the three weeks of rioting in France in 2005 were reported on pages 47–48 of the December 17, 2005 issue of ***The Economist*** under the title "After the Riots." Additional information on the riots is from page A18 of the November 13, 2005 issue of the ***Washington Post*** in an article titled "Police, Rioting Youths Clash in Central Lyon." The failure of the British security establishment to respond to threats by Muslim extremists in Britain is the subject of Chapter 3 of ***Londonistan*** by Melanie Phillips. The Turkish prime minister's urging of Turks in Germany to resist assimilation, and the poor performance of Turkish students in German schools were reported on pages 31 and 32 of the April 5, 2008 issue of ***The Economist*** under the title "Two Unamalgamated Worlds." The social fragmentation of the various ethnic cultures in Britain was reported on pages 74 and 76 of the February 23, 2008 issue of ***The Economist*** under the title "The Search for Social Glue." The assimilation of the Irish, the Jewish, and the Lebanese immigrants into American culture during their periods of immigration have been discussed, respectively, in pages 101–102 of ***The Irish*** *in America* by Carl Wittke; pages 229–235 of *World of Our Fathers* by Irving Howe; and pages 154–155 of ***The Lebanese in the World***, edited by Albert Hourani and Nadim Shehadi. Similar efforts toward assimilation among blacks are discussed on pages 36–37 of my ***Black Rednecks and White Liberals***. Support among Hispanic voters for the proposition ending bilingual education in California was reported on pages 57–58 of ***Heaven's Door*** by George J. Borjas. The distributions of immigrants and native-born Americans in various job classifications were reported on page 3, section 4, of the April 2, 2006 issue of the ***New York Times*** in an article titled "Immigrants and the Economics of Hard Work." The small share of agricultural labor in the price of fruits and vegetables was shown on page 3, section 4, of the April 2, 2006 issue of the ***New York Times***, in an article titled "Plentiful, Productive— and Illegal."

CHAPTER 7: THE ECONOMICS OF DISCRIMINATION

The admission of Jewish merchants into Russia during the reign of Catherine the Great was from pages 86–87 of ***Human Capital: The Settlement of Foreigners in Russia, 1762–1804*** by Roger P. Bartlett. W. E. B. DuBois' comments on the hiring of black workers in the nineteenth century were from pages 323 and 395 of ***The Philadelphia Negro***. The fact that never-married, college-educated women who have never had children and who were working full-time between the ages of 40 and 64 earn higher average salaries than men of the same description is from page xxiii of ***Why Men Earn More*** by Warren Farrell. The greater likelihood of hiring young black males by those employers who check criminal backgrounds was reported on pages 452 and 473 of the October 2006 issue of ***Journal of Law & Economics*** in an article titled "Perceived Criminality, Criminal Background Checks, and the Racial Hiring Practices of Employers." Bias against lower-caste people in India was discussed on page 553 of ***Competing Equalities*** by Marc Galanter. The comment that the Chinese could do everything better and more cheaply than Malays was from page 25 of ***The Malay Dilemma*** by Mahathir bin Mohamad, published in Kuala Lumpur by

Federal Publications in 1983. The comment about the more "thrusting" people of southern Nigeria was quoted on page 178 of ***Ethnic Groups in Conflict*** by Donald L. Horowitz. Similar comments from various other countries were quoted on pages 171 to 181 of the same book. The quoted paragraph about Japanese immigrants by an advocate of restricting their immigration was quoted on page 123 of ***East to America: A History of the Japanese in the United States*** by Robert A. Wilson and Bill Hosokawa. Pre-World War II discrimination against blacks and Jews by non-profit organizations was discussed on pages 695 and 705 of "Through the Back Door: Academic Racism and the Negro Scholar in Historical Perspective," which began on page 678, written by Michael R. Winston in the Summer 1971 issue of ***Daedalus***; on page 480 of ***The American Democracy*** by Harold J. Laski; and on page 323 of ***An American Dilemma***, Volume I, by Gunnar Myrdal. Anti-Semitism in American and European universities before World War II was noted on page 31 of ***Memoirs of an Unregulated Economist*** by George J. Stigler. The over-representation of Jews among physicians in Poland between the two World Wars was discussed on pages 23 and 27 of ***The Jews of East Central Europe between the World Wars*** by Ezra Mendelsohn. Discrimination by the telephone industry in the hiring of black women during the first half of the twentieth century was noted on pages 73 and 80 of ***Negro Employment in Public Utilities*** by Bernard E. Anderson. The reversal of previous discriminatory hiring policies in the telephone industry which led to the increase in the hiring of black workers during the late 1960s was noted on page 150 of the same book. A.T.& T.'s top ranking for promoting diversity was reported on pages 70 and 74 of a special section titled "Diversity to Work," in the April 16, 2007 issue of ***BusinessWeek***. Violations of apartheid laws by white employers were discussed on page 164 of ***Apartheid: A History*** by Brian Lapping; page 152 of ***Capitalism and Apartheid*** by Merle Lipton; and pages 78, 112–113 of ***South Africa's War against Capitalism*** by Walter E. Williams. Expansion of Jewish ghettoes during the Thirty Years' War was discussed in Chapter V of ***European Jewry in the Age of Mercantilism: 1550–1750*** by Jonathan I. Israel. The relationship between the Jews and the Poles in Chicago in the early twentieth century was discussed on page 229 of ***The Ghetto*** by Louis Wirth.

The fact that black young men from homes with newspapers, magazines, and library cards had the same incomes as white young men of the same description when they had the same education was from Chapter 4 of ***Black Elite*** by Richard Freeman. The similarity of blacks, whites, and Hispanics of the same age with the same IQs was reported on page 323 of ***The Bell Curve*** by Richard J. Herrnstein and Charles Murray. The fact that single women who had worked continuously since leaving school had slightly higher incomes than single men of the same description was from page 105 of ***The Economic Report of the President, 1973.*** The earnings of never married women in Canada in relation to the earnings of never married men were shown on pages 23, 25 and 26 of an article titled "Women's Earnings/Men's Earnings," which began on page 20, of the Winter 1999 issue of ***Perspectives***, published by Statistics Canada. The higher incomes earned by female faculty members who had never married compared to male faculty members who had never married were from pages 95–96 of a study of mine titled "Affirmative Action in Faculty Hiring," reprinted in ***Education: Assumptions versus History.*** The non-comparability of untouchable and caste Hindu students who seemed at first to be comparable was from pages 357, 366, 391, 396, 406, 414, and 418 of a doctoral dissertation at the Tata Institute of Social Sciences in Bombay (Mumbai) in 1982 titled "Inequality in Higher Education: A Study of Scheduled Caste Students in Medical Colleges of Bombay" by Padma RamKrishna Velaskar. The non-comparability of black and white faculty members in the United States was from pages 81 to 89 of a study of mine titled "Affirmative Action in Faculty Hiring," reprinted in ***Education: Assumptions versus History.*** Qualitative differences between students from different social groups in Malaysia, Sri Lanka, Israel, India, and the United States were documented in the following studies: Mohamed Suffian bin Hashim, "Problems and Issues of Higher Education Development in Malaysia," ***Development of Higher Education in Southeast Asia: Problems and Issues***, edited by Yip Yat Hoong (Singapore: Regional Institute of Higher Education and Development, 1973), pages 57–78; Chandra Richard de Silva, "Sinhala-Tamil Relations and Education in Sri Lanka: The University Admissions Issue— The First Phase, 1971–7," ***From Independence to Statehood: Managing Ethnic Conflict*** *in Five African and Asian States*, edited by R. B. Goldmann and A. J. Wilson (London: Frances Pinter, 1984), pages 125–146; Sammy Smooha and Yochanan Peres, "The Dynamics of Ethnic Inequalities: The Case of Israel," ***Studies of Israeli Society***, Volume I, edited by Ernest Krausz (New Brunswick: Transaction Books, 1980), page 173; Suma Chitnis, "Positive Discrimination in India With Reference to Education," ***From Independence to Statehood***, pages 31–43; Thomas Sowell, "Ethnicity in A Changing America," ***Daedalus***, Winter 1978, pages 231–232. The study on mortgage loans was reported in many places, including pages A1, A10, and A11 of the March 31, 1992 issue of the ***Wall Street Journal*** in a story titled "Behind the Figures: Federal Data Detail Pervasive Racial Gap in Mortgage Lending." The conclusion that residual differences in mortgage loan approval rates was attributed to discrimination was from a study by Alicia H. Munnell, et al., titled ***Mortgage Lending in Boston: Interpreting HMDA Data***, Working Paper No. 92–7, October 1992, Federal Reserve Bank of Boston, pages 2, 24, 25, 43, 44. Differences in wealth by blacks and whites in the same income brackets were shown on page 20 of the Census Bureau publication "Population Profile of the United States: 1991," ***Current Population Reports***, Series P–23, No. 173. The fact that whites were turned down for conventional mortgage loans more often than Asians was reported in the following studies: Glenn B. Canner, et al., "Home Mortgage Disclosure Act: Expanded Data on Residential Lending," ***Federal Reserve Bulletin***, November 1991, page 870; and Glenn B. Canner and Dolores S. Smith, "Expanded HMDA Data on Residential Lending: One Year Later," ***Federal Reserve Bulletin***, November 1992, pages 807, 808. The predominance of the Chinese minority in Malaysia in the study of engineering during the decade of the 1960s was shown on a table on pages 70–71 of the essay by Mohamed Suffian bin Hashim, "Problems and Issues of Higher Education Development in Malaysia," ***Development of Higher Education in Southeast Asia: Problems and Issues***, edited by Yip Yat Hoong. The great over-representation of people of German ancestry in the St. Petersburg Academy of Sciences was discussed on page 195 of ***The Volga Germans*** by Fred C. Koch; and the over-representation of southern Nigerians in the professions in northern Nigeria was shown on pages 40 and 41 of ***Northern Nigeria's***

Statistical Yearbook 1965, published by the Ministry of Economic Planning in Kaduna. The statement by an Illinois state official condemning the use of tests that were harder to "disadvantaged" minorities to pass was quoted from pages 3133 and 3134 of a compendium compiled by the U. S. Equal Employment Opportunity Commission under the title, ***Legislative History of Titles VII and XI of Civil Rights Act of 1964.*** Evidence indicating that Japanese companies setting up businesses in the United States tend to locate away from concentrations of blacks was revealed on pages 9 to 22 of the Fall 1988 issue of the ***California Management Review***, in an article titled "Racial Factors in Site Location and Employment Patterns of Japanese Auto Firms in America"; and on page 704 of the January 1992 issue of the ***Southern Economic Journal***, in an article titled "Locational Determinants of Japanese Manufacturing Start-ups in the United States." Similar findings for domestic companies were reported on page A14 of the February 15, 1983 issue of the ***New York Times***, in a news item titled "Businesses Said to Have Barred New Plants in Largely Black Communities." The effects of preferential admissions on black law school students were examined in the study "A Systemic Analysis of Affirmative Action in American Law Schools," written by Richard H. Sander, and published in the ***Stanford Law Review***, November 2004, Volume 57, Issue 2, pages 367–483.

CHAPTER 8: THE ECONOMIC DEVELOPMENT OF NATIONS

International comparisons of Gross Domestic Products by purchasing power are from page 26 of ***Pocket World in Figures***, 2007 edition, published by ***The Economist*** magazine. The Gross Domestic Products for the states of New Jersey and California are from page 124 of the July 2007 issue of ***Survey of Current Business***, under the title "Gross Domestic Product by State." The ranking of the top 70 countries by per capita GDP is from page 29 of ***Pocket World in Figures***, 2007 edition. Comparisons between Argentina's economic standing in the world in the early twentieth century and in the early twenty-first century were from page 27 of ***The Economist*** of

March 2, 2002, under the title, "A Decline Without Parallel." The sharp decline in income per capita in Argentina between 1998 and 2002 was reported on page 16 of the August 17–18, 2002 issue of the ***Washington Post National Weekly Edition***, in an article titled, "In Argentina, Dignity Turns to Despair." Changes in the relative positions of India and China were reported on page 28 of ***The McKinsey Quarterly***, issue number 4 in 2001, in an article titled "India— From Emerging to Surging." Estimates of the proportion of the world's total output produced in Asia and in Western nations at different times in history were from pages 30 and 344 of ***Thunder from the East***, 2001 paperback edition, by Nicholas D. Kristof and Sheryl WuDunn. The changing locations of the leading achievements in various fields in the Western world are discussed on pages 299 to 304 of ***Human Accomplishment*** by Charles Murray. The tenuousness of property rights in many Third World countries was discovered in an international study reported in ***The Mystery of Capital*** by Peruvian economist Hernando de Soto, published in 2000 by Basic Books. The lengthy processes required to get legal title to real estate in Egypt and Haiti were from pages 20 to 21 of that book. The enormous value of legally unrecognized economic assets in various poor countries was discussed on pages 32 to 35. The illegal buses, taxis and food vendors in Third World countries were discussed on page 28. The role of property rights in enabling strangers to combine their assets for corporate ventures beyond the reach of any given individual was discussed on pages 56 and 61. Another analysis of the same phenomenon appeared in ***The Economist*** of March 31, 2001 under the title "Poverty and Property Rights," pages 20 to 22. The greater accessibility of San Francisco from China than from the banks of the Missouri was mentioned on page 65 of ***The Chinese of America*** by Jack Chen. The importation of kerosene by the city of Tiflis from America was discussed on page 60 of ***The Prize: The Epic Quest for Oil, Money, and Power***, by Daniel Yergin. Similarly huge disparities in costs between land transport and water transport in Africa, Japan, and England were mentioned on page 5 of ***The Geography of Modern Africa*** by William A. Hance; page 515 of ***East Asia: Tradition & Transformation***, revised edition, by John K. Fairbank, Edwin O. Reischauer, and Albert M. Craig; and on page 72 of "Coal and Steam Power," by Nick von Tunzelmann in ***Atlas of Industrializing Britain 1780–1914***, edited by John Langton and R.J. Morris. The cost of shipping wheat in the Ottoman Empire was from page 184 of "Imperial Borderlands or Capitalist Periphery? Redefining Balkan Backwardness, 1520–1914," by John R. Lampe, in ***The Origins of Backwardness in Eastern Europe***, edited by Daniel Chirot. The relative costs of shipping oil by various modes were from page 124 of ***Ethnonationalism: The Quest for Understanding*** by Walker Connor. Samarkand's role as a crossroads of desert routes was mentioned on pages 176 and 178 of ***Before European Hegemony: The World System A.D. 1250–1350*** by Janet L. Abu-Lughod. The manpower used to carry cocoa by porters and by train was discussed on page 54 of ***The Economic Revolution in British West Africa*** by Allan McPhee published by Frank Cass & Co., Ltd. in 1971. The dramatic decrease in the cost of shipping goods brought about by railroads and steamships was quoted from page 5 of ***Global Capitalism*** by Jeffry Frieden. The fact that every one of the early industrial regions in Europe had the benefit of navigable waterways was discussed on pages 492–493 of ***An Historical Geography of Europe: 1800–1914*** by Norman J. G. Pounds, published by Cambridge University Press. The lack of fossil fuels, urbanization, railroads, and rivers in the Balkans, and its cultural fracturing, were mentioned on pages 43, 132, 178–179, 430, 459, and 485 of the same book. The characterization of the Balkans as "self-sufficient" was from page 488 of the same work. The locations of Russian rivers were discussed on page 2 of ***The Industrialization of Russia: An Historical Perspective***, third edition, by William L. Blackwell, published by Harlan Davidson in 1994. The role of waterways in Genoa and Mombasa as sole outlets for productive regions was discussed on pages 263 and 283 of ***Influences of Geographic Environment*** by Ellen Churchill Semple. On the role of the port of Dubrovnik, see page 147 of "The Geographical Setting of Medieval Dubrovnik," by Josip Roglic in ***Geographical Essays on Eastern Europe***, edited by Norman J. G. Pounds. The role of the Gulf Stream in Europe's weather was discussed on pages 14–15 of ***Europe: A Geographical Survey of the Continent*** by Roy E. H. Mellor and E. Alistair Smith. The dearth of navigable rivers in Spain was mentioned on page 365 of ***An Economic History of Spain*** by Jaime Vicens Vives and the dearth of rainfall in Sicily was mentioned on page 35 of ***The Sting of Change: Sicilians in Sicily and Australia*** by Constance Cronin. The incomes of immigrants from Southern and Eastern Europe in the United States were discussed on page 15 of ***The Economic Status of Americans of Southern and Eastern European Ancestry***, published by the U. S. Commission on Civil Rights in 1986. These immigrants also took more years to reach the average income of native-born Americans. See Barry R. Chiswick, "The Economic Progress of Immigrants: Some Apparently Universal Patterns," ***The Gateway: U. S. Immigration Issues and Policies*** (Washington: The American Enterprise Institute, 1982), page 147. Illiteracy among these immigrants was discussed on page 72 of ***Ethnic Patterns in American Cities*** by Stanley Lieberson, published by the Free Press of Glencoe in 1963. The lag of their children in education and IQ was discussed in Paul Fox, ***The Poles in America*** (New York: Arno Press, 1970), page 96; Leonard P. Ayres, ***Laggards in Our Schools: A Study of Retardation and Elimination in City School Systems*** (New York: Russell Sage Foundation, 1909), pages 107–108; Reports of the Immigration Commission, 61st Congress, 3rd Session, ***The Children of Immigrants in Schools***: Vol. I (Washington: Government Printing Office, 1911), pages 48–49, 89, 90; Thomas Sowell, "Race and I.Q. Reconsidered," ***Essays and Data on American Ethnic Groups***, edited by Thomas Sowell (Washington: The Urban Institute, 1978), page 207. That many Southern Europeans tended to speak local dialects, rather than the official languages of their respective countries was discussed on page 58 of ***Southern Europeans in Australia*** by Charles A. Price, published by the Australian National University, 1979. Their geographic origins were mentioned on pages 16, 17n, and 24 of the same book. The earnings and occupations of various Southern European groups in Australia were discussed on pages 47, 63, and 68 of ***A Profile of the Italian Community in Australia***, by Helen Ware, published by the Australian Institute of Multicultural Affairs in 1981. Differences in rainfall on different sides of mountain ranges were discussed on page 31 of ***The Mountains of the Mediterranean World*** by J. R. McNeill and on pages 132 to 133 of ***Physical Geography of the Global Environment*** by H. J. de Blij and Peter O. Muller, published by John Wiley & Sons, Inc. The fact that Germans ate dogs and cats to avoid starvation during the blockade in the First World War was mentioned on page 79 of ***Against the Dead Hand: The Uncertain Struggle for Global Capitalism*** by Brink Lindsey. The classic study of Stalin's man-made famine in the Soviet Union is ***The Harvest of Sorrow*** by Robert Conquest. The ratio of people to land in India was from page 72 of ***Asian Drama*** by Gunnar Myrdal, abridged edition, published in 1972 by Vintage Press. The emptiness and fertility of the lands of Eastern Europe during the 12th century were noted on pages 135–137 of ***The Making of Europe: Conquest, Colonization and Cultural Change: 950–1350***, by Robert Bartlett. British preeminence in international investment in the years before World War I was described on pages 16 and 48 of ***Global Capitalism*** by Jeffry Frieden. Foreign investment in Australia and Argentina in 1913 was noted on page 20 of the same book. The fact that private capital greatly exceeds foreign aid in the emerging world was reported on page A18 of the October 19, 2007 issue of the ***Wall Street Journal***, under the title "World Bank Weary." The value of global remittances for the year 2007 was reported on page 106 of ***The Economist*** dated December 15, 2007, under the heading "Remittances." The dramatic economic transformation of South Korea from one of the poorest to one of the most prosperous nations was discussed on pages 110–111 of ***India: The Emerging Giant*** by Arvind Panagariya. The mistaken predictions of development "experts" regarding India and Africa were noted on page xiii of the same book. The use of cellular phones by Africans living in mud huts was reported on page 75 of the February 9, 2008 issue of ***The Economist***, under the title "Of Internet Cafés and Power Cuts." Differences between the cultures formed by Spanish and British conquerors in the Western Hemisphere were discussed in Chapter 1 of ***The Pan-American Dream*** by Lawrence E. Harrison. The decline in poverty levels in Latin America from 2002–2006 was reported on page 22 of the August 18, 2007 issue of ***The Economist***, under the title "Adiós to Poverty, Hola to Consumption," which began on page 21. The reduced margin of profit in trade in West Africa in the early twentieth century was from pages 65–66 of ***The Economic Revolution in British West Africa*** by Allan McPhee. Historian Ulrich Bonnell Phillips' quote can be found on page 269 of his ***The Slave Economy*** *of the Old South: Selected Essays in Economic and Social History*, edited by Eugene D. Genovese.

INDEX